Jena to Eylau

Jena to Eylau

The Disgrace and Redemption
of the Old-Prussian Army

Colmar,
Freiherr von Der Goltz

LEONAUR

Jena to Eylau: the Disgrace and Redemption of the Old-Prussian Army
by Colmar, Freiherr von Der Goltz

Leonaur is an imprint of Oakpast Ltd

Material original to this edition and
presentation of text in this form
copyright © 2010 Oakpast Ltd

ISBN: 978-0-85706-367-0 (hardcover)
ISBN: 978-0-85706-368-7 (softcover)

http://www.leonaur.com

Publisher's Notes

The views expressed in this book are not necessarily
those of the publisher.

Contents

Author's Preface

Unlike my previous book, *Von Rossbach bis Jena und Auerstedt,* the present work is not as a whole based upon personal research, although as regards the battle of Eylau itself, and especially as regards the part played by the Prussian troops therein, this is to some extent the case. I think that by thoroughly examining the ground itself and comparing it with the received accounts of the battle, I have brought forward some new suggestions that should be of use to the student who tries to clear up the doings of L'Estocq's corps on the 8th of February 1807.

My main object has been to provide a general and non-technical account of events between the double battle of Jena-Auerstedt on the 14th of October 1806 and the next great decision in arms at Preussisch Eylau on the 8th of February 1807: a narrative which I myself felt to be a necessary supplement to the more comprehensive work which preceded it.

Those of my readers who have followed my account of the Old-Prussian army in *Von Rossbach bis Jena* and my contention that history has been unfair to this much-maligned army, which yet had within itself the essentials of Old-Prussian worth and Old-Prussian valour, will ask—Where in the later stages of this unhappy war did this intrinsic worth manifest itself? Blücher's retreat from Boitzenburg to Lübeck evidenced it, but his force and his combats alike were on a small scale only, and the opportunity for a greater and more decisive act was lost when the old man suffered himself to be dissuaded from giving battle to Bernadotte on the 31st of October.

The opportunity did not return until the day of Eylau, when, however, it came in the most brilliant and honourable form that can well be imagined. It was reserved for the weak, but brave and tenacious East Prussian corps to retrieve the honour of the Prussian arms, and it was given to them to succeed. I have always held that it was at Eylau in 1807, and not in the War of Liberation in 1813, that the old army vindicated itself before the tribunal of history, and my aim in the present work is to set forth the evidence in support.

Convictions need time to mature, and particularly in the unfavourable environment of a general prejudice they present themselves but timidly to the light of day. All the more luxuriantly do they spring up and flourish when the time is ripe. In this way, just before the completion of my own study, I heard by accident of the admirable work of the pastor of Schmoditten, Dr. J. Hildebrand, and I was astonished to find that it was the outcome of a feeling identical with my own.

Only too long has the great mass of our people allowed the dark and unpleasant side of the events of 1806-7 to divert its sorrowful gaze from what was true and noble in those years. Only too completely has the name 'Jena-1806' cast into shadow and oblivion the name of 'Preussisch Eylau, 1807.' . . . Here, at Eylau, was the place and the opportunity wherein the glory of the Prussian arms, forfeited wholesale by the neglect and senility of its leaders at Jena, was most honourably retrieved in detail.

So says Dr. Hildebrand in his preface.[1] That the battle of Eylau did not end in complete victory, that indeed no serious attempt was made to seize the laurels half won, was no fault of the Prussian corps. It was dependent upon the decision of a foreign commander-in-chief, and had to submit to the unfortunate consequences of this decision. Its own leaders at least were for fighting on, and had fate allowed them to do so, and led them to success, then would the victors of Eylau have been recognized and honoured by history as the men who revenged the disasters of Jena and Auerstedt and restored the military glory of Prussia.

That fate ordained otherwise detracts nothing from their merit. Their just claim to the undying gratitude of the Fatherland cannot be contested and must not be ignored. Honour to their memory!

The Author
Königsberg
E. Prussia

---

1. Dr. J. Hildebrand, *Die Schlacht bei Fr. Eylau* (Quedlinburg, 1906. H. C. Huch).

Das Eisen

Lang genug als Dichter und Denker priesen
Oder hohnten and're das Volk der Deutschen;
Aber endlich folgten des Wortes Taten
Taten des Schwertes.

Nicht des Geistes, sondern des Schwertes Scharfe
Gab dir alles, wiedererstand'nes Deutschland . . .
Ruhm und Einheit, auss're Macht und Wohlfahrt
Dankst du dem Eisen!

Lass die Harfen tonen von Siegesgesangen!
Aber halte mitten im Jubel Wache!
Unter Lorbeerzweigen und Myrtenreifern
Trage das Schlachtschwert!

Denn die Zeit ist ehern, und Feinde drau'n dir
Wie am Hofe Etzels den Nibelungen;
Selbst zur Kirche nur in den blanken Brünnen
Gingen die Helden.

And're Zeiten, and're Geschlechter kommen . . .
Und dem spaten Enkel, der deine Taten
Dankbar segnet, werden des Krieges Waffen
Weider zur Pflugschar.

Leuthold

Translator's Note

In preparing the English translation of this work it has been thought advisable to recast the maps. In those of the original, several successive positions of the troops are shown on one sheet, by different conventions and colours; in the present volume separate maps in black and white are employed for each situation shown. Three additional maps are included, one to show the territories of Prussia in 1806—her eastern frontiers then being very different from those of today—and two of the Jena operations, to indicate the initial situation from which the narrative starts.

C. F. A.

CHAPTER 1
From Jena to Magdeburg

At the Webichtholz, before the gates of Weimar, a fierce charge of the French cavalry had dispersed the remnants of the Prussian army that had escaped from the field of Jena on the afternoon of the 14th of October 1806. Half dazed, Prince Hohenlohe, the general who for the first time had undergone decisive defeat, let himself be borne away in flight by his staff. Grief over the disaster so mastered him that his officers scarcely recognized their once cheerful and vigorous leader. The tension of the great crisis was over, and left him, sixty years old as he was, the prey of physical weariness. Only youth's elastic courage can be expected to recover itself when Fate has dealt it a blow like Jena. Narrowly escaping from the French horsemen, who pursued the crowds of fugitives through Weimar, and captured one of the generals, the prince and his suite, accompanied by some few regiments of cavalry, reached Schloss Vippach at about 10 p.m. Of his army, part fled in rout to Erfurt and past Erfurt to Langensalza; part, led by one and another general, retreated northward.

Meantime, the Prussian main army, retreating in tolerable order from Auerstedt, had headed for Weimar, expecting to join Hohenlohe, whose disaster was as yet unknown. Suddenly encountering the French,[1] who had already passed the Ilm, the Prussians swerved and gradually broke up. Only the "advanced guard" division[2] of the Duke of Weimar, which was retiring from the Thuringer Wald and had not been engaged in the battles, was in complete order; this force was now near Erfurt.[3]

---

1. Bernadotte's corps from Apolda.—Tr.
2. The division forming the original advanced guard in the projected southward movement through the Thüringer Wald.—Tr.
3. There was further a small mixed corps under General von Winning, farther west, near Eisenach.

However, during the night that followed Prussia's appalling disasters, some 60,000 were by degrees reassembled about Sömmerda, Sondershausen, and Langensalza. Some sort of a retreat over the Unstrut and some sort of renewed resistance on the other side would have been possible, had there been but a single man capable of seizing authority with a strong hand, of electrizing the masses, and of lifting the leaders and the troops from the Slough of Despond. But there was no Frederick to be hard and pitiless to the poor in spirit. Monotonous attention to small details had killed the capacity for great resolves in the generals and senior officers of the Prussian army.

During the retreat that followed, all the routine forms were observed. Regular orders were issued, dealing with the usual minutiae in the usual pedantic way, and the watchword was given out in due form. But all this was only a salve to the conscience that red tape had enslaved, and a drug for the individual's own anxious heart. "An unimaginable despondency had mastered the souls of the higher war leaders,"[4] says von Lettow-Vorbeck.

It was not merely the army that was beaten. The spirit that had lived in it and, now if ever, should have shown its vitality, began to ebb away. Discipline vanished. Everyone had known his duty in the battle—to play the man and to follow his general—but now the demand upon him was something different from this. In spite of anxiety, confusion, and fatigue, he was called upon to put forth great efforts, to freeze in the cold October nights and to endure bare hunger. Such things could not be borne, such demands were more than the soldier could fairly be asked to meet, for in those days there were no manoeuvres "under service conditions" to teach the troops endurance.

> Habit gives strength to the body in great exertion, to the mind in great danger, to the judgment against first impressions. By it a valuable circumspection is generally gained throughout every rank from the hussar and the rifleman up to the general of division.[5]

It was not that the demands of peace-time were small: on the contrary, the strictness and precision exacted at the crucial moment of a review-manoeuvre were quite extraordinary. But this was not the same thing as the stubborn endurance of the perpetual alarms and

---

4. *Der Krieg 1806-7*, ii. 44.
5. Clausewitz, *On War* (English translation), book i. chap. 8.

excursions of campaign life. Things happened that to our ears sound fabulous, and this not merely with the rank and file, but with officers and even generals as well.[6]

The events of this night of 14th/15th October 1806 stand for all time as a warning against the mistaken kindness of sparing an army in peace, and against harbouring the erroneous notion that even fighting efficiency suffices by itself to meet the stern necessities of war.

In the old army discipline and order were dependent upon the supervision of sharp-eyed superiors. When this was absent—as here in the darkness of the night and the press of vehicles and men on foot— then discipline and order ceased, for it became evident to the rank and file that the punishment no longer followed upon the heels of the crime as hitherto. The doctrine that "the soldier should fear his officer more than the enemy" was bankrupt, for the enemy had proved the stronger. Wagons came to a standstill, guns were abandoned, arms were thrown away, rascals fired their muskets at hazard, to increase the confusion and so to get a chance of plundering the baggage-wagons. In short, phenomena never before seen in the Prussian army and believed to be absolutely impossible in its well-ordered ranks, now made their appearance to an alarming extent.

The king had intended to make for Erfurt. On the road thither, however, he soon encountered the enemy and, besides, received the news of Jena, upon which he altered his mind and gave orders to move on Sömmerda; it was no longer possible, however, for these orders to reach all the troops. On the 15th, at 7 a.m., the king was at Sömmerda in person, and resolved to continue the march by Nordhausen on Magdeburg, which implied, of course, a detour to the westward. At all costs contact with the enemy was to be avoided, and therewith all idea of reaching the middle Elbe in advance of the enemy, and of uniting with the Duke of Württemberg's reserve corps near Halle, to make a fresh stand, was *ipso facto* abandoned.

In the French army, too, the exhaustion of the troops after their great exertions made its influence felt. It settled down in two main

---

6. In the evening at Vippach, there was a discussion in the Prince's staff as to whether it would not be better to go on to Sömmerda, in order to get clear of the stream of fleeing baggage-wagons which would make resistance impossible in case of attack. On the other hand, the enemy might very well be all about Sommerda, if not actually in the place. Now, a staff officer could easily have gone to investigate— Sömmerda was only five miles away—but, instead of this, the local bailiff sent a "trustworthy messenger," who naturally saw ghosts and came back with a false tale. The consequences of this were very serious.

groups, on the Saale and near Erfurt.[7] For the moment, only the cavalry followed up, and at first they were without information as to the state of the Prussians and the direction of their retreat. Thus it befell that on the 15th even the road from Sömmerda to Halle by Querfurt was clear. It was natural enough that a route running so close along the enemy's front as this should not be used. But no such reason prevented the Prussians from taking that by Sangershausen and Mansfeld—as in fact was done by some of the fugitives (Prussians and Saxons, under Generals von Tschammer and Zezschwitz).

But consternation dimmed their vision, and they failed to see the shortest way to safety. Obsessed by the one idea of escaping from the French and their Emperor, the mass of the army streamed away northwards towards the Harz.

The king sent a representative to his victorious opponent, hoping to obtain terms of peace by a frank admission that the game was up. It must not be forgotten that he had previously felt great confidence in Napoleon's character. Not very long before the war he had said straightforwardly that the Corsican had never deceived him. How little he knew the great demi-god! Psychologically, however, it is easily explained. Frederick William, whose simple, quiet, and peace-loving soul found its highest satisfaction in the conscientious performance of the day's work and the happiness of his people, and knew neither ambition nor the thirst for glory, could not possibly comprehend the conqueror whose devouring impulse for action and insatiable greed of power drove him from one war to another. That Napoleon would give up the enormous advantage that he had won—and could see that he had won—on the 14th, it was vain to expect.

Worse was to come. Orders were issued to the troops that if the French were encountered, hostilities must not be begun—this at a moment when nothing but a stout resistance could impose respect on the pursuers and save the remnant of the army! What wonder if the rumour spread that the war was over and peace concluded? In the minds of the leaders and the hearts of the soldiers such orders could only heighten the existing confusion and paralyse all energy.

Field-Marshal Kalckreuth, whom the king had appointed to the command of the main army,[8] had after the battle collected part of

---

7. Davout, Bernadotte, Lannes, Augereau, and the Guard between Naumburg, Jena, and Weimar; Soult and Murat about Erfurt and Sömmerda. Napoleon went to Weimar on the 15th.
8. The Duke of Brunswick had been mortally wounded at Auerstedt.—Tr.

his troops at Sömmerda. With these he intended to follow the king towards Nordhausen on the morning of the 16th, and to that end he drew up in the correct official form a long-winded "disposition" (operation order). At Weissensee, some four miles on, he found a weak French cavalry division barring his way. He had 10,000 men of all arms under his orders, and the enemy, 2000 strong and cavalry alone, had the worst of the ground. What an opportunity Fortune offered him! To advance boldly to a brilliant success, and to put fresh life into the whole army by the news of the *first Prussian victory,* into which rumour would instantly have magnified it! But no more blood was to be shed; under a flag of truce a sort of armistice was arranged, and in the end Kalckreuth marched round the enemy. Even this was something gained, for it is said (though Kalckreuth denied it) that there was talk of capitulation, the field-marshal imagining himself to be surrounded. And yet this is the same Kalckreuth who was soon to win for himself a place of honoured remembrance in our nation's history as the manly defender of Danzig.

The same sort of thing happened in the afternoon near Greussen. Marshal Soult with the cavalry of his army corps met the Prussian column. Negotiations began, Soult consenting thereto because he had not enough troops in hand to attack and wished to gain time. As if the war were a thing of the past, Kalckreuth gave the French marshal a detailed and accurate account of the state of the Prussian army, stating that it was to reassemble about Magdeburg, and that the Duke of Weimar—of whose movements the French had hitherto had no information—was still considerably in rear owing to supply difficulties, etc. etc. When Soult had sufficient troops in hand, he attacked and inflicted heavy loss on the Prussian rearguard.

Meantime, on the 15th, Erfurt had, disgracefully and without the least necessity, surrendered to Murat's cavalry. The old Marshal Mollendorf,[9] the senior officer amongst the fugitives who had reached this place, had had to be carried to his room owing to extreme exhaustion. In his stead the Prince of Orange signed the capitulation, though as the king's brother-in-law and the king's general it was doubly his duty to hold out. The fortress commandant, a weak man, agreed, and none of the generals present protested. Some troops, well in hand, were standing ready to march off towards Langensalza. This movement was judged to be impracticable without an attempt to carry it out, and the worst that could

9. Mollendorf was eighty-one years of age, and had distinguished himself as a *general officer* at Torgau in 1760.—Tr.

have happened if the attempt had failed was, gratuitously and without a thought, accepted in advance. Nor did the Duke of Weimar, who was approaching with his corps, make any serious effort to disengage the troops crowded in and about the fortress. And yet what boldness could achieve, even at this stage, was shown by Lieutenant von Hellwig of the Pletz Hussars, who on the 18th, between Gotha and Eisenach, rescued some 4000 prisoners who were being marched from Erfurt. Today the name of this hero is almost forgotten, and yet it deserves immortality, for a great deed in the midst of a great misfortune has a double merit.[10] Such crises as this sound the hour of deliverance for the man of latent power whom the adverse conditions of peace service have kept down in obscurity, and who, suddenly released from captivity by the ruin of his prison, can give wings to his soul.

The armistice, as was to be expected, was curtly and promptly refused by Napoleon (16th). "I hope to end the war sooner in Berlin than in Weimar," was the emperor's reply. Yet even in the insolence of success he did not disdain at the same moment to detach Weimar and Saxony from the Prussian cause by personal negotiations. A woman had impressed him. The Duchess Luise, Karl August's wife,—of whom in his astonishment he is said to have remarked that "Here is a woman whom not even our two hundred guns can frighten,"—had by her firmness extracted from him a promise to preserve the duchy. Here and always, fearlessness obtains more than subservience from the great men of history.

Prince Hohenlohe, meantime, in the despairing search for his army, had reached Sondershausen on the afternoon of the 15th. The cavalry regiments that he had had with him up to his arrival at Schloss Vippach had vanished in the darkness, and only a few troopers were still with him. His staff had great difficulty in preventing him from turning back, for he imagined that he was the only one who had retreated so far to the rear. "A general, and riding away without his army------" he said to his officers repeatedly.

On the 16th, at 9 a.m., the king entered Sondershausen. Such was the confusion of his surroundings that he was without a penny. Prince Hohenlohe lent the king what he had, and borrowed some more from the prince of Sondershausen. A consultation was then held, and the king decided to leave the army. There was undoubtedly a good deal to be said in favour of this, for the commander-in-chief would be better

---

10. Gustav Freyteag has done homage to his memory in the last volume of *Die Ahnen*.

able to bring fresh forces into play, and to supervise and make full use of the country's means of resistance if he were clear of the turmoil of the retreat, than he could be in the midst of it. Notwithstanding all this, he would have been better advised to stay with the army. The news that the king—regarded by all as the actual commander-in-chief—had left the army meant, for the exhausted and disordered troops, that the game was really up. Of course no merely nominal command would have sufficed; at this grave crisis the baton of command would have had to be grasped with a firm hand, if the necessary unity was to be re-established in the army. And, above all, it was desirable that he should not leave Magdeburg until the army reassembled there was reorganized and in a fit state to move.

Incidentally his stay there might very likely have had the desirable result of his seeing that the governor, von Kleist—formerly a stout soldier but now too old—was not fit for serious work, and his appointing a younger man in Kleist's stead.

On leaving Sondershausen the king ordered Prince Hohenlohe to assemble the army at Magdeburg and to cover the capital, or in case this were no longer possible, to seek to join the East Prussian troops. But even in this extremity of distress personal considerations were as powerful and as insistent as ever. Kalckreuth received the independent command of the troops of the main army that he had collected around him. In so doing the king's idea was undoubtedly to avoid further offending the sharp-tongued critic who already felt that he had been set aside, and was disposed to claim that events had borne out his predictions in every particular. But in war blunders induced by such considerations are frequently the worst. Fortunately, however, a change soon came.

Equally vague was the position of the general staff. Scharnhorst, as chief of the staff of the main army, should now have belonged to Hohenlohe, and fortunate indeed would it have been for Prussia had he been permanently attached to the prince. But he was only with that general at Nordhausen long enough to sketch out the orders for the passage of the Harz, for at that moment Massenbach appeared, after wandering hither and thither, and claimed his former position with the prince. In the prevailing uncertainty Scharnhorst had to give way in Massenbach's favour. Filled with disgust at the sight of witless and spiritless generals, he betook himself to the rearguard and remained with it.[11]

---

11. Max Lehmann, *Scharnhorst,* i. 446.

The general movement of the principal groups on the 16th of October was towards Nordhausen, while the whole countryside, from Halle (where the Duke of Württemberg's corps was), by Mansfeld, Nordhausen, and Sondershausen, to Mühlhausen (which point the Duke of Weimar had reached), was covered with fragments of the Prussian and Saxon armies. As a matter of fact there was no immediate danger. Soult and Ney had only reached Greussen and the district N.W. of Erfurt respectively, while Murat had pushed on towards Mühlhausen in search of the Duke of Weimar, instead of passing round the east end of the Harz to forestall the Prussians at Magdeburg.[12]

Nevertheless, it was in ever-increasing disorder that the march went on. Excessive precaution against the enemy frequently led to the day's marches being begun needlessly early and continued into the night. Guns and wagons broke down, units were broken and scattered, quantities of supplies were abandoned because no orders had been given for their destruction. To obtain some refreshment for the hungry troops, extended cantonments were allotted to them with all the pedantry of elaborate peace-time instructions—cantonments that it was impossible for the troops to reach. Clumsiness and indecision everywhere!

The crossing of the Harz range at least brought some sort of system into the retreat, as the columns had to thread their way along four roads in order not to block up the narrow mountain defiles in one spot.

On the 17th of October a rearguard action was fought against Soult's advanced light cavalry, but this was the only incident, and in the Harz all contact with the enemy ceased. And yet this day proved noteworthy in the history of Prussia.

The westernmost road, the longest but easiest, was allotted to the heavy artillery, for under the conditions of those days the Harz was impassable for heavy guns. There were still forty of them—a priceless asset for the reconstitution of the army, if such a reconstruction had been tackled in real earnest, for this arm could least of all be improvised in haste. A force was naturally told off to cover its march, but in the prevailing confusion we are not surprised to learn that this force failed to appear. Scharnhorst, who as usual was with the rearguard, heard of this and went at once to Blücher to request him to take over the duty of protection. At the moment the latter had but few troops in hand, but he did not belong to the insufferable class of difficulty-makers of whom the army in those days produced so

---

12. Map No. 4.

20

plentiful a crop. He was ready. Both men, posting themselves at the point of danger, accompanied the artillery column in person, and during the toilsome days that followed there was cemented between them that close bond of friendship that was to contribute so powerfully to the weal of Prussia. Hitherto they had been regarded, the one as a rough old blade and reckless gambler, the other as a pedantic schoolmaster. The enlightened ones—the learned strategists of the Massenbach school—looked askance at Blücher, the stiff soldiers of the Old-Prussian type—the tacticians of "heads right, eyes left," the neo-Salderns—at Scharnhorst. But at this moment and thereafter it was given to both to show their real powers.

Under their guidance, order was brought into the march. The undismayed bearing of the two leaders visibly affected the troops. Fear and anxiety vanished. Needless efforts being spared them, the work that was really necessary, however heavy it might be, was willingly performed. The brave grenadier battalion Rabiel many times victoriously repulsed the rushes of French cavalry, kept off the French skirmishers by the fire of the third rank, and *always* managed to rejoin the column, although "officers and men dropped and went mad from over-exhaustion."[13]

Horses were requisitioned for the transport of the guns in good time, and not a gun was left behind, whereas those with the other columns stuck fast in the hills. For five days a daily average of 22-24 miles was maintained. For that epoch it was a fine performance. It does not of course represent the limit of what is humanly possible—man and horse can endure more than the theoretician's fancy imagines. No good infantry regiment of today would think a march of 24 miles extraordinary. Cavalry and artillery, even on bad roads, can be asked to do more than this—as Napoleon showed the Old-Prussian army in his pursuit of it. Nevertheless, the example of this march in the midst of the general chaos, slackness, and discouragement was most inspiring, and incidentally it showed what the Prussian troops could still do, in spite of their inadequate preparation and poor equipment for field service.

Undisturbed by the enemy, the foremost Prussian troops soon reached the northern edge of the Harz at Aschersleben and Blankenburg (evening of the 18th); the main bodies were at Stolberg, Hasselfelde, and Benneckenstein, in the mountains. Away to the left rear near Scharzfeld (which point he reached next morning) was

13. Lehmann, *Scharnhorst*, i. 450.

Blücher with his artillery train, and at Heiligenstadt, far back and on the left flank of the French pursuers, was the Duke of Weimar. The enemy pursued, but in general only followed up directly by the Nordhausen road.

Thus, considering the circumstances, things had gone tolerably well in this quarter. Elsewhere, on the contrary, this day brought two fresh misfortunes.

The Saxon commander, General von Zezschwitz, had separated from the eastern column of the retreat near Aschersleben and moved to Hettstedt with a view to reaching the districts of Barby and Gommern, outlying Saxon possessions. There he proposed to await the result of the negotiations that had already been opened with Napoleon, but finally he decided to send an officer of his own to the emperor. The latter, who had from the first openly announced his intention of treating the Saxon alliance with Prussia as a forced one, willingly met these overtures. Saxony parted company with Prussia, and Zezschwitz conducted his troops home to their garrisons. Zezschwitz was no Yorck—and yet, considering the standards of the time, he must not be too harshly judged.

More serious than the defection of a half-hearted ally was the overthrow of Duke Eugene of Württemberg at Halle—a disaster which might perfectly well have been avoided. The reserve corps under his command had assembled at Fürstenwalde[14] and was moving thence in the direction of Magdeburg when an order from the king diverted him towards Halle. The Duke reached this point on the 14th October. A fresh message directed him to take up a position at Merseburg, in order to keep open the Saale passage there for the king in case of emergency. The cannon-thunder of Auerstedt was distinctly heard in Halle, but no one hastened to the battlefield to find out what was going on or which way the decision had fallen, although the distance was but 30 miles. Only late on the 15th and in the night that followed did accurate information reach Halle—the army beaten and retreating on Nordhausen, the Duke of Brunswick wounded, and Marshal Davout at Naumburg and Weissenfels with 30,000 men!

The situation was now clear, and it was equally clear that the only thing to be done was to defend the Elbe about Wittenberg and Rosslau, so as to cover the roads leading to Berlin—the heart of the monarchy. But the Duke, like all other Prussian leaders, hungered for specific orders, and sent a staff officer to Eisleben, as he expected that the

---

14. E.S.E. of Berlin.

wounded commander-in-chief would pass there. The orders, however, did not come, and the Duke remained at Halle, taking utterly inadequate measures of security. His idea was that the French army would follow up the Prussians directly towards Nordhausen (as in fact had hitherto been the case), and that consequently he himself was in no sort of danger. He remained in this blissfully confident frame of mind when on the morning of the 17th he received an accurate account of the disasters of Jena and Auerstedt; the pressing advice of von Bergen, his chief of staff (quartermaster-lieutenant), to fall back on the Elbe was ineffectual, for in the first place he by no means realized the seriousness of his position, and in the second—prince and senior general as he was—he dared not form an independent resolution upon his own responsibility. To await orders and to obey them was apparently, for him too, the highest of all soldierly principles.

One thing, however, he did, and that was the worst of all—he assembled his generals to take counsel with them. By 8.30 a.m. they were actually all agreed as to the necessity of a retreat when a trumpeter of the Herzberg Dragoons rode up with the urgent news that his regiment had been surprised by the enemy in Passendorf, only a mile and a half from the town.[15]

Napoleon, the master of concentration, knew how to employ dispersion as well when the circumstances demanded it, above all when the fruits of victory were to be gathered. Already his clear vision had seen that his double victory implied the conquest of the whole country as far as the Oder. For the present he reckoned upon meeting no resistance, and it was therefore unnecessary to keep his army concentrated.

While Murat (cavalry), Soult (IV Corps), and Ney (VI Corps) followed the disjointed remnants of the Prussian-Saxon main army, Davout (III), Bernadotte (I), the Imperial Guard and Lannes (V) had been given the direction of Berlin. Augereau (VII) was still far back, at Weimar.

Bernadotte reached Querfurt with his corps (I) on the 16th, and moved thence upon Halle next day. It was his advanced guard that effected the surprise at Passendorf above mentioned. The unsuspecting Duke, even after the first alarming message, had no expectation of a surprise on a large scale. The position that he took up with his corps seems to us simply extraordinary. He occupied the heights S.E. of Halle,[16] facing about N.E., and with his back to Leipzig. Some few troops under General von Hinrichs were

---

15. As the town stood in 1806.
16. At that time Halle was a small town tying close upon the Saale bank.

pushed forward on to the left bank of the Saale; these had the bridges behind them and, according to the "scientific" fashion of the time, were widely scattered.

The inevitable followed. When Bernadotte came on in superior strength, General von Hinrichs could not bring himself to draw back his weak force behind the protecting river. He had no orders to do so! Consequently, he stood to be attacked, and the most gallant resistance did not save him from being crushed, unit by unit, by his powerful opponent. The General himself was taken prisoner.

Meantime the main body under the Duke had at last begun to draw off. But nothing whatever was done even to prevent the oncoming French from issuing out of the town, and ere long the Prussian corps was attacked in flank, thrown into disorder, and cut in two. The separate fractions made off towards Bitterfeld and Dessau respectively.

The disaster that befell the Tresckow Regiment was a separate affair. This regiment was advancing from Magdeburg by the left bank of the Saale to join the Duke's corps. Having merely been ordered to come to Halle, it had no suspicion of its fate. It marched into the enemy's midst and was broken and captured, only a small remnant escaping.

The losses in this utterly purposeless and senseless fight were exceedingly heavy—87 officers, 5000 men, 11 guns, and 4 colours is the probable figure.[17] Unhappily, by far the greater part of the casualties in the rank and file was in prisoners.

But even this was not enough. Thus rudely awakened, the Duke might at least have thought of barring, with the remnant of his troops, the otherwise completely uncovered roads to Berlin. But no, he must needs make an entirely unnecessary forced march to reassemble his corps on the farther bank of the Elbe, in a camp between Zerbst and Gommern, a process that cost him as many men from exhaustion and desertion as he had lost in the fight of the day before.

And so this corps, too, that in better hands would have formed the kernel of a fresh defence, that might even have ensured the re-erection of a field army, perished shamefully, and its fragments disappeared without leaving a trace into the flood of the general retreat.

The Duke, we may mention, resigned his command "for reasons of health," and left the army.

****

---

17. Lettow-Vorbeck, *Krieg 2806-7*, ii. 113.

The wreck of the main army moved on towards the longed-for haven of Magdeburg. During the 18th it reached the line Wernigerode-Aschersleben, entirely clear of the Harz. Blücher on his way round the mountain track reached a point halfway between Osterode and Seesen; the Duke of Weimar followed him as far as the district between Osterode and Gottingen. The foremost of the pursuing troops approached the line of the Bode.

A new order from the king, which reached Hohenlohe in Quedlinburg, at last cleared up the question of command. The prince was to have sole control west of the Oder, Kalckreuth east of that river.

At midnight on the 18th/19th Prince Hohenlohe summoned his staff, acquainted them with the new situation, and *asked every officer present to give his views.* The majority were in favour of continuing the retreat to Magdeburg and there resting for some days. Major von dem Knesebeck (afterwards the king's *aide-de-camp* general) alone suggested that they should throw themselves into the western provinces, in order to unite with Blücher, the Duke of Weimar, and an entirely fresh corps that was at Hameln under General Lecoq. By offering a new and vigorous resistance on that side, and drawing the French thither, they would give the king time to form a new army which should take the field against Napoleon in concert with the Russians.

With the capitulation of Prenzlau before one's eyes, Knesebeck's scheme is in many ways tempting. It deserved consideration for its boldness alone, and indeed, once uttered, it met with great approval. Massenbach, however, opposed the scheme, and it must be admitted that for the responsible leaders the most natural course was at least to attempt to reach the Oder at Stettin. There was no Ernst of Mansfeld or Bernhard of Weimar amongst them, and the march on Magdeburg continued.

In the king's entourage illusory hopes of obtaining peace at the cost of some small sacrifices were still entertained. On the 18th, at Magdeburg, he sent Marquis Lucchesini to Napoleon with the offer of "everything west of the Weser"[18] and a war indemnity. He then travelled by Ruppin, Oranienburg, and Wrietzen to Cüstrin, which fortress he reached on the 20th. It is easy today to see how vain were these hopes of obtaining peace from the devourer at the price of such morsels.

And, indeed, it was fortunate for the Fatherland that Napoleon rejected the proposal. Had he taken the offered hand in friendship, then Prussia and her grateful King would have been chained to the

---

18. Map No. 1.

triumphal chariot of the emperor, like little Saxony and her Elector, and with similar results. Never would there have been that resurrection that, sooner than anyone could have imagined, was to come out of shame and tribulation. Napoleon forced Prussia into a desperate resistance, forced her to become his bitterest enemy and, unwisely harsh, brought about thereby the deliverance of Germany.

On 19th October part of the army had already reached Magdeburg, while the bulk of it was at Gross Wanzleben and Gross Oschersleben. Blücher and his artillery column was at Salzgitter, the Duke of Weimar at Clausthal, Osterode, and Seesen. Neither, at this stage, could attempt to rejoin the main body at Magdeburg, for the way thither was barred by the leading French corps (IV), which had already reached Halberstadt.

On the 20th the main army streamed on to Magdeburg. But Magdeburg then was by no means the great and spacious city of to-day; it was a cramped town of narrow streets shut in by the *fortress enceinte*, and, possessing but 38,000 inhabitants, was, relatively to its condition today, poor in resources. Magdeburg had been to the eyes of the fugitives as the mirage of an oasis—the place that should afford them safety, rest, renewal of strength, refilling of depleted ranks—the place whence the struggle could be resumed with fresh power. Bitter was the disillusionment. Prince Hohenlohe, who had ridden forward to arrange for the reception of his army, could not blind himself for an instant to the terrible truth. Magdeburg was in irretrievable confusion. No steps had been taken to check the inflow of fugitives or to direct them to proper places of assembly. There was no provision for the orderly issue of supplies, arms, and ammunition. No arrangements had been made for the reconstitution of tactical units. Above all, there was no attempt to divert the fleeing wagon-trains. No one had thought of throwing bridges across the Elbe outside the fortress to enable them to stream away without blocking the road for troops. Wagons of all kinds poured through gate and street, and even the glacis was so completely covered with them that nothing could move forward or backward, not ten men in rank and file could pass without climbing or crawling, and not a gun on the *terreplein* could fire otherwise than into this mass of vehicles. "According to fancy one stayed in Magdeburg or ran out again by the back way."

At first rations were served out casually to individuals as they presented themselves. But soon the Governor began to be alarmed for his own garrison's supplies, and refused to give the field troops any more. Of requisitioning in the well-stored environs he would not hear. Major von dem Knesebeck, who had been sent in ahead, was told roundly that the army must "clear out." Everyone had to fend for himself. There was so marked an absence of readiness to oblige the troops that Prince Hohenlohe, who had recovered from the paralysis of defeat and was once more unweariedly active, had some trouble in obtaining two small rooms for his headquarters. Difficulties of the meanest kind beset the mere business of commanding the army, orders having to be given out in the passages or in the streets. We of today shake our heads and cannot imagine why his staff did not seize upon the finest house and the amplest accommodation in the place for the work of the headquarters, for nothing less than the fate of the country was at stake, and it was no time for considering private interests and private rights. But we forget that our ideas are not those of 1806, and that what we should consider reasonable self-help would have seemed to them acts of brutal violence. Clumsiness and the force of habit had the army at their mercy. It was impossible to stay in Magdeburg. Onward, then, to Stettin over the Oder!

The choice of this point was sound. To take the shorter road to the Oder, Berlin-Cüstrin, would have meant imposing on the troops marches that they were no longer fit to perform, and it was impossible to allow them further rest, for very soon the enemy appeared before the fortress. On the 20th, moreover, Napoleon was already nearer to Berlin than the Prussian army.

Stettin was now, as Magdeburg had lately been, the goal upon which the eyes of the fugitives were set.

The haste of departure, of course, brought many evils in its train. Even now Hohenlohe did not know where to find the various units that were henceforth to form his sadly shrunken army. Some of them he told off to reinforce the Magdeburg garrison, which he believed would thereby be brought up to a strength of 9000. Yet in the event, when the town was cleared at the capitulation, no fewer than 24,000 presented themselves—so numerous were the men who, either in malice or in ignorance, stayed behind when their comrades marched. Had the prince been able to face events with 15,000 more men at his back, many things would have happened differently. Napoleon was a true prophet indeed when he called Magdeburg "a mouse-trap into which everyone that could get away after the battle would walk."

Massenbach, the chief quartermaster (chief of staff), refused to take any part In working out the orders for the march—these were details with which he would not be troubled. All the same, it was the details that were all-important in the circumstances. This opportunity of re-organizing the shattered fragments of the army into solid units under proper command was the last that came, and the time for practising grand strategy had passed away once and for all. This was the view of mere common sense, only it was not that of a man who intended to win by mind and art, and considered all else as beneath his dignity.

At last, somehow or other, a tolerably appropriate set of orders was drafted, it seems, without Massenbach's assistance. At dawn on the 21st the cavalry was to pass through Magdeburg and thence to beyond Burg. The infantry of Hohenlohe's army was to follow as far as Burg, accompanied only by the smaller part of the train, *viz.* treasure-wagons and *commanders private carriages*. The former reserve corps of the Duke of Württemberg, now commanded by General von Natzmer, was to follow the above as far as Grabow (5 miles S.E. of Burg). The bulk of the cavalry and some of the infantry crossed the Elbe below Magdeburg and went into quarters. The prince ordered field states to be sent in to Burg by all units, as a basis for further orders, and as it was uncertain whether all the troops would in reality march out, a general staff officer was posted on the bridge of Magdeburg to check the units as they passed and to direct them to their next halting-place. Officers, accompanied by a civil official, were sent forward on the route to Stettin to provide for supplies and billets. Thus at least the most urgently necessary arrangements were made. All this the prince reported that night in a simple and dignified letter to the king.

Blücher briskly continued his march; the Duke of Weimar followed more slowly. The two generals met at Wolfenbuttel and decided to march on Stendal and to pass the Elbe at Sandau.[19]

---

19. Map No. 5.

CHAPTER 2

From Magdeburg to Prenzlau

If we examine the positions reached by the French on the day on which the Prussians left Magdeburg, it will be evident that Hohenlohe's march to the Oder, if it had been executed with less haste and more forethought, must have been successful. The French left wing (Murat with the cavalry and Soult's and Ney's corps) following the Prussians directly, could indeed drive Blücher and the Duke of Weimar away in a divergent direction, but the main army was beyond their reach as soon as it had reached the shelter of Magdeburg. The other corps of the *grande armée* had also to cross the Elbe before they could be dangerous, and for this operation they were poorly equipped. Their bridging train was scanty and had had to be left far behind. The pontoons captured by Davout had been sent to Leipzig and were equally unavailable when the heads of the corps marching in the general direction of Berlin (Davout, Lannes, and Bernadotte in first line, Augereau and the Guard in second) approached the river. The emperor in person had gone to Halle. He urged on the passage of the Elbe with all energy, knowing well that if he wasted time his prey would escape him. His adjurations to the marshals were incessant. Bernadotte was told to collect boats and to cross the Elbe on the 20th at the mouth of the Saale, but the attempt failed. Lannes, who had advanced by Dessau to Rosslau, reported that he would have the bridge there repaired after forty hours' work, and the emperor at once directed the second-line corps to the same place, himself coming to Dessau on the 21st. But here, too, he was disappointed. Only a small part of Lannes' troops was got across, and the bridge was not yet ready.[1] Great was the wrath of the emperor at being delayed by such a simple obstacle. But at this moment news

---

1. It appears that the bridge was completed on the 23rd, but even then it was so untrustworthy that Murat was uneasy about allowing his artillery to pass it.

came that the permanent bridge at Wittenberg had fallen almost intact into Davout's hands the day before. A Prussian detachment had set fire to it before marching off, but the nearest inhabitants had extinguished the fire, and thus enabled the enemy to cross the river. Napoleon thereupon resolved at once to cross with the bulk of the army at Wittenberg, leaving the bridge of Rosslau free for the left wing.

This was at least a respite—for the movement by Wittenberg necessitated a detour—and fortune was kinder still to the conquered. Murat, giving up the idea of driving away the Duke of Weimar, marched on the 21st October to his right, reaching the Elbe at Barby. Here, however, he was quite unable to cross, and so he closed in upon Bernadotte. Thus for a moment actual pursuit ceased, and Hohenlohe temporarily regained, his freedom of action. It appears that the emperor no longer really believed in his retreat to the Oder.

Involuntarily we reflect that things might have been very different if the Duke of Württemberg, instead of aimlessly exposing himself to the disaster of Halle, had chosen the simple course of retreating to the Elbe and using his intact troops to defend the crossings.

****

Hohenlohe's transfer of his army to Burg was accomplished without interruption or observation by the enemy, although seriously delayed by the disorder in Magdeburg.[2] For the continuation of the march the army was to form three columns. The main column under the prince was to follow the route Genthin, Rathenow, Friesack, Ruppin, Zehdenick, Prenzlau; on his right the light troops under General von Schimmelpfennig moved by Plaue-Fehrbellin; and the rearguard, composed chiefly of the former Reserve Corps, followed. The main body of the cavalry, which had crossed the Elbe below Magdeburg and was still scattered over a wide area, was to assemble at Havelberg, whence it was to move by Wittstock and Pasewalk—i.e. on the least exposed flank—to Stettin.[3] A far more natural course would have been to push it out to the south-east, where it could have watched the enemy's advance on the roads from Rosslau and Wittenberg towards Berlin, at the same time veiling the movements of its own side, and, by moving on a wide front, would have utilized the accommodation afforded by a large area.

The light troops, too, would have been better placed on the road

---

2. Map No. 6.

3. The total force of these various columns was still 50 battalions, 121 squadrons, and 6½ batteries.

Brandenburg-Nauen-Cremmen. The main column would thus have been spared the necessity of marching on to the rendezvous and out to their quarters every day, the route would have been shortened, the effort would have been lessened, and the supply work would have been made easier. The enemy had been shaken off, for the moment there was nothing to fear, and therefore there was absolutely no necessity to be always in a state of "instant readiness." But these very simple measures occurred to nobody, for the wondrous influence of the "rules of the art" blinded everyone to the obvious.

On the 22nd the main column reached Genthin, the light troops Plaue; the rearguard followed; the cavalry was farther back at various points nearer the Elbe.

On the 23rd Rathenow was reached. At this point the simple soldierly instinct of the prince conceived the sound notion of marching straight through to Ruppin without a halt. The troops had had two easy marches and were fairly rested and restored. The effort of a thirty-mile march could well have been demanded of them. One such a march and the army, or what now called itself the army, would have been saved. But just as the prince was about to give the orders himself, Prussia's evil genius brought Massenbach before him. This officer who, when confusion was at its height in Magdeburg, had considered it beneath his dignity to draft march-orders, changed his mind at this grave and pregnant moment, and urged the prince to move not north-east towards Ruppin but north towards Neustadt and Wusterhausen, representing that it was an act of strategical madness to march on Friesack between the marsh-lands of the Rhin-Luchs and the enemy. The prince replied, very justly, that the French were nowhere near; but it was of no avail, the prophet stuck to his word, and Hohenlohe, instead of shaking off the intolerable wiseacre and following his own excellent notion, was unhappily weak enough to give in.

Thus it was that the Prussian army was deflected in order to avoid an enemy who, exhausted by very heavy marching, had only reached the Berlin and Potsdam region, over 40 miles distant, that very day! Rarely indeed has strategical sophistry won a more tragic victory. Quite apart from the fact that the entirely unnecessary detour cut off the prospect of escape, the abandonment of the route upon which preparations had been made for the sustenance of the troops meant fresh privations at a moment when the restoration of the wearied men had become more urgent than all the rules of strategy and tactics put together.

On the evening of the 24th, therefore, Hohenlohe found himself at Neustadt and Wusterhausen instead of at Ruppin. Not a yard had been gained towards the Oder. Yet nothing, of course, was to be seen of the enemy, who did not interfere even with the march by Priesack, which General von Schimmelpfennig and his small flank-guard carried out unmolested.

At Neustadt Blücher, who with his artillery had crossed the Elbe on this day near Sandau, presented himself at the prince's headquarters. With him was Scharnhorst. The Zehdenick-Templin-Prenzlau route was again adopted. Blücher took the heavy task of leading the rearguard, the guns that he had rescued being handed over to another command.

The Duke of Weimar was still far back. He reached Gardelegen, 25 miles short of the Elbe, only on this day, while Soult from Magdeburg made a vain attempt to head him off from that river. Yet even now, in spite of the fateful detour by Neustadt, the army might have been brought off safely had it not been for an unlucky accident.

Napoleon meant to give the right column of his army a well-earned rest at Berlin and Potsdam. He seems already to have turned his thoughts to the coming campaign against the Russians, ignoring Hohenlohe. But at that moment it was—falsely—rumoured that a strong Prussian column of all arms had passed through Brandenburg. A girl who had fled from that place was the originator of the story. Military history can furnish many parallel incidents even in modern times. MacMahon's march to the northern frontier, for example, was talked about by the country-people of the Metz region before any authentic news of it could have reached them. Coming events cast their shadow before, and the "wish that is father to the thought" generates rumours that give a hint of the facts. Such indications are not to be despised by a general, and Napoleon immediately took measures to deal with the situation should the vague rumour prove to be well founded. The idea of a rest was given up, and the pursuit of Hohenlohe was resumed on the night of the 24th/25th.

The most advanced cavalry received orders to hasten forward from Charlottenburg on Oranienburg, and to send in to the emperor all news that it could gather of the movement of a Prussian column supposed to have passed through the district. At Oranienburg it was said that Hohenlohe with 18,000 men had left Magdeburg to march to Stettin *via* Kyritz. More cavalry was to push up to Hennigsdorf on the Havel.[4]

---

4. N.W. of Berlin.

The French appeared before Spandau on the 24th. The fortress was weakly garrisoned and in a neglected state, but the citadel was capable of defence. The commandant, however, unfortunately chose to follow the evil example of Erfurt, and opened the gates to Marshal Lannes upon a mere empty threat, even before terms of capitulation had been formally concluded. Lannes, too, had news of the march of a Prussian column on Stettin, but wrongly supposed it to have passed by Spandau and made its escape on the previous night. A servant of Prince August, seized in Charlottenburg, spoke of a retreat on Cüstrin, where the king was. Then Bernadotte, who had marched to Ziesar on the 24th, reported in turn that Hohenlohe had retreated with 45,000-50,000 men by Nauen and Oranienburg.

Thus the rumours of Hohenlohe's attempt to get away to Stettin gained more and more consistency, and now the emperor's orders followed in quicker succession. Lannes was to march on Zehdenick, Bernadotte to search for the enemy by Brandenburg; Soult was set free to cross the Elbe on Hohenlohe's track, Ney alone remaining before Magdeburg. Murat and the cavalry were set in motion north-eastwards. Davout made his formal entry into Berlin; Augereau reached Teltow, 9 miles S.W. of the capital; and the Guard went to Potsdam.

Meanwhile the prince and the Prussian army (25th October) wearily continued their movement. The foremost troops indeed got as far as Lindow, but the rearmost were scarcely clear of Neustadt; for, in spite of the burning need of haste, the army was still widely distributed into quarters for supply reasons, and no one dared to set custom at defiance by requisitioning supplies from the surrounding country and enforcing close billets.

Schimmelpfennig's flanking column reached Falkenthal (between Zehdenick and Oranienburg). Blücher's rearguard did not get much beyond Wusterhausen. The cavalry column made Wittstock, the artillery bent away northward heading for Rheinsberg, and the baggage-train passed into Mecklenburg territory. A small mixed force under General von Wobeser remained behind near the Elbe at Sandau, to give a hand to the Duke of Weimar. Not even bitter experience could eradicate the evil practice of dispersion.

Next day, 26th October, Hohenlohe heard that the enemy was not merely at Potsdam but had reached Spandau, and that they had even entered Cremmen and appeared at Gross Mutz.[5] The prince therefore wrote to tell Blücher to come in by forced marches, and

---

5. Six miles south of Gransee on the road from Cremmen.

to the Duke of Weimar to say that he must shift for himself. He then moved on to Schoenermark (S.W. of Gransee), where about 9 o'clock he called a halt and spoke a few stirring words to the troops. "There was not a trace of bad feeling anywhere, and some corps indeed appeared to be in the best spirits."[6] But this good feeling was not turned to account. Instead of going on to Zehdenick (only 8½ miles farther), and there crossing the Havel and heading for Prenzlau, the column remained halted short of Gransee. Disquieting reports came in that the French cavalry in great force was coming on by Liebenwalde and Oranienburg, followed at full speed by the corps of Lannes and Davout; and soon the peasantry brought a rumour—false at the moment, yet only premature—of a disaster to the flanking column of Schimmelpfennig which was supposed to be keeping open the passage of Zehdenick for the main body.

Nothing at all was done to verify this report, although it was only 8½ miles—not an hour's ride for a well-mounted officer of today—from Schoenermark to Zehdenick. Three full hours the column stood inactive, and then, once again on Massenbach's advice, it swerved north towards Fürstenberg. It is only too easy to understand how the troops little by little lost confidence in their leaders, when time after time, in spite of their manifest readiness, they were compelled to evade the enemy (who had not even shown himself) as timidly as if they no longer dared to look him in the face.

From Fürstenberg the march was to be by Lychen and Boitzenburg to Prenzlau, a route that seemed to offer the advantage—the enormous advantage, according to the canons of the time—of having on its exposed flank a chain of small lakes, ponds, and marshes. And yet if the Prussians had simply moved straight on Zehdenick, they would undoubtedly have gained that point. The enemy had only cavalry there, and was still in no great force, and they would not only have successfully cleared the passage of the Havel, but also inflicted on the pursuers a check that would have had an excellent effect upon their own *morale*.

Massenbach's contention that Hohenlohe halted to wait for Blücher is a poor excuse, for it was impossible for Blücher to catch up the main body that day. Blücher himself wrote to the prince to that effect, adding the noteworthy remark that he was more afraid of night-marches than of the enemy, and would sooner expose his corps to danger than reduce it to sheer impotence by over-driving.

6. Lettow-Vorbeck, *Krieg 1806-7*, ii. 239.

The disaster to General Schimmelpfennig's small corps at Zeh-denick, that had been mere rumour on the 25th, was hard fact on the 26th. The importance of this point, that Hohenlohe had overlooked, was grasped at once by Murat, who rapidly pushed out Lasalle's cavalry division thither, himself following with two more. The total of this cavalry indeed was but 3800, and the prince could easily have driven them out of his way by a sharp and straightforward attack. But he could not rouse himself to do it. Schimmelpfennig, after waiting for him in vain till midday, gave up hope and departed, leaving this important passage open. Soon afterwards, the enemy coming on with great rapidity, a part of the Prussian cavalry turned to face them, and for a time offered an effective resistance. But delaying its retreat too long in view of the enemy's ever-increasing superiority, it was driven back and routed, part of the fugitives making for Schwedt, the rest for Stettin, whither their general had already preceded them.

Hohenlohe's column had now lost its flank guard, and had moreover made another unnecessary detour. Only one thing perhaps excuses the prince's conduct, *viz.*, a letter from the king which arrived just at the moment of uncertainty, warning him that any engagement with the enemy was undesirable in the general interest.[7]

On this day, the 26th, Hohenlohe reached Fürstenberg, Blücher Alt-Ruppin. The Duke of Weimar crossed the Elbe at Sandau, and his rearguard, under the stern Yorck, bravely repulsed an attack of the French upon the ferry—the first encounter in this luckless campaign that was a Prussian victory.

On the 27th Hohenlohe's mournful march continued. At Lychen, once again, there was an entirely unnecessary halt of three hours, which can only be accounted for by the indecision of the commander. It is true that the cavalry column, now told off to replace Schimmelpfennig as flank-guard, had to be given time to get into position, but, in fact, this cavalry, except one heavy regiment (Gensdarmes) failed to appear. At last the main body resumed its march on Boitzenburg. At that point Hohenlohe's *aide-de-camp*, von der Marwitz, and the squire[8] of the place, Count Arnim-Boitzenburg, had had plenty of potatoes cooked in the brewing vats, and in other ways made ready for the feeding of the hungry soldiers. Oats and brandy were ready for issue, and bread was expected from Templin, where it had been collected before the army's

---

7. Lettow-Vorbeck, *Krieg 1806-7*, ii. 211.
8. Literally, the "owner of the lordship." Rural Prussia was thoroughly feudal, and the local lord exercised the powers, influence, and jurisdiction of a mediaeval baron.—Tr.

change of direction. But when the column finally arrived the enemy had already come upon the scene—the points of Murat's cavalry. Fresh hesitation, an indecisive cannonade, while cavalry was sent for. It took the unhappy prince two hours to make up his mind to attack. A few battalions moved forward with bands playing—and, lo! the enemy vanished. Some prisoners were taken and some captive Prussians officers released, and all that was now necessary was to move on, to serve out the food—or what the French had left of it—and then to cover the few remaining miles to Prenzlau, which was still clear of the enemy.

But this first ebullition of courage bore no fruit. The prince had only seized and occupied Boitzenburg in order to screen his further movements from the enemy's eyes. In addition, there came a Job's messenger with the news that the Gensdarmes regiment had unsuspectingly ridden into the arms of the enemy (Grouchy's division) and had been forced to surrender. Once more—for the third time in this fateful retreat—the column was deflected northward.

High authorities[9] have approved this detour upon tactical grounds, considering that a flank-march by night, from Boitzenburg straight on Prenzlau, was altogether too dangerous and that an attack would have disbanded the whole column. As if things had not already come to such a pass that one danger more or less did not matter! The column was on the verge of a break-up in any case, for exhaustion and disheartenment had now reached the highest point, and a fresh night-march, or night-flight, was bound to give the *coup de grace*. Battle could not have made things worse than they were, and the army would at least have gone down with colours flying. The soldier who knows that he cannot face this alternative had better not aspire to the baton of command.

Passing round Boitzenburg, the procession drifted on, in hunger and weariness, by bye-paths to Schoenermark[10] near Prenzlau. The march was very severe, a deep brook had to be passed, and a steep gradient to be climbed. The columns straggled apart, the bad characters availed themselves of chaos and darkness to slip away, others fell down from sheer exhaustion. Hunger drove away many a man whose hopes of appeasing it at Boitzenburg, as so often before, had been cheated. What the enemy had not done, prudence and tactical scruples had done for him—the last particle of resisting power was gone.

---

9. For example, Lettow-Vorbeck, ii. 255.

10. Not to be confused with the Schoenermark near Gransee, where Hohenlohe spent the morning of the 26th.

Late in the night the column assembled at Schoenermark. The march had covered 26 miles—nothing excessive for good troops well handled, but absolutely ruinous in the present miserable conditions of hunger, depression, and prolonged halts, not to speak of darkness and the bad roads. Not one of these things, however, exercised so baleful an effect on the hearts of the men as the perplexed attitude of their leaders, now patent to all.

About 4 a.m. the prince himself arrived at Schoenermark, and betook himself to the castle of Count Schlippenbach. A discussion arose as to which route should be taken in order to get to Stettin without meeting the enemy. If only the Ucker River, close by, could be reached at Prenzlau, the worst of the danger was practically over; for this river runs in a wide marshy depression parallel to the Oder and empties itself into the Kleines Haff. Only a few embankments traversed the depression, which was reinforced as an obstacle by a chain of lakes. Besides the Prenzlau crossing, there was indeed another, 7 miles farther south, at Seehausen, but by good luck the bridge here had been destroyed by Schimmelpfennig's cavalry in their retreat, and the grass track joining Nechlin and Nieden, 9 miles below Prenzlau, was protected both by its distance and by its bad state. If, then, the eastern bank of the Ucker could once be reached at Prenzlau, there would be no further need to fear that the force would have its retreat cut off by an enemy passing round it. A further advantage was that beyond the Ucker there was yet another obstacle which, though not so important, would afford a certain amount of protection, *viz.*, the line of the Randow or Landgraben.

In fact, Prenzlau was still free of the enemy, and this time the prince rightly decided upon the shortest line, although voices were raised in favour of yet a fourth detour by Nechlin and Nieden. Only the cavalry, which had not yet managed to come up, and Hagen's brigade of light infantry that accompanied it, were assigned to the Pasewalk route.

Meanwhile the men were lying, utterly exhausted, by the wayside, and it was only by persuasion and force that they could be induced to move. Soldiers pressed the muzzles of their muskets to one another's breasts and fired, rather than have to march farther—to such a pass had prudent strategy and the fear of catastrophes and combats brought the army! Up to this point, the main column had in fact met with no reverse. And yet it was helpless, and the courage that even in a hopeless fight would have found some sort of a way out, was broken by indecision in the command and unnecessary toil.

A military writer has very justly compared the army as it wended its way from Schoenermark towards Prenzlau to a long funeral cortege. It is a warning for all time that he who makes war must not forget its wastage, and that even the most disastrous issue to an engagement may be less ruinous than the fear of it and the consequences of that fear. In Prenzlau the coming of the troops was awaited with tense anxiety. Supplies were collected, and a portion of them was sent to meet the army; this, however, was captured by the hostile cavalry. From the tower of the Marienkirche were seen the march columns approaching from Güstow, and two bodies of French cavalry on the Templin road. Delay was not yet dangerous. (Map No. 7.)

The approach to Prenzlau over the flats was an embankment, 1¼ miles in length; along this, in those days, there were but few houses and gardens. A swerve was impossible, for a fair-sized brook (Der Strom) ran along the north side of the embankment. To the south lay the wide marshes on the left bank of the Ucker. At the entrance to the Neustadt a gate and a palisade successively presented themselves, and farther in, around the old town, there was a wall. There was therefore plenty of opportunity for a stout defence, and once the marching column had passed the defile, the pursuers could have been held at bay for long. Here would have been work for old Yorck and his Jägers—but unhappily they were far away.

In the town was Lieutenant Count Nostitz, who had ridden in ahead with a small body of horse. The French general Lasalle, who had come on the scene with his 5th Hussars, had not ventured to attack, but had sent word to Murat of Hohenlohe's coming. Murat had believed that the fighting would be at Boitzenburg, but Lannes, who was following him, had succeeded in converting him to the view that Hohenlohe would continue his march, and Murat thereupon started off for Prenzlau with the two cavalry divisions he had in hand. Lannes followed up with the V Corps, but only arrived at noon, when all was over.

It was still possible for Hohenlohe to win through. The fortune of war had against all expectation turned in his favour. But, alas! no recognition of this could now penetrate the cloud of despondency which had settled on all men's spirits. The embankment was still held, and the troops had begun to pass into the town. But the prince allowed himself, in the most irresponsible fashion, to be kept in play by a French flag of truce, which for his benefit depicted the place as surrounded on all sides by large forces. He lost time in making dispositions, and so enabled Murat to come up. A brief cannonade began. The prince rode in person to his artillery, which had driven up on the left side of the Strom, posted himself in front of his cavalry escort and calmly faced the fire, in the secret hope perhaps that a kindly shot would free him from the burden of responsibility that was too heavy for him to bear. Only when his staff suggested that his presence was required on the other side of the town—where meantime General Count Tauentzien was forming up the troops as they arrived—did he ride away thither. General von Tschammer remained behind in his stead to hold on until the last troops should have passed.

The French meanwhile began to press on, and as the Prussian guns were presently compelled by want of ammunition to cease fire and limber up, the enemy's cavalry succeeded in passing the Strom and cutting off the rearmost Prussian troops, the Prince August Grenadier Battalion amongst them. Some few squadrons broke away, but raced down the embankment alongside the marching column, hunted by the French. The latter, whom success and the recent strange timidity of the Prussians had made recklessly daring, broke into the ranks of the column. The paralysing cry of "Down with your arms!" resounded. A Prussian officer was struck down without a hand being raised or a shot fired to defend him. One soul only, and he a boy of fourteen, Ensign von Petersdorff, fought like a man in defence of his colour, which he would not let go until the stave had been hewn in pieces and himself repeatedly wounded. Finally the men threw down their arms; the rearmost covering troops were broken by a *voltigeur* battalion of Lannes' corps—the only French infantry that reached the field—some of the guns were seized as they drove off, and General von Tschammer was captured. Only at the town gate was the pursuit temporarily checked, and it was but for a moment, for in the universal chaos even the walls were abandoned. The enemy now drove on into the town. The prince himself was rescued with difficulty by his staff. Rejoining the troops deployed beyond the town, he busied himself with the minor details of placing them in position—the infallible sign of embarrassment in a general at a critical moment.

Yet withal, sadly diminished as it was, the Prussian corps was not cut off. The French had still no means of passing the Ucker flats above or below Prenzlau to outflank it. The retreat could not indeed be continued without fighting, for the enemy pushing directly through Prenzlau could follow up on Hohenlohe's heels; but there was no need to be afraid of fighting, for it was only a question of keeping off cavalry.

But Prussia's baleful star was in the ascendant. During his conversation with the enemy's flag of truce west of the town the prince had sent Massenbach to verify the Frenchman's assertion that the Prussians were surrounded. Now, Massenbach was unaccustomed to severe personal exertions, and the strain of these last days had brought his excited fancy into a state bordering on sheer madness. As a rule he travelled in his carriage, and riding not only wearied him, but appears to have entirely bereft him of the power of reasoning. After leaving the prince on the north-west side of Prenzlau, he rode to the Thiesorter Mill (about 2½ miles from the town) and crossed the Strom. This brook, however, he mistook for the Ucker itself, and when south of it he met Murat and Lannes with their troops, he assumed that they were over the Ucker, *viz.*, close upon the Prussian line of retreat, which the advancing columns of the French were in a position to intercept. With this Job's message he returned to headquarters just at the critical moment when the unhappy prince was interviewing a French general (Belliard) who this time had really been sent in by Murat to demand the surrender of the Prussians. By this time Hohenlohe had lost all capacity for resistance, otherwise he would have closely examined Massenbach's information and detected the mistake in it. What a commander, to depend so slavishly upon a subordinate's ideas! Indeed, even at Schoenermark the prince had come to be considered as a cipher. "To the overclouding of the spirit there was added extreme physical exhaustion. He had eaten nothing for thirty-six hours."[11] In these conditions his heart accepted with culpable readiness the idea that neither retreat nor fighting was now possible.

Presently Murat himself appeared, and in a long conversation worked up still further the hallucinations that already darkened the prince's soul. It was all over with the Prussian army. A capitulation was agreed upon. There was one more formality, according to the custom of the time, a consultation of general officers; but when the prince—the general of highest reputation, the victor of many a fight—saw no way of escape, it would have needed a man of nothing less than extraordinary force of character to make the venture, and even had such an idea been entertained in the group who surrounded the prince, the rigid discipline of literal obedience and the systematic repression of initiative set a barrier that it was impossible for a subordinate to transgress.

---

11. Report of Major von der Marwitz, in *1806: Das preussische Offizierkorps* (Prussian Great General Staff), p. 229.

Thus, without effective pressure from the enemy, the army, still ten thousand strong, laid down its arms. It was all over with the Old-Prussian glory "Many a man's heart was broken, but it was too late. The prince with his suite rode back to the town in silence."[12] In the country at large, the news had a far worse effect than the double disaster of Jena-Auerstedt. "Prince Hohenlohe and the army have surrendered!" The game was up at last, it appeared, and its calamitous consequences made themselves felt immediately.

The grenadier battalion Prince August, that had been pressed by the French cavalry towards the Ucker marshes below Prenzlau, perished gloriously.

Led by their Prince, they not only steadily refused all proposals for surrender, but beat off seven successive cavalry attacks. Only when the French had succeeded in bringing up guns and were pouring case-shot into the little troop (whose ammunition had been wetted in wading the deep ditches) did this gallant body give in,[13] and even then a handful managed to break away and to reach Stettin in safety. About a hundred grenadiers were left when the surrender came. On the contrary, the needless night-march had of itself cost the battalion 276 men—tragic evidence of the fact that pale fear of fighting is more deadly than fighting itself.

The cavalry column, in so far as it had not come up with the main body, marched on the 28th, along with its attached light infantry, to Pasewalk. In the evening there came the bad news from Prenzlau. Instead of acting, the generals debated. The defile of Lockenitz, which was close at hand on the Stettin road, offered security. Some were for continuing the march, others gave up all hope. "On one point only was there unanimity, and that was, that in any circumstances a conflict with the enemy was to be avoided."[14] The French cavalry under General Milhaud, which from Boitzenburg was pushing on towards Pasewalk, was diverted by the cannon-thunder on the Ucker. The defile of Lockemtz was occupied on the 28th alternately by the French and by a Prussian detachment sent out from Stettin. The passage could unquestionably have been forced. And yet the column stood inactive at Pasewalk, and next day its bewildered generals positively sent out officers in search of an enemy to take their formal surrender. One of

---

12. Lettow-Vorbeck, ii. 277.
13. Clausewitz, *Preussen in seiner grossen Katastrophc,* Appendix (Great General Staff), *Kriegsgeschichtliche Einzelschriften,* No. 10.
14. Lettow-Vorbeck, ii. 283.

these officers met the French general Lasalle on his way to Stettin, and the latter proposed to send back a squadron to make prisoners in due form of five cavalry regiments and a fusilier brigade. But it was too late, for General Milhaud appeared before Pasewalk on the morning of the 29th with 700 sabres and finished the business. One hundred and eighty-five officers, over 4000 men and 2000 horses surrendered.[15] Many men of the Leib-Karabinier Regiment—still four hundred strong—wept as they defiled before General Milhaud. "The sure sign of the ruin of the Prussian monarchy," he reported, "is despair. This evidence confirms us in our belief that there were many brave officers and men in the regiments thus scandalously surrendered to the enemy who would have preferred an honourable soldier's death to the shame of surrender."

There was even worse in store. After Hohenlohe's capitulation on the 28th the whole of Lannes' corps had installed itself in Prenzlau. Grouchy's cavalry brigade lay north-east of the town, and Hautpoul's division of heavy cavalry from Templin had reached Mittenwalde. There were now enough troops in and about Prenzlau to undertake further operations. On the morning of the 29th Murat went in person to Lockenitz. It was thought that Stettin was only held by some few stragglers and also ill-provisioned, and an officer conceived the bold idea of inviting her fortress to surrender then and there. In reality the place was capable of sustaining a formal siege, held by 5000 men and well supplied, and 100 guns were mounted on its walls.[16] The first suggestion of surrender was, moreover, rejected.

But the incredible happened after all, for when General Lasalle, at four in the afternoon, repeated the demand, the aged governor,[17] Lieut.-General von Romberg, agreed to it. The great fortress was lost, and with it the line of the Oder.

Yet even this was not enough. A part of Hohenlohe's cavalry, under General von Bila II, was to have formed the prince's rearguard from Schoenermark, but arrived at that point so late at night of the 27th/28th that it could not follow the main column, from which it was presently-separated by Milhaud's advance. On the 29th Bila II, with 18½ squadrons, by a northerly detour reached the environs of Stettin, and requested permission to pass through the place. This

15. Only the small advanced guard, under Lieut.-Col. von Stülpnagel, who had not taken part in the Pasewalk debate, and had started again on the evening of the 28th, successfully made its way to Stettin.
16. In all 281 guns were available.
17. He was eighty-one years old.

was refused by the Governor, who was then negotiating with the French—whom doubtless he did not wish to vex by succouring the new-comers. All this is not legend, but the unvarnished truth. Von Bila II thereupon got away northward to Uckermeinde, and thence to Anklam. There he unexpectedly met his elder brother, General von Bila I, who, with one battalion and 120 men of the Baillodz Cuirassiers, was bringing in the contents of the Hanoverian and East Friesland treasuries. At Anklam, besides, there was a detachment that had been sent forward from Lindow with the military treasure, and the baggage column[18] and its escort, which had pushed on from Genthin. The river Peene was successfully crossed, and all went very well for one day. But through indecision the time was wasted instead of being turned to account in transferring everything to Usedom Island, which could easily have been arranged; and when the news came that Stettin had capitulated the brothers Bila decided to do likewise. On the morning of the 1st of November they surrendered with 1100 infantry and 1073 cavalry to a weak force of French cavalry under General Beker.

The artillery column that after the disastrous battles of the 14th had been rescued with such infinite pains by Blücher and Scharnhorst, had already met its fate. In accordance with Massenbach's advice, it had been sent by Alt-Strelitz to Friedland. Beside the artillery proper, the column comprised baggage and a mobile park, so that the total number of guns, horses, and vehicles was considerable. Twenty-four cuirassiers only were told off as escort and police. When, however, the column entered Mecklenburg *it was met by a refusal to supply forage,* and thus the compounder, Major von Höpfner, found himself compelled to make for Prussian territory at once. He crossed the frontier and moved to Boldekow, on the road to Anklam. General von Bila II had told him not to come any nearer, but the French pursued him through Mecklenburg, and he too could think of nothing better than to surrender the 25 guns that were still with him. The tiny escort had gone on beyond the Peene, and one cannot understand why the gunners and drivers could not have done the same, after destroying the *matériel.*

Pusillanimity spread like an infectious disease. On 1st November Cüstrin, exceedingly strong in itself and protected besides by the Oder, surrendered without the least necessity. It is a significant fact that the commandant, Colonel von Ingersleben, had himself to send boats to

---

18. *i.e.* of Hohenlohe's army.—Tr.

the west bank of the river to bring over the French who were to occupy the fortress that they had so unexpectedly conquered.

On the 8th of November came the worst blow of all. General von
Kleist opened the gates of Magdeburg to the far inferior forces of the
besiegers, and 24,000 men laid down their arms. On the 20th, the
strong place of Hameln and with it the field force of General Lecoq
capitulated to insignificant forces of the enemy, and when six days
afterwards Nienburg followed its example every single fortress west of
the Oder, save in Silesia, had passed into the enemy's hands.[19]

---

19. Even the insignificant fort of Plassenburg in Bayreuth was surrendered to the
Bavarians on the 25th.

CHAPTER 3

Observations

So incredible do these events appear when brought home to our mind that we are as men in a dream. Yet no suspicion either of cowardice or of treachery attaches to the parties concerned. We have only to read the judgment of that sternest of all critics, Clausewitz, on the personal character of Kleist, the chief offender:

> It is a pity that he should owe his fame to the surrender of Magdeburg, for he deserved to be known for better reasons.... He had a quick and not uncultivated mind; as a soldier he was keen and thorough, and his calmness in battle was conspicuous...Although old and frail, his whole personality still bespoke the energetic soldier, the experienced general, and his career judged by the standard of the day was among the most brilliant.... In figure General Kleist was short, crippled, and shrunken, but the expression of his face was both soldierly and dignified. He was among the best of our military personalities of that time.

Lecoq was another who proved a bitter disappointment to the Fatherland. He was the man who brought Scharnhorst into the Prussian service,[1] and was apparently himself a kindred spirit. His former achievements fully justified the general expectation that he would do great things, and yet at Hameln, like all the rest, he failed miserably.

Less is known of the past life of the others, but they too had rendered great services in their time. That these men should, one with the other, *all* have proved equally weak and foolish amounts to a psychological puzzle. The similarity of these widely disseminated phenomena drives us to conclude that they had a common origin.

The stupefying effect of the terrible defeat on 14th October ex-

---

1. From the Hanoverian.—Tr.

plains much, but not all. The events of that day should, according to preconceived notions, have been so utterly impossible that the calmest mind might well be shaken, the clearest brain confused. But all this should only have affected the first few days, and ought never to have led to such shameful submission to the enemy's will.

Physical cowardice certainly played no part in it. The subsequent searching inquiry in no case revealed the least trace of ignoble motives.

To explain the quick succession of catastrophes so similar in type, we are, then, thrown back on the degenerate, insipid, and artificial conception of the nature of war, of the soldier's calling and the soldier's responsibilities, and also on the general mode of thought and sensibility of the period.

Prussia had gone into the struggle without making any special effort—without indeed calling upon the whole of the ordinary military means available even in peace-time. In spite of the crushing superiority of the enemy she left, as is well known, a quarter of her army at home, and garrisoned her fortresses on their peace-footing so that the expenses of the war should not be too heavy.

It is perhaps too much to say that the magnitude of the danger had been underrated. Rather was it that all were alike too timid to draw the obvious conclusion from their knowledge of that danger and to make unsparing use of all means and all forces to oppose the giant. They wished to fight, but without strengthening the army by a general levy—without, indeed, having recourse to *any* unusual expedient, for experienced men of the old school regarded such measures as intrinsically unsound.

Above all, the country was not to be allowed to suffer, either at the hands of the enemy, or for that matter by participating in the contest at all, even to the extent of meeting an increase in the army estimates. And this represented not only the popular feeling, but also the Government's will.

Woe betide the Cabinet which, half-hearted in its policy and fettered in its ideas of war, meets an opponent whose crudely elemental principles acknowledge no law but that of inborn strength.

The opponent they now had to face was, alas! of precisely that order.

What was apparently intended was a frontier war in the Elbe and Saale regions, in which the splendidly drilled Prussian phalanx would again, as at Rossbach and Leu then, display its proved offensive power

46

in brief, brilliant battles, and once more assert the "godlike army's" former fame. They had no thought of a life-and-death struggle. Had anyone prophesied that the finale would take place on the far distant Memel River he would have been ridiculed.

People's heads were still full of the idea that war was a game of chess between kings, in which victory depended on skill and reflection, and not on brute force; a game in which the winner is quite satisfied with victory for its own sake. They readily admitted that in this case the king had lost his game on the Saale, but could not understand why the opponent was not satisfied to let it rest there. No better proof of this mental attitude could be adduced than the childish hopes of a *cheap* peace with which the Court circle deluded itself after its terrible disaster.

To allow the country to be devastated, its prosperity ruined, its calm shaken to the foundations, or its population sacrificed by continuing the hopeless struggle, seemed to the worthy and humane men who were in high favour at the time the very extremity of rashness and folly, in fact a crime. Nothing of the sort could be expected of any thoughtful general who had penetrated the secrets of the art of war and also infused the necessary element of diplomacy into his soldierly sentiment—or so it seemed to these enlightened minds.

There is hardly a doubt that the disloyal commandants, one and all, honestly believed that they were acting from the highest sense of duty when they signed their capitulation and their shame. The "law of humanity" justified them in their own eyes.

Kleist, the general once known for his brusque severity, declared it was a doubtful sort of glory for a commandant to suffer "the devastation of a stretch of such beautiful and prosperous country," merely to prolong the resistance, when "*dure necessite*" must shortly involve surrender in any case. He himself surrendered "to avoid greater misfortune to the State.... to preserve the royal interests and the commercial town of Magdeburg," regarding these probably more in their relation to the terms of settlement when peace should be concluded rather than as a military end. The commission of inquiry when judging his conduct expressed its opinion that this motive alone was responsible for its anxiety about reducing the town to ashes and his unwillingness to have the suburbs burnt down.

"Reduce the town to ashes, and the inhabitants to misery! That I cannot, dare not, do!" was Ingersleben's excuse at Cüstrin. His brave wife implored him "for God's sake not to cross over to the enemy and give up the fortress;" but certain enlightened and humane men of rank and distinction, such as Kammerpräsident von Schierstaedt,[2] gained the upper hand with him, and contrived to remove the courageous woman at the critical moment. The disloyal Governor was declared worthy of a memorial column in his honour. Hard pressed by the civil authorities and by the inhabitants, he lost his head, and "the few who were ready to make any sacrifice were easily silenced by the multitude."[3]

Consideration for towns and populations played a great part everywhere, even at Hameln, which did not even belong to old Prussian territory. Foreseeing, as he explained, that if he defended the capital it would suffer incalculable misery, Count Schulenburg withdrew his troops from Berlin. And one finds practically the same wording each time the shameful abandonment of a town or a fortress occurs.

When, at Prenzlau, Massenbach was advising surrender, he declared that he would "give himself up to save the poor fellows" who stood armed and ranked in front of him. This need not be taken too seriously, for his bombastic self-glorification led this poor dreamer to be generous with such speeches. But when a man of Prince Hohenlohe's chivalry and courage can say similar things, that is, that he thinks it nobler to sacrifice his own fair name for the general welfare than to preserve it by the sacrifice of so many good lives that could otherwise be preserved for the country, then indeed we see a perversion of soldierly sentiment which could only have been the result of a general deterioration in the military spirit of the army and the nation alike.

As if, indeed, it were a question of the prince's reputation, and not rather of a desperate attempt to save at least a remnant of the army which, however small, might have served as the nucleus of a new army to be formed! Had they fallen like heroes they might have awakened the spirit of resistance throughout the country. But there was no question of that.

So little had this spirit been aroused among the soldiers that a glance at their faces was enough to show the utter hopelessness of any suggestion to form a body of men who with no hope

---

2. It is said that Schierstaedt and Kammerdirektor von Lüdemann had attempted to get into communication with the French commanding officer at Berlin to ask his protection and to inquire where the board of revenue was to go.

3. An assertion made by Thynkel, a lieutenant of engineers, at the court-martial held on the surrender of Cüstrin (1806: *Das preussische Offizierkorps und die Untersuchung der Kriegsereignisse,* published by the Great General Staff, Berlin, 1906).

of a happy issue were yet ready to face death before disgrace. It was the sort of thing that would have been stigmatized as rash and quixotic, and refuted with the assertion that in a few days peace would surely be declared.

Thus did blunt, uncompromising Marwitz express himself on the subject of Prenzlau.[4] Where was the spirit of Frederick, who, when in desperate case, flung these ever-memorable words at his friend, the Marquis d'Argens:

You are always talking to me of my person when you ought to know that there is no need for me to live, but every need for me to do my duty, to fight for my Fatherland and to save it if there be still a means to save it![5]

The heroic standard of the Old Prussians had been perverted by a long period of peace, and by the effeminacy which had come over their mode of life, condemning passion as brutality, daring as folly, and finding the greatest wisdom in art, moderation, and comfort. This misguided generation had lost the power to understand that the highest wisdom is often found in a desperate deed which may save the situation when the superfine mind detects no way out.

****

But we must not look back on those dark days with the pride of the Pharisee, however culpable these men may seem to us, and although we see them laying down their arms without compulsion before a weaker adversary when for the country's good they should have laid down their lives as a solemn warning. It would be impious on our part to pride ourselves overmuch on our immeasurable superiority. The men of Magdeburg, Prenzlau, and Stettin were of the same stock as ourselves. In early life they were as brave and as bold as the youth of our own generation. They were undone by a dangerous influence which crept in stealthily, and gradually enveloped them, overpowering at the most fateful moments the victims that it had rendered defenceless. It was their misfortune to be no longer soldiers pure and simple, but politicians and courtiers who from considerations without number were incapable of making the plain

---

4. In his report of the capitulation (Great General Staff, *1806: Das preussische Offizierkorps,* p. 236).
5. At Reussendorf, 18th September 1760 (*(Euvres de Frederic le Grand,* Tome xviii, *correspondence de Frederic avec le marquie d'Argens,* p. 193).

decision which their duty as soldiers demanded. There is no doubt whatever that Kleist, like the other governors and commanders, supposed himself to be acting upon a reasonable and justifiable policy in handing over his charge to the French.

Germany is experiencing just such another long period of peace. She has become rich, and her riches increase daily. She grows in culture, but this growth in culture is unfavourable to the warlike development of the people. It compresses the army more and more into barracks and parade-grounds. Ground is more valuable; unused stretches, once available for troops, are rarer; the damage which may be inflicted by them is greater; the derangement of industrial life by the soldier's period of service is felt the more keenly in proportion to the strain created by the general competition and the increasing value of time.

All classes live in greater comfort than of old. The capacity for enduring privation and hardship disappears because it is no longer necessary, and in consequence compulsion and exertion appear to lose their point. To many, the careful distribution of the day's work rendered necessary by the short period of army service and by the many-sidedness of modern training which is the inevitable consequence of modern improvements in armament, seems merely a vexation inflicted on the soldier by the officers' military ambitions.

Some great danger visibly threatening us from abroad, as in the days before 1806, when the existing danger might have served as a useful corrective, is what we lack, and the lack of it lulls to sleep our sense of the practical utility of a strong army and of the need of intense activity in the service itself.

The idea, or rather the shibboleth, expressed by the word *militarism* is a product of our time. We speak of it as thoughtlessly as if it were a parasitic thing that existed for its own sake and fed upon the vitals of the people. This idea is dangerous, for it inevitably suggests that this excrescence on the body of the nation ought to be cut off, whereas in reality the question is rather, Are we doing enough in view of the secret envy which Germany's rapid growth to maturity has aroused?

Present-day philosophy teaches free development of personality. Everything which stands in its way should be put aside, the barriers imposed by the State reduced to a minimum, and in accordance with this tendency the authority of officials and superiors is becoming daily more restricted. This state of things on the one hand increases the difficulty of organizing and directing the masses, and on the other renders them more resentful of superior influence.

Our milder-mannered time regards with distaste the application of force, and dislikes the outbursts of a strong temperament. Those in command are required to execute their difficult task by methods of moderation, by imposing conviction, and not by exercising the full powers of authority. It is obvious that this tendency is not favourable to the rise of such strong characters as are essential to us in war. The integrity of the citizen, the principle of moderation which disposes him to resist all promptings to violence, is given a disproportionate value as compared with rugged worth of character. But the "poor man" whose feeble shoulders are to be spared their load, the nursling of public opinion whose "baccy" and "nip "have become inviolable, whose wages constantly increase while his hours of work are shortened, and who hears of nothing but his rights in the state and in society, never of his duty towards either, can only become more and more unsuited to sacrifice his all for the Fatherland in the hour of extreme need. Training is as necessary a preliminary to devotion in a great cause as to courage and bodily strength. It is this sort of training, however, which our modern existence tends to eliminate, and the result will in the nature of things be felt at the moment when the mass of the nation is called upon to meet an exceptional strain for an exceptionally great effort. But at the same time, without the mass of the people there will be no great effort. The empire's independence cannot be maintained by a handful of men of high rank.[6]

Involuntarily the question arises, Will the spoilt multitudes, after a course of unmixed flattery, be willing to respond to the stern call to sacrifice life and property in the defence of the Fatherland? That

---

6. We may quote here from an essay which, though it deals exclusively with the way in which the State is financially affected by the masses, may well be applied to the moral side. " The fundamental cause of the present unsatisfactory state of affairs is to be found in the fact that while the people's representatives in the *Reichstag* and *Landtag* are only too fond of enlarging on the claims their constituents have on empire and State, they leave practically un-mentioned the claims of the latter on the constituency. Given so new a system of government as our own, it is not of the least use depending on Jubilees and other public occasions such as the unveiling of statues for the opportunity to speak of duty to one's country. We must have as the chosen or potential representatives of the people men brave enough and conscientious enough to tell them the truth even though it may be less palatable than the perpetual promises in which each party surpasses the other." "One of the greatest drawbacks to the so-called new, now old, economic policy, is that it deals ever with the duty of empire and State towards citizens, treating the obligations imposed on these by the bounties of empire and State as quite a subsidiary matter" (Prof. Gustav Cohn, *Die deutsche Finanzreform der Zukunft,* p. 5. Zurich, 1907).

they should be so is an essential condition, if the fighting portion of the population is to go into the field in joyous confidence of victory. The warlike spirit must have its root in the nation if it is to flourish in the army.

Then, again, there are the false apostles of today who condemn war as in itself reprehensible. A universal peace in which wolf and lamb shall dwell together in unity is proved possible by means of a multitude of misleading and seductive arguments. Thus do the shadows deepen over the ancient Germanic ideal of a proud nation of warriors, an ideal which is bound to lose its power to attract, particularly in a prolonged peace, when even the most martial-minded see that all chances of testing their prowess are fading gradually away.

The trend of events with us, since our great victories in the middle of last century, is only too natural.

> Victory brings might, might riches, but prosperity luxury. It is a matter of experience that after any war there sets in a fever of speculation, a tendency to corruption, a way of life that is, to say the least, lax. The more civilized, the more wealthy a nation becomes, the greater the capacity for pleasure and indulgence. It shrinks from effort, and comes gradually to estimate property and ease more highly than the brutal pursuit of war.[7]

These currents are no more to be stemmed than the floods of mighty rivers, and it does little good to lament over them; for in fact they always ebb again, somehow or other. In all probability, every age has within itself some seeds of corruption. But one false idea, pushed to its extreme development, brings both itself and its age to destruction. Into a cycle of this sort egotism, the true daughter of today, has drawn us; but the cycle will work itself out, and external pressure will force into a new path those who have pursued no object but their own satisfaction. This was the experience of our ancestors a hundred years ago. From fear they lavished on the enemy with enforced smiles what had been sparingly and grudgingly conceded to the defenders of the Fatherland.[8] Every age stands in need of stringent self-criticism. It is the duty of its own generation to expose the seeds of corruption and make every effort to stop their abundant growth, It is undeniably in the general tone of the age, and not in

---

7. Dr. A. Wirth, *Hemmungen ties Imperialismus (Der Tag,* Nov. 21, 1906, illustrated number).

8. For details see J. G. Fichte's *Eeden an die deutsche Nation* (copy of the 1st edition, 1808, Berlin, 1869), Erste Rede, p. 10.

the sphere of military administration or training[9] (where the vulgar crowd chiefly looks for it), that the resemblance exists between our own time and the peaceful pre-Jena days. The prevailing ideas of an age exercise a powerful influence upon military development.[10] It behoves us, therefore, to have a sharp eye for, and to guard against, half-heartedness in our military effort, the hidden working of heresies which hypnotize our common sense by a parade of pseudo-scientific arguments, against any adulteration or dilution of the warlike spirit and of warlike passion, against diplomatic generals, against the interference of political considerations with strategical and tactical decisions, and above all against the tendency to value more highly the art of war and perfection of technical training than the soldierly virtues. And may the army never again foster that timidity in the face of civil law which, in 1806, spared the country, to the great detriment of its own troops, only to leave it unconsumed for the enemy to devour. Let us be spared also the false humanitarianism which would shrink from a desperate fight and give up the attempt to escape in order to save the king his soldiers or his fair cities. The warlike spirit must not be allowed to die out among the people, neither must the love of peace get the upper hand, for all the greater would be the consternation at the moment of awakening. If the Fatherland is to remain victorious we must not let our old ideals of manly courage, fearless scorn of death, and knightly virtue be destroyed, but must cherish and uphold them to the utmost both in this generation and in all that are to come.

Nicht des Geistes sondern des Schwertes Scharfe
Gab dir alles, wiedererstand'nes Deutschland!—
Ruhm und Einheit, aussre Macht und Wohlfahrt
Dankst du dem Eisen!

---

9. Von Boguslawski, *Armee und Volk im Jahre 1800. Mit einem Blick auf die Gegenwart* (Berlin, 1900. R. Eisenschmidt).

10. The systematic efforts of the Social Democrats and kindred organizations to undermine the two main supports of the army, loyalty and obedience, and build up on the ruins their own despotism, will not be touched upon here, the state of affairs being so evident as to render warnings superfluous. We restrict ourselves here to speaking of those expressions of the spirit of the age, which though secret and more obscure, are none the less exceedingly widespread.

CHAPTER 4

From Prenzlau to Lübeck

We turn now to Blücher, and the scene is changed. The stage has been cleared of those learned and enlightened leaders who would have won by art without bloodshed, who would have overcome the enemy by the overpowering force of their strategic calculations and scientific conceptions of warfare, had war not been too rude to pay the least respect to their angles and their lines, their barriers and their spheres of effect.

On the night of the 27th/28th, following Hohenlohe, Blücher entered Lychen and Fürstenberg after a severe march, part of his troops only reaching their quarters at 3 a.m., after covering 28 miles. Hostile cavalry (belonging to Lannes' corps) had followed upon their heels. Weary as they all were, the troops started again in the early morning of the 28th—the day of the capitulation of Prenzlau—with the French cavalry in chase. The latter pressed forward, hot on the scent, and overtook the rearmost Prussians at Lychen. But the rearguard, the Blücher Hussars, turned sharply upon the audacious hunters, the Usedom Hussars of the flank-guard joined in, and together they flung back the French, taking well over a hundred prisoners. This was a first sharp lesson.

Towards evening the column passed Hardenbeck[1] and appeared before Boitzenburg. Here, like the main army on the previous day, it met the enemy. But, unlike Hohenlohe, Blücher did not halt irresolute for several hours. Along with the other generals he had been advised by Hohenlohe to make the northward detour by Schoenermark. Instead, he attacked at once, and the enemy vanished.

There was no news of the fate of the main column ahead of him, and the night passed in tense anxiety. At 4 a.m. (Blücher himself says

---

1. A few miles "west" of Boitzenburg.

3 a.m.), in darkness and thick fog, the column stood ready to move on towards Prenzlau. Then, just as the advanced guard was setting off, stragglers came in with the news of Hohenlohe's capitulation. Blücher himself confessed that they "grieved and depressed him sorely."

His little corps was now alone in the midst of the enemy, for even of Weimar's corps there was no news (Map No. 7). When Hohenlohe laid down his arms he was neither surrounded nor cut off. Blücher was both, for in front of him were the troops assembled under Murat's orders at Prenzlau, and in rear of him, besides Lannes' cavalry, was Bernadotte's I Corps, which after crossing the Elbe at Rosslau had marched by Zerbst-Ziesar-Brandenburg, and on the 28th had already reached the zone between Gransee and Fürstenberg. Unfortunately, the gossip of the inhabitants of Brandenburg had put him on Blücher's track, just as previously the peasantry of Weimar and Erfurt had put Murat's horsemen on the track of the enemy's retreat to the Harz.

> I had to make up my mind without loss of time to turn about at once and go back towards the Elbe, which I did, taking the direction of Strelitz in Mecklenburg. As to what should be done next, I consulted with Colonel von Scharnhorst. . . .

So runs Blücher's report[2] of this memorable moment. Unlike the commanding officer at Pasewalk, he did not send out an officer in search of an enemy to take his surrender. His resolve was fixed at once, and he set his face towards his first objective, the only remaining path of escape. That done, he considered the future. Thus acts the man of courage and common sense.

Presently, Blücher and Scharnhorst agreed upon one of the boldest plans that could well have been conceived in so dangerous a situation. This was, to double back, join Weimar's corps, recross the Elbe and throw supplies into Magdeburg and Hameln, and by this foray in the rear of the enemy to draw upon themselves so many of the latter's troops that the king would be enabled with the aid of the Russians to organize a new defence on the Oder.

Officers and guides were sent out to find the Weimar corps, and to acquaint it with Blücher's intentions and orders for the recrossing of the Elbe at Boizenburg.[3] Unfortunately, they had to return with their

---

2. Before the commission of inquiry.
3. Not to be confused with the Boitzenburg that has figured in the narrative so often. Boizenburg is on the Lower Elbe, in the Luneburg country.

mission unfulfilled. The corps could not be found; it only reached a point between Wittstock and Mirow on that day (29th). Blücher reached the neighbourhood of Feldberg unmolested. His swift resolution had put the enemy completely off the track. Next day he marched by Neu-Strelitz towards Waren, halting at Dambeck, unpursued as yet.

When I arrived at Strelitz, I posted a guard of 1 officer and 30 men at the gate, and issued orders to my corps that no one was to be allowed, on pain of death, to enter the town. I hoped thereby to induce the enemy to behave with consideration.

Even Blücher, it seems, did reverence to the idol of the time, exaggerated respect for private rights. The resources of the little capital would have been very welcome to the hungry troops; the Duke, moreover, was the king's father-in-law, and thus had a double incentive to furnish the king's troops with all that they needed. Massenbach subsequently made it a reproach against Blücher that he had not spared his own country while moving into Mecklenburg, and the old soldier actually felt compelled to defend himself against this absurd charge. So powerful are the prejudices of the time! Yorck alone was free from them, and "failed to understand why one should let one's men go hungry in order to feed the enemy."[4]

On the evening of the 30th, a French flag of truce, which came to Blücher at Dambeck to demand his surrender, was met with a calm and dignified refusal. Marshal Bernadotte had followed up Blücher by Fürstenberg and Boitzenburg. At this point he assumed that the Prussian general had moved on Pasewalk in order to escape to the Oder—like other Prussian columns. On the 30th, therefore, he marched north-eastward. But, reports of a march of the enemy by Feldberg having reached him in the day, he swung round to the W.N.W., and reached the neighbourhood of Stargard, 16½ miles from Blücher's quarters at Dambeck. His advanced cavalry had already caught up the Prussian rearguard. The hunt had begun.

One event, however, came on the evening of the 30th to rejoice the hard-pressed Prussians. Quite unexpectedly, the Duke of Weimar's corps, now under General von Winning,[5] was found to be at Speck, only a short distance from Dambeck. This corps had at first headed

4. Lettow-Vorbeck, *Krieg 1806-7*, ii. 300.
5. The Duke was not only a Prussian general but a sovereign prince, the same who was Goethe's friend and the champion of liberalism in the years after Waterloo. Napoleon's treatment of the duchy of Brunswick (continued on next page)

for Stralsund, but receiving tidings of general disaster, it had turned towards Rostock, with the intention of taking ship there.

Blücher at once assumed sole command of both columns, and now disposed of 22,000 men. For the moment his situation was by no means unfavourable. Frederick the Great had won Rossbach with no greater force, and Bernadotte, his closest opponent, was far weaker than the Franco-German[6] army that had faced Frederick on the 5th of November 1757. One of Bernadotte's cavalry regiments had entered Neu-Brandenburg. Blücher believed him to be still closer, and assumed besides that the French troops at Prenzlau, now free to move, were with him. He calculated, therefore, that the enemy's combined forces were superior to his own, and that they would come on was a fact that admitted of no doubt. Nobody in the French army at this stage expected the Prussians to make any serious resistance. Lannes, for example, wrote to Berthiér on this day that "the Prussian army is so thoroughly terrified that it throws down its arms at the mere sight of a French soldier." The emperor assumed the capture of Blücher and Weimar as immediate and certain. Indeed, after what had happened lately, it was perfectly reasonable for the French marshals to believe that all they had to do was to prevent an easy prey from escaping.

A new appeal to the decision of arms would have utterly surprised them. And this is exactly what Blücher at first proposed. He desired to fight, and trusted that the superiority of his cavalry, both in quantity and in quality, would have neutralized the French superiority in infantry.

In reality, Bernadotte advanced on the 31st of October *alone*. Assembling his corps at Neu-Brandenburg by 7 a.m., he left his exhausted men and a great part of his artillery there, and moved forward with (by his own account) only 12,000 men, 700-800 horse, and 18 guns. In the course of the day he advanced to within some four miles of Dambeck. Had he encountered Blücher, or had the latter marched out to meet him, he would unquestionably have attacked without

showed that he would not allow the same man to be neutral sovereign and hostile general. In the case of Weimar, he had, as already narrated, given the duchess a promise to respect the duchy, and in consequence he naturally demanded the duke's resignation of his Prussian command. With the permission of Frederick William III, the duke therefore handed over the command to Winning.—Tr.

6. A French army and the contingents of the smaller German states forming the army of the Empire, not to be confused with the Austrian "Imperial "army, which was the army of the emperor.—Tr.

waiting for supports; Murat indeed had told him on the evening of the 29th that Blücher had only 12,000 or 14,000 men, and that it was only necessary to find him to bring about his surrender.

In all three arms Blücher was superior to his adversary. In spite of the clumsiness that crippled the Prussian troops, in spite of the spell of past defeats, and even in spite of the marches—or flights—that Prince Hohenlohe had demanded, victory was possible. Exhaustion was no greater a factor on one side than on the other. In the interests of our national history, it is deeply to be deplored that Blücher at this crisis allowed himself to be dissuaded by his entourage and gave up the idea.

Wiseacre strategy could undoubtedly argue that Bernadotte would very likely not accept battle, that if he did so the Prussians might lose it, and that Blücher's army would then cease to possess the attractive force which was to draw the enemy away into the west.

Soult, too, had entered the lists. Kleist's inactivity in Magdeburg had allowed him to cast loose from that place, to cross the Elbe at Tangermünde, and to march in pursuit of Weimar's column by Rathenow towards Wittstock. He had selected this route because he foresaw this very possibility of the Prussians doubling back to the Elbe, and he would presently come up to the west of the Muritz-See. Should Blücher's blow against Bernadotte fail, Soult would be in a position to cut off his retreat, while even if it were successful Soult's appearance in superior force would rob it of all its effect.

These were the arguments with which the old man was assailed, and which led him to give up—with what a heavy heart we can imagine—the project of fighting. Even Scharnhorst advised him that it was more important to gain time than to gain a victory.

Nevertheless, the venture ought to have been made. The old army should not have been denied the satisfaction of showing that even at this stage it was a match for the French. There would have been two things in Blücher's favour—his wholly unexpected determination, which would have had the effect of a surprise, and his superior numbers, factors of great, if not indeed of decisive, importance. The effect that a Prussian victory would have had upon public opinion and upon the enemy's conduct is not to be estimated. In war one must act with foresight, but one must not on that account foresee too many of the possible consequences of a venture. A first success often quite unexpectedly breeds a second, and events take a wholly unforeseen turn. What Murat would have done, what route Soult (who only reached

Wusterhausen on the 30th) would have taken, on the news of a disaster to Bernadotte, it was impossible then, and it is equally impossible now, to say with certainty.

Even if Blücher had failed to turn the course of fate, the pursuit would have been brought to a full stop, and he would have been free to escape by sea and to present his victorious army to the king in Prussia. There, on the Vistula, his appearance would have been an event of high importance.

As it was, prudence only prolonged the existence of his corps for eight days, and it influenced events on the Oder not at all, and those on the Vistula but little.

From the events of this memorable day, we may learn that, for the bold, even in the most desperate circumstances, there is almost always *one* road to safety—and to victory.

****

The continuance of the retreat westward was decided upon. Unnoticed by the enemy, Blücher, who had divided his little army into two corps,[7] reached the neighbourhood of Waren and Alt-Schwerin, with the Müritz-See and Plauer-See to the south of him. And yet on this day his fate was sealed, for the hounds took up the scent from all sides.

Murat, who had hitherto obstinately clung to the idea that Blücher could only move towards the Oder and Hither-Pomerania, now swung in. On the evening of the 31st October he was with the bulk of the cavalry at Friedland. Bernadotte reached Ankershagen near Penslin; forced marching brought Soult to Zechlin; two cavalry regiments under Savary, sent out by the emperor himself, were at Neu-Strelitz; and even Sahuc's dragoon division of Soult's corps, which had been employed on the other side of the Elbe, came to Rathenow. More than 50,000 men set themselves to take Blücher. Unity of command indeed was lacking to this mass, for Murat, the responsible chief, was still distant. But unity of aim and singleness of purpose in pursuit of the object that their Emperor had given, was enough of itself to hold them together so long as no sharp blow severed any link of the chain.

---

7. Each of these corps consisted of an advanced guard of light troops and two divisions of varying strength. Lieut.-General von Winning commanded the 1st Corps, with General von Pletz in charge of the advanced guard; the command of the 2nd Corps Blücher retained in his own hands—an example that is not to be recommended for imitation—and his advanced guard was under General von Oswald. The movement being one of retreat, the two "advanced guards "were in reality rearguards.

Blücher was only imperfectly informed as to the positions of his opponents. But, so far from his desiring to escape, it was actually part of his plan of operation that the enemy should be at his heels. This was, however, a dangerous game, for it meant perpetual fighting in retreat, struggling only to give way, and engaging without letting himself be really overtaken and brought to action. There is hardly a single operation of war that is more ticklish than this. It calls for great skill and resolution in the leaders of all ranks, and great endurance and steadiness in the rank and file. It may bring even fresh troops, well equipped with all necessaries, to the verge of dissolution, and here it was to be carried out by an army already exhausted by a long retreat, and suffering every sort of privation. In order not to break down this army utterly, it was distributed each day into widespread billets, for this country has but few localities of any size. For the next day's march an initial point of assembly was chosen as far back as possible. In the afternoon, if it was certain that the enemy could not attack any more, the columns broke up again. Often night overtook them in the process. Thus were their exertions multiplied—and yet what alternative was there, in the prevailing ignorance of the ways and means of self-help? Then, too, a strong rearguard had to keep the enemy in sight, and *ipso facto* to submit to the enemy's observation itself. Thus there was bound to be serious fighting.

In this fashion the retreat was to continue on the 1st of November, in two columns, the 1st Corps to the south, the 2nd to the north, behind the defiles of the Plauer-See. The march began, but almost at the outset there was a disaster. The French pursuit was chiefly directed against the southern column, and the weak body of cavalry forming its rearguard was cut off in Waren, and surrendered.

Bernadotte, whose deficiency in cavalry had been remedied by the arrival of Savary's regiments, pushed forward at once. Half-way to Nossentin, at Jabel, his advanced guard caught up the Prussian rearguard. Old Pletz, whose fine soldierly figure has been vividly portrayed for us, commanded the latter, and under him Yorck led the rearmost troops. He turned about and deployed in good time, and without delay attacked the French cavalry, as it pressed forward out of Waren, with a half-regiment each of the Pletz and the Kohler Hussars.

It was one of those rare occasions in which nobody wheeled about before the shock. Blade struck upon blade.[8]

---

8. Malachowski, *Erinnerungen aus dem alten Preussen* (Leipzig, Grunow, 1897, p. 41). The Kohler Hussars were recruited in Poland, which shows that the Poles in the Prussian service were not always so unreliable as they are usually assumed to be.

The French were hurled back, and fled into Waren again, leaving numerous prisoners[9] on the Prussians' hands.

Indescribable was the jubilation and delight of all of us. We had seen that the French were not invincible. I am firmly convinced that at that moment our men would have flung themselves upon the strongest enemy and beaten him, and I shall therefore go to the grave with the conviction that the Prussian army of 1806, well led, would have been as victorious as the Prussian army of 1813.[10]

Meanwhile the Prussian infantry had occupied a defile on the route and were holding it against Bernadotte's oncoming infantry. A second brilliant charge, delivered by several squadrons of the Pletz Hussars under Major von Katzler, won them a breathing space. Then they retired step by step, and frequently delivering powerful counter-strokes, through the Nossentiner Wald. The engagement was very brisk, and eye-witnesses said that never save at Wachau[11] in 1813 had they heard so furious a roar of musketry. Behind Nossentin General von Pletz halted again and steadily awaited the enemy. The latter soon appeared, and the engagement reopened with great violence. Meantime Pletz sent to Blücher requesting a reinforcement of a few battalions, with whose assistance he hoped to be able to hold on till evening, "to give the main body a good night's rest for once, after its eternal marching." Instead of the reinforcement, however, there came Captain von Muffling of the general staff, and presently Blücher himself appeared. What followed may best be told in Malachowski's words:[12]

Blücher and Pletz had served together in the Seven Years War as cornets under Belling,[13] and had spent their whole service together in the same regiment. Intimate friends from their

---

9. Malachowski says 300.

10. Malachowski, p. 43. Yorck rode with the attack, and frequently referred to it afterwards with delight. To Malachowski, who had been with him, he said, "We can get home, too, eh?" (*"Nicht wahr, wir können auch einhauen?"*). (Yorck was an infantryman.—Tr.)

11. Battle of Leipzig.—Tr.

12. *Erinnerungen*, p. 42-3.

13. The Prussian general who, in the Seven Years War, held the Swedish army of Pomerania in check with a small containing force. Blücher, then a Swedish officer, was taken prisoner, and joined the service of his captors, Belling procuring him a cornetcy in the Hussars.—Tr.

youth, they conversed in a fashion that was at least blunt, if not actually coarse, while to all other men Pletz was invariably calm and dignified.

The moment he came up Blücher called out, 'Good morning, Pletz. I can't send you[14] any infantry. The fellows are lying all about like dead men and couldn't be got out of the village. You must just show the *canaille* over there your claws—show them well, too—and then they will soon clear off.'

Whereat Pletz, 'If you only came to tell me that, you might have saved yourself the ride, because that will be done anyhow without your advice. They always turn tail at the mere sight of your great moustache, eh? *Ha, ha!* You know very well that there are times when they don't.'

'Well, well! I was only joking,' replied Blücher propitiatingly; and the two old comrades rode forward into the midst of the musketry, discussing trifling matters, joking and teasing one another.

Pletz, in the event, succeeded even without support in checking all onsets of the enemy. It was a glorious day for the Prussians. But, alas! it was only a day's work in retreat, and not a victorious advance.

To the great disgust of Yorck, who would have liked to attack the hesitating enemy once again, the rearguard retreated after nightfall to Alt-Schwerin, where other troops of the southern column stood in support. The enemy followed on, and the opposing forces spent the night in close proximity.

Four names stand out prominently in these days—Blücher, Scharnhorst, Yorck, and Katzler. Yet it was no strange coincidence that brought together on this field these four men who were to play so great a part in the war of liberation. They were present in their ordinary capacity and in the regular line of duty; only of Scharnhorst can it be said that he joined Blücher on his own initiative. There were others, too, of the same stamp, the undismayed Winning, old Pletz, Oswald, and others who were too old for field-service after the war, and we may regard this as a proof that the unfortunate army of 1806 was certainly not destitute in strong characters. When the leadership was resolute and energetic, gave them scope for their action, and freed itself from the mists of a topsy-turvy war-theory, then they came to the surface.

---

14. *Dir* and *du* throughout this conversation on both sides.—Tr.

Bernadotte followed up in the night to Malchow, Soult to Waren. The two came to an understanding. They both assumed that Blücher was retreating on Schwerin, and they agreed to follow him up on a broad front, so as to be able to envelop him on both flanks should he offer serious resistance on the line of the Stör.

The Prussians, however, were on the move again even before daybreak. The enemy failing to follow up, they were able to go into quarters in the region east of Crivitz. But what the French had not done was accomplished by weariness, hunger, and distress. Dead and exhausted men were left lying in the road, and the regiments were thinned without the disintegration of battle. Many of the former errors repeated themselves, bitter experience notwithstanding. The troops left their outlying quarters for the rendezvous of their columns very early, often marching to the starting-points in the dark. Then followed hours of needless waiting, against the contingency of a hostile attack. Only when this anxiety was over and a good march accomplished besides, were the columns broken up and the units sent to the widespread and often hardly discoverable cantonments assigned to them for a brief rest. Even this was frequently broken by alarms on the outpost line that led to needless midnight parading and fresh long waits under arms, after which the column would start on its next day's march wearied to death at the outset. More and more fiercely did old Yorck inveigh against the endless retreat, and the folly of destroying the army in this fashion, instead of risking a battle.

The pursuers had lost touch with the Prussians, and they only advanced again late on the 2nd of November, and with caution. The previous day had made them prudent, and Bernadotte wished to wait for Soult's arrival before attacking in earnest. He therefore marched only to Welzin, north of Lübz. Soult, for his part, was in doubt as to whither Blücher would turn, and, judging by the stubborn resistance that the Prussian leader had hitherto made, it was certain that he would hold on to the bitter end. On the evening of the 2nd Soult reached Plau, and his cavalry Lübz, thus more or less coming into line with Bernadotte. From these points he intended to advance on Parchim and Neustadt, so as to envelop Blücher's right flank on the Stör and to cut him off from the Elbe should he be moving in that direction.

This day, too, unhappily, did not pass without a fresh misfortune for the Prussians, one of whose battalions, belated, allowed itself to be surprised and lost 4 officers and 50 men prisoners as well as a gun.

On this day Murat reached Malchin.

Great was the surprise in Blücher's headquarters at the cessation of pressure, and the old man at once conceived the idea of falling upon the French in order to hold them. But the piteous condition of his troops imposed caution, and he resolved to fall back, first of all, behind the Stör between the Lewitz-Bruch and Schwerin, there to give his men some rest and refreshment. If then the French resumed the pursuit, he would march, slowly skirmishing, to Boizenburg on the Elbe. If the French held off, he would attack them.

On the 3rd of November the main portion of the Prussian army crossed the Stör and went into quarters behind that river, the flourishing little town of Schwerin being, however, as little burdened by their presence as Strelitz had been on the 30th, and for the same reason of dynastic policy. The rearguard still stood fast at Crivitz. Bernadotte again followed up cautiously, even calling up Soult from the route that the latter wished to follow. Then he attacked Crivitz, a low-lying locality, and captured it. But as his cavalry—just as at Waren—pushed through the village into the country beyond, it was unexpectedly charged by the Prussians and flung back with considerable loss, a colonel and one of Bernadotte's own *aides-de-camp* being amongst the prisoners. Nevertheless, this day, too, cost Prussia dear, for on the left flank a mixed column under General von Wobeser and the Usedom Hussar Regiment, falling back on the Stör too late, were attacked by Bernadotte, and driven in upon the east bank of the Schweriner-See. One battalion which missed its way was captured. These things were the natural and practically invariable consequence of continuing to retreat in scattered columns for the sake of scattered quarters.

Bernadotte's corps reached the southern point of the Schweriner-See the same evening, Soult following as far as Crivitz, where also Sahuc's dragoon division arrived after heavy marching. Savary went in quest of Murat, who, under the impression that the Prussian general could have no other object but to escape either to Stralsund or by sea, was still sweeping the country to the north-west, determined above all to head off Blücher from Rostock and the coast. On the evening of the 3rd, however, being now informed as to Blücher's real whereabouts, Murat moved to Güstrow.

On the Stör, at the point where it flows into the Schweriner-See, a bold attack succeeded in wresting from the Prussian grenadiers the important defile of Fähre, and the assailant pushed on to Zippendorf, only 2½ miles from Blücher's headquarters at Ostorf. The two Prussian corps, lying as they did to the north and the south of the breach, were now in imminent danger of being separated, and in any case the line of the Stör was no longer tenable. A continuance of the retreat was inevitable, and now the final decision had to be made as to its direction.

In reality, owing to Soult's having been called up to the northern road, Blücher's right flank and the country Elbe-wards were free from all danger. But unhappily the Prussians remained in ignorance of this turn in Fortune's wheel. All that they knew was that touch with Soult had been lost. Probably they supposed him to be advancing south of them by Parchim, whence he could head off Blücher from the Elbe, and in any case they had become anxious for their right flank. For another thing, the troops that had been forced away on the other side of the Schweriner-See could only be extricated if the army moved north-westwards. Then, fresh anxiety was aroused by the appearance of a small Prussian mixed detachment which, marching in from Hameln, had lately been at Wittenburg and had left that place in order to join Winning's corps. A rumour became current at headquarters that this detachment was being pressed in by the French. A new demand for surrender was sent in to Blücher, and the bearer of the flag of truce, in ignorance or guile, gave out that Murat was actually north of the Schweriner-See. Thus was woven a network of false information and mistaken assumptions to grip the imagination of Blücher and his staff—baleful was the star that presided over every Prussian enterprise in these dark days. It was resolved to march on Gadebusch, and by night into the bargain. And yet the road to Boizenburg was open, and Major Count Chasot, who had been sent thither, had with the aid of the Wittenburg detachment assembled materials for a bridge, which in fact he built in thirty-six hours. Nay, more, it would actually have been easier to march to the Elbe than to Gadebusch. But Blücher believed that his flanks were already turned at the same time as his front was pressed by very superior forces, and he had given up the idea of crossing the Elbe.

Gadebusch was reached on the 4th without mishap. Thither too came the Wittenburg detachment (Colonel von Osten) and General von Wobeser with his troops. A small and scattered detachment (the Tschammer Regiment and battery) was indeed overtaken by the French, but it beat off all attacks. Only the Usedom Regiment of Hussars strayed towards Wismar in the expectation of meeting General Wobeser there, and, not finding him, turned east towards Swedish Pomerania, to fall next day (5th November) into the hands of Savary's cavalry brigade.

On this day (4th November) Bernadotte stayed with his wearied troops just west of Schwerin, while Soult moved on Gadebusch. The French were now certain that Blücher had given up the idea of marching to the Elbe. Murat, too, was at Schwerin, so that the enemy was concentrated in full force. All the same, there was entire uncertainty as to Blücher's further intentions.

Unfortunately, Blücher, even at Gadebusch, believed himself to be surrounded by the enemy on three sides, assuming Bernadotte to be in front, Murat on his left, and Soult on his right. Their force he greatly over-estimated, supposing it to be six or seven times his own. The exhaustion of his troops was extreme. He had already lost 4000–5000 men—more than a battle east of Waren would have cost him. In these conditions the idea of accepting battle was once more given up, although the ground was favourable at Gadebusch. "Farther back still" was the word.

Yet, strange as it may seem, it was just at this moment that for the first time Blücher had really succeeded in imposing respect on his opponents. Murat's report[15] to the emperor, who was growing more and more impatient, breathes something like discouragement. He spoke of the good order in which Blücher withdrew, and said that he had at least 25,000 men, including 5000 cavalry, whereas Bernadotte had but 12,000 foot and 600 horse. "I consider it wise, therefore, that we should concentrate and bring unity into our operations if we are to annihilate him at one blow. His troops are not yet beaten, and Blücher commands their confidence. We must therefore unite and overpower him in mass."

The renewed retreat could be made either towards Lübeck or on Hamburg. The latter city possessed the larger resources. Blücher, however, chose Lübeck, as the road thither was shorter and the town itself more defensible. There was no question that it was in his power to reach it. Within its walls he hoped to obtain a few days' rest and refreshment for his utterly exhausted troops. This gained, he would then risk the last and decisive battle.

On the morning of the 5th, accordingly, the army set out for Lübeck. Following it up, the French found Gadebusch clear, but a little way beyond there they encountered Prussian rearguards, which after skirmishing awhile drew off in the direction of Rehna and also in that of Ratzeburg. The pursuers thereupon divided also, Soult going by Roggendorf to Ratzeburg, Bernadotte taking the Rehna route. Murat himself was with Soult, but the bulk of his cavalry joined Bernadotte.

15. Evening of 4th November, Schwerin.

Blücher had originally intended to halt at Herrn-burg, a few miles S.E. of Lübeck. But it proved impossible to quarter there, and so the march was continued to the city itself. Blücher himself hurried on, and was at Lübeck with the foremost troops by noon, asking the assembled senate[16] to provide large quantities of supplies. Everything now depended upon the attitude which the Danish general Ewald, who commanded a force on the adjacent frontier, meant to observe towards the contending parties. Blücher, therefore, at once placed himself in communication with him. Ewald declared that he would resist by force any infringement of the frontier by either side, and Blücher made his calculations accordingly. The district that he would have to defend presented a very narrow front along the Trave, on either hand of Lübeck, and this he might confidently expect to hold. Lübeck itself was no longer indeed a fortress, but the old ramparts with their broad wet-ditches would be an effective support for the defence. Before nightfall nearly all the little army had come in, and for the first time in these exhausting days was housed in comfortable, concentrated quarters.

On the morning of 6th November Blücher made his arrangements for the defence of the town. The gates were provided with guns, the troops distributed to guard the approaches, commanders told off to the various points, and, confident of being able to deal with any attack, he was so firmly resolved to give no more ground that no line of retreat was named.

All these measures were sound and appropriate. Nevertheless, one mistake was made that was destined to have serious consequences. Blücher himself had allowed General von Oswald and the rearguard of his own (II) corps to remain in front of the town. It was unfortunately the custom in the Prussian army, when a defile had to be traversed, to keep not only cavalry but troops of other arms as well in front of it until the enemy arrived. Herein lurked always the danger that the enemy would enter the defile on the heels of the retiring troops, and so it befell in this instance. When, on the morning of the 6th, Bernadotte attacked Oswald's force, the combatants became intermingled, and Prussians and French pressed on in wild confusion towards the Burgthor, the north gate of Lübeck. The officer in charge of the defence here, the Duke of Brunswick-Oels, unfortunately advanced to disengage Oswald with part of the force guarding the gate. This only added to the confusion. The artillerymen of the guns posted at the

16. Lübeck, it must be remembered, was one of the independent Hanse towns.—Tr.

gate did not dare to open fire upon friend and foe indiscriminately, and the officer in charge, losing his head, actually tried to get the guns away. Driven into the middle of the streaming tide of infantry, these only augmented the confusion, and before anyone could prevent it the enemy was in the town. The key of the defence was lost.

At this very moment, about noon, in the town which he had believed to be absolutely safe for the day at least, army orders were being issued at Blücher's headquarters. The first hint of what had happened was the sound of the firing. Blücher instantly hurried out, flung himself upon a horse that stood ready and, with such troops as he could collect about him at a moment's notice, strove to check the inflowing enemy, while the assembled staff officers dashed away in all directions to warn and assemble their various corps. There was furious fighting in the streets, but the French cleverly spread out, each gate in succession was opened by an attack from the rear, and gradually the whole town was mastered. With a heavy heart Blücher rode out by the last remaining exit, the Holstein gate, narrowly escaping capture. His devoted Scharnhorst was taken prisoner. The fighting was fierce throughout. In the words of Bernadotte's report:

> . . . . the enemy entrenched in the streets and houses made incredible efforts to repel us. Every square, every street was a battlefield. General Blücher himself made several charges with his cavalry in the streets.

But the fate of the brave little army was sealed. Blücher with the remnant of his troops marched to Schwartau, a few miles beyond Lübeck. More than once, as the sound of heavy firing came from the town, he was on the point of turning back again to attempt the rescue of the gallant bands that were fighting still. But this idea, and also the notion of winning back Lübeck by a night-surprise, were given up in the end, as the infantry that had been brought off seemed to him too few and too weary for the enterprise. He therefore stood fast with all that was left of his army at Ratkau, north of Schwartau. Yet not all his officers shared his opinion that an attack on Lübeck was impossible— as witness Malachowski.[17]

> Here stood at least 10,000 good Prussian troops penned between the Trave and the guarded Danish frontier. No one had an inkling of what was going on. From the heavy firing in and

---

17. *Erinnerungen aus dem alten Preussen,* pp. 45-6.

about Lübeck we simply argued that a big fight was in progress, and every moment we expected the order to advance. But no order came, and instead, as night came on, we were told that we had capitulated. My God, who could describe the impression that this accursed word made upon us all? We were dismayed, perplexed, simply stupefied! Most of our men in their rage smashed their muskets and threw them away. And so this night too, the most terrible of my life, passed. . . . Blücher's later renown will never die; yet at Lübeck we had the feeling that strength and resolution had failed even in him. This is one more example of how unjust was the universal condemnation of the army of 1806. It was in great part these very same men who accomplished the heroic feats of 1813.

Scharnhorst, too, as is well known, did not approve of Blücher's action. The latter, indeed, on the morning of the 7th, meant to leave Ratkau and throw himself into Travemünde, which was in those days a fortified place. When, however, the Duke of Brunswick-Oels appeared in company with a French flag of truce and informed him that Travemünde too was in the enemy's hands, he submitted to his fate and signed the capitulation offered him. Once more mischance played its part. The news as to Travemünde was untrue. It was no more than a mere rumour that had come to the ear of the Duke, yet in his excitement he told it with such conviction that Blücher had to accept his evidence as verified and vouched-for fact. Had Scharnhorst been there, the idea of making for the little fortress would not have been tamely let drop. Yet another act of the great tragedy was over. But this act had been of a very different character to its predecessors. This time it was only after heroic efforts and stern fighting that the relic of the army of Jena and Auerstedt and its brave leader had succumbed. With his own hand Blücher added to the act of surrender these words, "I capitulate, because I have no bread and no ammunition," meaning thereby to place it on record that it was neither fear of fighting nor the recognition of the enemy's superiority that brought him to this fateful act. He had taught the French that the Old-Prussian army could fight, and the news from Lübeck spread over the land not merely the renown of Blücher and of Scharnhorst, but even a first faint hope of a better future.

The moral significance of Blücher's expedition must not be undervalued. Not yet indeed was the moment for a general uplifting of hearts. But Blücher's men came forth with a very different spirit from that of the others. Many escaped from the prisoners' convoys and made their way back to the army. Of the Blücher Hussars not one man crossed the Rhine; little by little they reassembled under the Prussian colours.

> Three brave sergeant-majors of the regiment succeeded in getting 300 of the men through to the province of Prussia in a closed body, in reward for which the king made them officers.[18]

The expedition failed because it involved a contradiction in terms. It was conceived in the likeness of the campaigns of one of the great leaders of the Thirty Years War, who used to traverse Germany from end to end. But for this neither the army nor its leaders were fitted by constitution or by habit. Only well-nourished and well-equipped troops, who, when forced marches became necessary, knew how to subsist comfortably at the expense of the country they traversed—only such troops could accomplish exploits of this kind. Blücher's force might indeed have reached the Elbe in good time, crossed it, and by raiding hither and thither in the west, kept the enemy busy for a long time to come. But if they were to do so, they would have had to put aside all ideas of sparing the country as they had spared Strelitz and Schwerin, and unhesitatingly made use of all available resources, for only in this way could they have moved with the freedom and celerity requisite for success. That the men and their officers could fend for themselves, when emancipated from the tutelage of higher authority and from the fear of responsibility learnt in the school of repression, was proved by everyone of the many men who, alone and left to their own resources, made their way through to the Vistula.

If, on the other hand, the principle of "making war support war "was unacceptable, it would have been infinitely better to risk a battle at the outset, when the conditions were favourable, than to embark upon a series of disintegrating retreats and stubborn rearguard rights, which must inevitably end in ruin, and that soon. So it proved in the event. But the event detracts nothing from the glory of the troops that took part in it: it is to be set to the account of their leaders.

---

18. Lettow-Vorbeck, iii. 25.

CHAPTER 5

On the Vistula

King Frederick William reached Cüstrin on the 20th of October, still intending to come to terms with Napoleon immediately. Not so the Queen, who wrote to him on the 20th from Stettin, "For God's sake, no shameful peace! "and at his call, hurried to Cüstrin to join him. There the king received from Lucchesini, whom he had sent to Napoleon on the 18th from Magdeburg, the first account of the terms of peace offered by the emperor. These were—the cession of all Prussian territory on the left bank of the Elbe except Magdeburg and the Alt-mark, an undertaking not to form an alliance with any other German state, and a war indemnity of 100,000,000 *francs* (£4,000,000). An answer was to be given by the 26th.

In the unwarlike entourage of the king the majority was in favour of submission. On the very same day General von Zastrow was dispatched to Lucchesini with the acceptance in principle of the French demands. According to eye-witnesses, the king had recovered his equanimity. He had been opposed to the war, the result had justified him, and his conscience was easier. The queen, on the other hand, was bowed down with grief. To her the country's woes were as a mortal blow.

On the 26th the royal pair set out for Graudenz. At Driesen a false report reached them to the effect that Hohenlohe had reached Stettin in safety and was on the march thence to the Vistula. At this they turned off to the north-west. But then came the tidings of evil, the journey was set eastward by Schneidemüuhl, and on the 3rd of November Graudenz was reached (Map No. 8).

Graudenz, according to an eye-witness,[1] offered a gay spectacle:

---

1. Letter of Count Lehndorff-Steinort from Ostrometzko, 16th November 1806. *(C. F. Reichsgraf Lehndorff-Steinort,* by Maximilian Schmidt. Berlin, 1903.) The original is in French.

The king is in Graudenz with the divine queen and a great number of generals, princes, and officers of all ranks and every corps that exists or has existed in the Prussian army. Almost all of them have escaped from these unhappy days of the 10th-14th of last month. Farther down stream, about Marienwerder, there is re-forming the relic of that superb and wonderful army of 150,000 men that four weeks ago aroused the admiration of Europe by its splendour, its discipline, its energy, its patriotism, and its high spirit. Never, certainly, in Europe had so brilliant an army been brought together at one spot as this, and never probably in the years to come will there be another like it. Nothing is left of it now but some 8000 disbanded wanderers, without arms, who have brought back nothing with them but their lives.

At Graudenz, too, came in the news of the fortress capitulations. "The peace cult spread its slow poison everywhere."[2] Major von Rauch arrived from Charlottenburg with the news that the preliminaries of peace were signed. Meantime Napoleon's demands had become harsher, and he now even demanded under certain conditions the participation of Prussia in his war against Russia. These terms were discussed at Graudenz on the 6th and 7th. Prince William, Prince Henry, Haugwitz, Stein, and some of the senior generals spoke with one voice in favour of peace, but against participation in the war against their late allies the Russians. The king ratified the preliminaries of peace. An attempt of Prince Ferdinand in Berlin to obtain more favourable conditions failed. Even the queen wavered at first, but she soon recovered her confidence. "Firm and patient resistance is our only chance," was her opinion. On the 15th of November the first French troops appeared on the Vistula opposite Graudenz. The king went to Osterode, and the Queen accompanied him thither in spite of the efforts of Haugwitz and Köckeritz to separate her from her husband.

Unhappily, these expectations of peace did serious harm to the military preparations for a renewal of the war. No extraordinary measures were taken, no proclamation calling the nation to arms was issued. The existing *Kanton-Reglement* with its numberless and wholesale exemptions remained in force. The opportunity for new formations on a large scale was allowed to slip. Even field regiments were left to guard

---

2. Paul Bailleu, "Königin Luise im Kriege 1806 "*(Deutsche Rundschau,* 33rd year, No. 1, October 1906), a fascinating and historically very important study, of which we have here made considerable use.

the fortresses, a duty for which the third battalions already told off to them, the numerous escaped prisoners of war, and the recruit depots were perfectly adequate. Three regiments from Silesia, five battalions from Danzig, and two battalions from Graudenz, in all thirteen line battalions, could have been collected, and these, with the troops of East Prussia and South Prussia,[3] would have brought the field force on the Vistula to a respectable figure.

These prolonged negotiations with the enemy moreover aroused distrust in Prussia's allies. In the political sphere as in the military, nothing was done to put affairs in a better condition. Even an agreement with England, valuable as that power's support would have been, was not sought at the price of a frank renunciation of Hanover.

Far otherwise did the victor prepare for the next act. Even on the Elbe, Napoleon had turned his attention to the approaching campaign against the Russians, so much so indeed that for a moment, as recorded above, he had neglected Hohenlohe and Blücher. Russia was now the only Continental enemy remaining that was strong enough to stand in his path. With the means immediately at his disposal, he could not expect to beat her. But even as early as September fresh drafts were on their way to join the *grande armée*, and if these had not yet filled up the gaps in its sadly depleted ranks it was only because of the rapidity of the campaign and the great distances that had to be covered. At the beginning of November he was doing all in his power to hurry up the drafts.

I have much territory to hold, and it is essential that the reinforcements should reach me in good time. The Russians are indeed distant yet, but it is possible that we shall meet them half-way and be at close quarters with them in a month. There is no time to lose. Nothing that came up after the battle would be of much use. Take your measures accordingly.

In these words he wrote on the 3rd of November to Marshal Kellermann., who at Mainz was charged with the duty of sending forward the reinforcements arriving from the interior of France. The dis-

---

3. "South Prussia" was the Posen-Kalisch region, annexed by Frederick William II in the second partition of Poland. Like "New East Prussia" (the Warsaw-Bialystok region), this same king's share in the third partition, it was lost at the peace of Tilsit, and went to form the "Grand Duchy of Warsaw." At the general peace of 1815 Prussia only regained the Posen district, and the name Prussia was henceforward applied only to the two provinces of East and West Prussia to which it historically belongs (Map No. 1).—Tr.

mounted dragoons who accompanied the army were to be mounted on captured horses. A new Grenadier Corps was formed under Marshal Oudinot, and a levy of 100,000 conscripts arranged for January 1807. The emperor dispensed with a thorough recruit training for these levies. He considered it sufficient when they had been put into uniform and provided with greatcoats. Their military education was to be taken in hand again in the fortresses which for the present they were told off to garrison.

In diplomacy, too, his activity was extreme. General Sebastiani was sent to Constantinople, there to raise up a new enemy for Russia, and unluckily the *tsar* Alexander played into his hands by an untimely declaration of war. The insurgent Poles who, through Dombrowski, solicited his help at Berlin, were armed, the emperor, however, on his side undertaking no definite obligation towards them.

Undeniably the French army was much too weak, relatively to the size of the theatre of war. With its allies, it numbered little more than 190,000 men, and it had to hold the whole of North Germany. Had there arisen a man endowed with the capacity and the power to set the masses in motion, its insufficiency would have been manifest. And yet a campaign was on the point of beginning on the far distant Vistula. The notion that Napoleon only knew how to win with the "big battalions" on his side stands in need of correction. At this, the very moment of his greatest triumph, the lack of sufficient forces for the new campaign immediately in prospect made itself most seriously felt.

But he did not hesitate to begin this new campaign. On the 2nd of November Davout was pushed forward on Posen, and the new corps of Jérôme, formed of the Bavarians and Württembergers and now on the march to Crossen-on-Oder, was placed under his orders. Later Davout was entrusted with the protection of the main army's right flank towards Silesia, and began operations by besieging Glogau. On 6th November Augereau marched out of Berlin eastward, on the 8th Lannes moved forward from Stettin. All the available cavalry, other than that employed in the pursuit of Blücher, followed suit; strong though the emperor was in this arm, more was to be brought up, even from Italy, for he was convinced that in his next operations he would have the most urgent need of it. "I am on the frontier of Poland, and in that country one fights for choice with one's cavalry."

On receiving news that the Russians had crossed the frontier into Prussia—prudence being wedded in him, here as always, to boldness—he decided to halt for the moment at Posen.

Comprehensive measures were taken for the subsistence of the army, and the systematic collection of supplies on the Warthe was ordered. In Posen Davout was told to form a great magazine, and in this task he was only too eagerly assisted by the Prussian Administrator *(Kammerpräsident)*, who, on the 13th of November, actually ordered the finance board at Warsaw—which was still occupied by Prussian troops—to send out commissaries at once to comply with Davout's demands as quickly as possible.

All these provisions, however, needed time for their fulfilment, and the emperor had now to deal with an enemy that had not confronted him in the late campaigns. These campaigns had led him through prosperous countries, but now it was very different. From Schneidemühl Lannes reported to him:

> The country from Stettin to this place is exactly similar to that which we traversed when we marched from Egypt into Syria except that here the sand makes the roads even worse. It is impossible to get one day's bread ration for an army corps here. . . .

This state of want induced a renewal of the advance to the Vistula. In the meantime it had become clear that the Russians could not be thinking of an offensive over that river, for all the bridges were destroyed. In mild, damp weather which, all the way to the Vistula, turned the heavy soil of the roads into quagmires, the march proceeded.

Lannes arrived on the 17th opposite Thorn, where was the Prussian advanced guard under General L'Estocq. The town was bombarded and invited to surrender, but in vain. L'Estocq had an interview with Lannes on an island of the Vistula. Judging by the marshal's report, he must have expressed himself with incautious freedom, for it appears that he alluded to the weakness of the Prussian forces, and said that the defence of the line of the Vistula was Prussia's only hope of obtaining tolerable terms of peace, that moreover nothing was known of the Russians or their whereabouts, and so on. It is said he went so far as to allow the French generals to enter the town as peaceful visitors. This story, and others of the like kind, would be incredible were it not that they harmonize only too well with the amazing cosmopolitanism of the epoch that followed the great Frederick's death—the epoch that conceived of war as a game of skill that ought not to spoil the comradely relations between the two sides.

The king himself expressly approved L'Estocq's conduct, and several times instructed Kalckreuth to convey this in writing. "It gives one the greatest pleasure to hear the true Old-Prussian ring again at last." L'Estocq was next authorized "to send over some wine and delicacies, as an act of courtesy" to the French officers. Kalckreuth, although he had complained bitterly of the enemy's lack of *délicatesse* added thereto, "please send Marshal Lannes personally, on my behalf, a big Thorn gingerbread."

In one point, however, this correspondence shows an advance:

If the French wish, by burning the town of Thorn, to heighten the reputation that they have already fairly established for themselves in this regard, then they must be left to do so, and we can only sympathize with the unhappy inhabitants upon whom the fortune of war bears so hardly.[3]

To this extent, at any rate, facts were now looked in the face.

Marching by frightful roads that imposed extraordinary efforts upon his troops, Augereau reached Bromberg on the 20th. Davout had already reached Sompolno on the Warsaw road on the 18th, with a considerable part of Murat's cavalry corps in front of him. The little fortress of Lenczyc was found ungarrisoned and occupied by the French. The Guard was still at Berlin.[4]

The total of Prussian forces now available for field service was 19½ battalions, 55 squadrons, and 8 batteries, in all 20,000 men, under the command of Kalckreuth. At the moment these troops were very widely distributed, their outposts holding the line of the Vistula from Warsaw (later, when the Russians arrived, from Plock) to a point opposite Mewe. Russia possessed at that time fourteen divisions in all, of which, however, five were told off to operate against the Turks, and one was left behind in St. Petersburg and Finland.[5] On the western frontier, therefore, she disposed of no more than eight. Of these, four under Count Buxhöwden, which had taken part in the campaign of 1805, had not had their losses made good and were very weak. The other four, under Bennigsen, crossed the Prussian frontier (as it then

3. Emil Schnippel, *Urkundliche Beiträge zur Geschichte 1806. I. Zum Hundertjährigen Gedachtnis an den Aufenthalt des Königs Friedrich Wilhelm III in Osterode* (Osterode, East Prussia, 1906).

4. Bernadotte was on the road thence. Mortier's VIII Corps pushing up from Holland, had meantime occupied Hanover. Later, Mortier advanced by Mecklenburg and Hither Pomerania.

5. The divisions were of 18-21 battalions, 30-35 squadrons, 5-6 batteries.

was)[6] on the 29th of October, at four widely separated points (Jurburg, Olita, Grodno, and Jalowka). Bennigsen himself hurried on in advance, reaching Pultusk on the 7th of November. He had received orders from the *tsar* to place himself on the Vistula between Thorn and Warsaw, and then to act as he judged prudent. King Frederick William, indeed, at Graudenz, on the 6th of November, arranged a concentration of the whole allied army on the line Osterode-Soldau, and intended for the present simply to observe the line of the Vistula. Bennigsen, however, continued to advance concentrically on Pultusk, notifying the king of his movements.[7] On the 20th his four divisions were at Plonsk, Pultusk, Prasnysz, and Warsaw. Buxhöwden followed by way of Bialystok, which point he reached in the middle of the month. His group was to serve as the reserve of Bennigsen's, but it was to regulate its own movements in concert with the other—a most vague and unsatisfactory arrangement. Kalckreuth collected his own forces about Osterode. Thither on the 16th came Frederick William; next day he approved Bennigsen's dispositions, and arranged for communication between the two armies.

At this point he was called upon to make a new decision, and one, too, of the most far-reaching importance. Napoleon's demands had adapted themselves to the news of Lübeck and Magdeburg. He announced that the terms that he himself had proposed no longer held good, and on 16th November he presented others to the Prussian envoys. These required nothing less than the evacuation of the whole Prussian monarchy up to the Vistula, with the exception of a few unimportant fractions, and of the Vistula fortresses to boot, as the indispensable preliminary to an armistice, while nothing was said as to what Napoleon would undertake to do in case the negotiations broke down. The king was, further, to take care that the Russian forces that had entered Prussian territory were withdrawn behind their own frontier. In spite of these unheard-of demands, Frederick William was at first still undecided. It was in his temperament to be afraid of sudden great resolves. Haugwitz and most of the generals around him were for accepting. A new conference was called (Baron von Stein[8] amongst others being present), which

---

6. See Map No. 8.

7. Map No. 8. The Russian divisions were generally known by the names of their commanders—2nd Ostermann, 3rd Sacken, 4th Galitzin, 6th Sedmoratzki. The positions of these units are given above in this sequence.

8. The famous statesman and reformer was by birth the independent sovereign of the little barony *(Freiherrschaft)* of Stein on the Lahn.—Tr.

discussed the question on the 20th and 21st of November. The ministers Voss and Stein, General Köckeritz, and Privy Councillor Bey me gave it as their opinion that in the circumstances the armistice should be rejected. The king was influenced also by an encouraging letter from the *tsar* Alexander which, written on the 3rd, and received apparently at Graudenz on the 14th, had weighed with him in choosing the direction of Osterode. We need have no doubt, either, that Queen Luise was in favour of refusal. Her influence on the king's decision cannot indeed be proved by documents, but it is clear that the suite felt it instinctively. Misfortune had but strengthened and ennobled this great woman, whose character attained its perfection in these dark days. Heinrich von Kleist wrote on 6th December:

> This war has been worth more to her than a whole lifetime of peace and pleasure. She has developed a truly royal character before our very eyes, and now she grasps the great object on which everything depends, she whose whole soul, but a short time back, seemed absorbed by the desire to please in the ballroom or on horseback. She has gathered around her those of our great men who, though slighted by the king, must prove our only salvation. She it is who holds together the elements which are not yet fused.[9]

According to a diplomat's report at the end of the war:

> From the very beginning of the campaign the Queen has never for one moment acted contrary to her instinct for heroism and tenacity. Everyone connected with the Court either by interest or devotion has followed her lead with enthusiasm.[10]

On the 22nd, then, the king definitely rejected the French proposals, and personally communicated his decision to Napoleon's envoy, General Duroc, who had come to Osterode to receive the ratification, but was sent away empty-handed instead. It was doubtless largely the demand that the king should entirely renounce the Russian connection that turned the scale. Such a proceeding would not only have been a breach of faith, but might also have brought down upon him the danger of a fresh war. But of still greater weight

---

9. See the above-mentioned essay by Paul Baillen.
10. From the same. It is in the report sent by the Swedish ambassador Brinckmann to his government.

was the new spirit which manifested itself in the king and in some of his advisers, now that they were fighting at the last ditch and for the last province. To the *tsar* Frederick William wrote:

> Accept, sire, the solemn promise of my unyielding resolution never to lay down the sword before the enemy of Europe's independence, unless your interests, from now onwards inseparably bound up with my own, should lead you to desire it. This is my steadfast resolve.

Lucchesini and Zastrow were recalled from the French headquarters. The die was cast, and the war was to proceed. It was fortunate for Prussia, for at the back of Napoleon's mind there were schemes that might well have involved her complete extinction. As he had indicated to the Prussian envoys, he intended to make a definitive peace dependent upon the further conditions that France, Spain, and Holland were to have their lost colonies restored and the complete independence of Turkey was to be guaranteed as against Russia. The proud monarchy of Frederick the Great was thus to serve him as a means of bargaining for minor and outlying concessions. It was evident that nothing less than Prussia's continued existence was at issue.

It is worth while to dwell a little longer upon these decisive days at Osterode, for in a certain measure the regeneration of the Prussian monarchy can be dated from them. Here, in this little country town of East Prussia, there were taken the most important resolutions of our national history. The disastrous policy of standing neutral between the world-powers was now at an end, and the king had definitely emancipated himself. Diplomatic activity assumed fresh vigour. The courts of Vienna and London were informed of the change. Haugwitz, the man of the old time who disputes with Massenbach the title of "Prussia's evil genius," retired from the foreign ministry to make way for Baron von Stein.[11]

The army, too, was to be reformed. There was, of course, no opportunity for a thorough reorganization. But its tactical methods were to be brought as soon as possible into harmony with the requirements of the new warfare. On the 16th and 18th of November the king sketched out with his own hand "Instructions and Suggestions for, and Principles of, Tactics" for the guidance of the general officers commanding in East Prussia.

---

11. The king had offered Stein this office as early as 20th November, *viz.* before the discussion on the armistice took place (Max Lehmann, *Stein,* i. 442).

I have already pointed out in another place that it is absolutely impracticable for the weaker side to gain the upper hand by means of skilful strategic manoeuvres. The enemy with whom we have to contend is far too experienced and sensible for things of the sort not to have long ago lost all effect on him. Care must always be taken to oppose the enemy with superior force; and as long as this is impracticable, one must go to work prudently and seek to resist all decisive engagements.

Simple as this sounds to us, it was for its time a most important departure from the filigree strategy which had hitherto dominated even the best minds of the army—the strategy in which the geometrical figure described by an army's movements had mattered more than its stored-up energy, and favourable ground been thought to be more important than numbers.

In the next place the king laid down that outposts should be pushed farther forward, and that they should consist only of cavalry, especially *cossacks* and partisans. This ended the unfortunate custom of posting infantry and artillery in rear of the cavalry and in front of the positions to be covered—the custom that, as we have seen above, brought about the deplorable mishap at the gate of Lübeck.

In advancing towards the enemy, independent columns were to be formed, each preceded by its own advanced guard. The columns, assuming them to be divisions, were to be disposed by brigades abreast, so as to be able to form up rapidly, "which is one of the most important things of all on the day of battle."

The defence was to be maintained by the use of good positions, and not by advancing to the attack in the way in which tactical salvation had hitherto been supposed—in theory at least—to lie. Extensive use of heavy guns for the defence of a position was recommended. For a prolonged defence the king pointed out the desirability of having a reserve corps, and also undisclosed flanking corps to right and left of the line. In attack, an envelopment in force of the enemy's wing was to be combined with a frontal attack; the artillery was to support the attack vigorously from positions in rear, the horse artillery alone accompanying the infantry advance.

As a rule two lines were to be formed, the task of the first being the skirmisher fire-fight, that of the second, which was to be formed in columns, to close with and break the enemy.

All irresolution and hesitancy is supremely dangerous in an attack. Once the decision has been made, let there be no tarrying after the troops are in line. A swift and resolute advance to close quarters is the one and only way to victory.

Victory achieved, it is the cavalry's work to bring it to fruition, and to that end the cavalry must be at hand.

Generals and field officers of the cavalry must be invariably on the alert to profit instantly by any weak point the enemy may present, *for here a moment often decides. Exhaustive instructions are not to be given before a battle.*

For how could they fail to evoke reminiscences of those orders for sham-fights that before the war had pretended to give a carefully pre- pared and faithful picture of the reality—orders that prearranged the minutest details, covered many sheets of foolscap and were elaborated with the utmost care—or of the sixteen-page pamphlet which, little more than ten years before, set forth Count Wurmser's dispositions for the attack of the Weissenburg lines?

Further, the manner of effecting the deployment, on which of old so much priceless time had been wasted, and which it had been usual to regard as the highest test of tactical art,[12] was now to be left to each division. "There is only one best way—the quickest." This meant a complete breach with the old linear tactics, which had clung desperately to the idea of the phalanx of 28-30 battalions movable *en bloc* at the command of one man. It meant that the troops were released from the rigid fetters and formalities that had hitherto bound them. The teaching of Saldern and Lacy had lost its charm. But above all, it set the official seal of justification on the independ- ence of subordinate commanders.

The commanding general cannot be omnipresent. He has to supervise and conduct the whole as a whole, and especially to direct the reserves properly.

It was impossible, of course, that these important principles should take instant effect. Inbred customs and long-standing traditions are not easily eliminated, especially in an army which held the past in such high reverence as did the Old Prussian. Such things die hard. A good deal of the former sealed-pattern methods, the clumsiness, and above all the lack of initiative, manifested itself still and for many days to come. A long period of time was required, and younger men

---

12. See the author's *Von Rossbach bis Jena*, 528 ff. 9.

had to reach the higher ranks, before the new spirit could really live. Kalckreuth and L'Estocq were too advanced in years and too thoroughly impregnated with the Frederician traditions to feel at home in, and adapt themselves to, so complete a transformation in the way of making war. But at any rate the king's orders paved the way for improvement.

Further measures followed.

The prince of Anhalt-Pless was named governor-general of Silesia, and, what was more important, Major Count Gotzen, the king's *aide-de-camp*, was appointed to his staff to conduct the defence of the province. Gotzen was destined to become the national hero of Silesia. Further, the king for the first time made up his mind to take extraordinary measures. The words of the prince's instructions ran:

> The critical condition of the state demands the employment of extraordinary resources, and these must be called upon, especially in Silesia, with military energy.

Recruits were to be levied, stragglers collected, the fortresses defended with energy. The formation of a field-force was recommended, and the prince and his *ad latus* invested with far-reaching powers. This last, at any rate, was distinctly an advance.

On the 25th of November the king journeyed to Pultusk to the Russian army. Next day he placed the Prussian troops under Bennigsen's orders. Field-Marshal Kalckreuth, who did not care to serve as Bennigsen's subordinate, was relieved of his command and appointed governor of Danzig, General L'Estocq taking his place at the head of the Prussian field forces. On the 27th the king returned, his headquarters being established at Ortelsburg. Thence, on 1st December, he issued the celebrated *Proclamation Regarding Various Abuses in the Army*, the preamble of which runs as follows:

> Whereas, unhappily, the almost complete dissolution of the various army corps[13] which took the field against France, has hitherto prevented his majesty from receiving any trustworthy information whatever which should enable him to distinguish the true from the false and rumour from fact, or to reward and punish according to the deserts of each; therefore all decisions on these matters are to be suspended until such time as they can be dealt with with more knowledge and certainty.

---

13. Meaning, of course, simply *corps of troops.*—Tr.

This was followed by a statement of the provisions of the law with regard to unfaithful fortress commandants, officers who capitulate in the open field, and all who leave their corps without good excuse, or have otherwise shown themselves wanting in loyalty, firmness, or courage. To these were appended new and stringent rules for the future which remind one vividly of the well-known exhortation of Frederick the Great before Leuthen. And, further, there was another new regulation of the highest importance:

In unforeseen emergencies, *e.g.* in forced marching, retreats, etc., a commander of any rank, in any place, has power to obtain by requisition the quantities that he may need for the men and horses of his command. A receipt will be given.

If such a regulation had only been made at the outset, how many things would have turned out differently! But how hard the king found it to give an order so entirely opposed to his own previous views may be argued from what follows: "If he requisitions more, he is to be shot to death."[14]

One more event is to be recorded. On the 28th of November Scharnhorst, having been exchanged, returned from captivity, and at Danzig once more set foot on ground still held by the troops of his own sovereign.

The paralysing effect of the thunderbolts of Jena and Auerstedt appeared to be wearing off. A new spirit, or rather the Old-Prussian spirit, began to awake.[15]

****

Napoleon had assumed the acceptance of his armistice conditions as a certainty, which shows how confidently he relied upon Frederick William's unalterable love of peace. He supposed that the terms would be signed at Graudenz on the 21st of November, and already began his preparations for taking over the Vistula fortresses. On the 24th he received word from Duroc that the latter had found the king gone from Graudenz and was following him. The emperor's impatience grew. On the 25th the headquarters set out from Berlin for Posen, and it was at Meseritz on the road thither that Napoleon received, with the greatest astonishment, the news that his terms

---

14. The manifesto is reproduced verbatim in *1806: Das preussische Offizierkorps* (Great General Staff, Berlin, 1906), p. 7.

15. Bailleu, "Königin Luise" *(Deutsche Rundschau,* vol. 33, i. October 1906), p. 51.

were rejected. His unavowed desire was to give his army the winter quarters that it so badly needed, and, spoilt child of fortune as he was, began to take the wish for the deed. Now, in his ill-humour, he decided to dethrone the house of Brandenburg, as evidenced by a half-written but never-finished document that he wrote.[16]

The news of the appearance of the Russians at Warsaw, whence they pushed forward an advanced guard to the Bzura, had already led Napoleon to set his available forces in motion thither. Lannes was to approach Davout, Ney to replace Lannes on the side of Thorn, Murat to go to the front and assume temporary command there. Augereau's corps was added to his forces.

Now that hopes of an armistice had proved baseless, further steps were taken. The Guard, Soult, and Bernadotte (the last named only reached Berlin on the 28th), and three cavalry divisions lately employed in hunting Blücher were ordered in. At first all these moved on Posen, which the emperor and his suite entered at 10 p.m. on the 27th.

> The man of force was once more at the head of his army. With one or two fierce blows he expected to send the Muscovites whirling back into their own distant land, to give his faithful followers winter quarters, and thus at a better season and with refilled ranks to begin a new campaign.[17]

He was still far from suspecting the bitter disillusionment in store for him, but the reports of his marshals began little by little to disquiet him. Lannes reported that it was just as impossible to subsist near Thorn as it had been at Schneidemühl. "The road from Bromberg hither is almost impassable; it goes through ground in which horses sink to their bellies." Augereau, speaking of his march from Bromberg past Thorn and up the Vistula, "We are traversing a waste that yields us no supplies. The men are bivouacking, and many of them have no greatcoats. . . . The roads are appalling, and the season is hard." He adds that his men had brought three days' bread with them from Bromberg, and that supplies for three more days were in the wagons, but that it was impossible for the latter to follow up. The difficulty of supplying the army on account of a possible offensive of the Allies from the Lower Vistula, caused uneasiness at times to the emperor, who had hitherto never been moved by such anxieties when he was aiming at a decision. He was not accustomed to be

---

16. Lettow-Vorbeck, *op. cit.* iii. 96.
17. Lettow-Vorbeck, iii. 58.

held up by such elementary obstacles, as these appeared to him to be, and he urged his marshals forward unceasingly.[18] Equally untiring was his activity in diplomacy and in the administrative work of preparing reinforcements for the army.

****

Meanwhile Bennigsen, who it will be remembered had been given the supreme command of the Prussians and Russians, had decided to evacuate the line of the Vistula and to fall back to Novogrod on the Narew. L'Estocq was to close in on his right flank. The Prussian leader, emboldened by some successful forays on the left bank, had desired to hold the line of the river longer, as indeed did the king. But as he had to retreat, he did so in the general direction of Angerburg,[19] in order to be able to check a French advance on Königsberg by threatening it in flank.

Warsaw, which had been held by Prussian troops up to the 28th, was evacuated by the Russian division of Sedmoratzki as soon as the French cavalry approached. On the 1st of December the Russians precipitately abandoned Praga[20] as well. The bridge connecting the two places was set on fire, but only half destroyed. The natural fear of being turned by a French movement through Galician[21] territory, and the consideration that the arrival of ice drifts on the Bug might sever this division from the main body, appear to have been the motives of this, from the Allies' point of view, regrettable episode. Napoleon indeed had expected it. He had already written to Murat:

> If the enemy commits the folly of evacuating Praga, you are to seize this suburb, re-establish the bridge, and prepare a good *tete-de-pont*. . . . Immediately thereafter you are to try to pass the Bug.[22]

But it was more difficult to carry out the order than he supposed. Murat occupied Warsaw and set to work, but only slow progress was made.

The general movement of the Russians began on the 2nd of December, in the first instance to Ostrolenka. The Prussian corps retired from Thorn to Gollup, cavalry, however, being left on the Vistula.

---

18. Lettow-Vorbeck, iii. 96.
19. Map No. 9.
20. The suburb of Warsaw on the right bank of the Vistula.—Tr.
21. *i.e.* Austrian. See Map No. 8. Neglect of the possibility of Napoleon's violating neutral territory had contributed largely to the disaster to Mack's army at Ulm.—Tr.
22. The united stream of the Bug and Narew below their confluence is called indifferently by either name. In the present work, in conformity with Lettow-Vorbeck, it is called the Bug.

At Posen, Napoleon, perplexed by the course of events, at first thought that the Russians were going into winter quarters, and hoped that his own army would be able to do the same. Varying news evoked in him varying schemes, and bitterly he realized the distances and the difficulty of conveying reports. On the 2nd of December, receiving word from Murat that Warsaw had been evacuated by the enemy, he jumped to the conclusion that Murat's cavalry divisions must already be on the Bug, Davout across the Vistula, Lannes in the Polish capital, Augereau throwing a bridge at the mouth of the Bug. Ney's crossing at Thorn he expected to take place on the 2nd. But all this was illusion. The emperor's wishes raced ahead of possibility. The days were frosty; ice drifts had appeared on the Vistula. Even on the 9th, a whole week later than Napoleon expected, Davout had not yet got his troops across, and effective work on the damaged bridge was only just about to commence.

Meantime, Bennigsen too was disconcerted by the enforced delay of the French on the Vistula. He realized that he had far too lightly given up that broad, and at this season easily defensible, river and on the 4th at Ostrolenka he decided to turn back, telling L'Estocq, who on the 6th reached Strasburg, to retake Thorn. But this sudden fit of enterprise was soon followed by a return of apprehensiveness. Bennigsen halted on the Ukra, and entirely let slip the precious opportunity of attacking and crushing the French detachments on the right bank of the Vistula, which were not only scattered but, further, divided by the lower Bug. Not only this, but he did not even guard the ground between the Vistula and the Ukra.

L'Estocq for his part only advanced as far as Gollup. There he received erroneous information that Thorn was already strongly garrisoned by the enemy, and he fell back to Lautenburg.

All this marching and counter-marching passed wholly unperceived by the French.

****

Napoleon meantime anxiously awaited at Posen the establishment of a passage over the Bug, for he seems to have taken it for granted that the bridging of the Vistula must have been successful. But the news did not come, and now he inclined to the idea of facilitating the advance of his right wing on the Warsaw side by pushing his rearward corps over the river at Thorn. His first operation orders on the 13th were drafted accordingly. At this date, moreover, the Thorn bridges were ready.

Out of the cavalry divisions that had been directed towards Thorn he formed a II Reserve Cavalry Corps under Marshal Bessiéres. This was ordered to march by Rypin and Biezun. and ultimately to reconnoitre the line Pultusk-Willenberg, where the emperor's rich and restless imagination placed the Allies. Ney was directed on Strasburg and ordered to push out his light horse on the Königsberg road. Soult was to cross the Vistula at Thorn and Wlocklawek, and the Guard and Bernadotte were directed upon Thorn, whither Napoleon himself proposed to go. This division of his army into two widely separated groups, so contrary to Napoleon's usual practice, was forced upon him by the difficulty of crossing the Vistula and the want of supplies. If the Russians gave ground and retired into winter quarters he proposed to follow them up with the whole of his numerous cavalry, but no other troops. A report from Murat that the Russians were really retiring seemed to him on the night of the 13th/14th to confirm his hypothesis.

At last a French detachment got across the Bug at Okunin and maintained itself on the other side. Napoleon assumed from this that the bridges were finished both at Warsaw and on the Bug. He was right as regards the first, but the unfinished Bug bridge had been carried away by floating ice, and the Vistula bridge at Zakroczyn was not even begun.

On the 15th Napoleon altered his plans. The news from Warsaw decided him in favour of passing there with the bulk of his army. The retreat of the Russians was now evident. Bessiéres, Soult, and Ney, therefore, as well as Bernadotte, who was following them by Thorn, were to take a more southerly direction. The emperor himself marched with the Guard for Warsaw. Pultusk was named as the common objective, with the idea of bringing the two army groups closer together and having them in hand for a battle. At 2 a.m. on the 17th, receiving a report that the Russians seemed to have really come to a halt at this point, he ordered Soult to join the Warsaw group by the left bank of the Vistula. The command of the far-distant left group he handed over to Bernadotte. Augereau was told to urge on the bridging operations at Zakroczyn. "It is high time for us to extricate ourselves from our present situation and to drive away the Russians and go into winter quarters." Murat was to assist him, and he hoped to bring off the desired battle on the 20th or 21st. His latest experiences, however, might have told him that this was impossible, and yet he calculated upon bringing up Jérôme's corps from Silesia and so bringing his available total to 140,000—an idea which still further outran the facts.

The frost had meantime given place to thaw, and the roads had become bottomless mires. Napoleon himself was delayed, although he travelled in a light country cart. It was midnight on the 18th/19th ere he entered Warsaw. He found his brother-in-law Murat ill with fever. His reports of the marshals had a gloomy ring; food was lacking for the men's sustenance, timber for the bridges. There was no news from the left group, and uncertainty as to the enemy's positions and purposes. Winter quarters were the one universal desire, but events would not be hurried. Bernadotte was not able to draw in rightwards as fast as Napoleon desired. Augereau's building operations were very slow. Soult was looking for a new point of crossing, which he eventually found at Drobrzykow, just above Plock. Three weeks had already been wasted on the Vistula—for Napoleon an unheard-of stoppage.

At last, on the 22nd, came the welcome news that the Bug bridge at Okunin was ready, and the worst of the danger was over for the troops on the right bank of the Vistula. At once there went forth the orders that were to rid the army of its troublesome opponent. Davout was to cross the Bug and extend along the Ukra, attacking the Russians behind that river if they were not too strong. The whole of the cavalry at Warsaw—I Reserve Cavalry Corps—was put in motion, Nansouty taking over the command owing to Murat's illness. Augereau was to advance on Plonsk by the right bank of the Ukra, and Soult had already named that point as his own objective. The Guard was moved up from Warsaw. The left army group under Bernadotte was given Biezun as its point of direction.

During this time the Prussians stood fast at Lautenburg, the old-fashioned mixed detachments being pushed out to the front. The Osterode decree had evidently produced no effect as yet, for 25 squadrons stood idle with the main body. A detachment sent out to Biezun to connect with the Russians was driven off on the 20th by the French cavalry, and General von Diericke was dispatched to support it with reinforcements. Arriving before the town on the 22nd, he first refrained from attacking and then, in planning a surprise assault for the 23rd, allotted to the task no more than two small mixed columns. One of these was suddenly attacked and captured by the French cavalry, whereupon Diericke gave up the enterprise, not daring to use the rest of his troops, who had stood idle spectators of the mishap. This was leadership of the sort that characterized the disastrous October days.

L'Estocq's advanced troops were likewise expelled from Gurzno, and the Prussian general thereupon retired on Soldau. In thus taking the direction of Königsberg this small force sacrificed its connection with the Russians for the sake of covering Prussian territory, just as the Prussian headquarters had intended on the 9th of October to separate Tauentzien's corps from Hohenlohe's army and to send it to Dresden for the reassurance of the Saxon court. At Soldau L'Estocq broke up his force into seven groups and distributed it between Neumark and Mlawa, in a broad zone measuring 28 miles front and 9 depth. Thus even at this stage the disastrous practice of dissemination which had already done so much harm still figured in the armoury of Prussian strategists.

Bennigsen, therefore, was left to his own devices in the angle between the rivers Ukra and Narew. He awaited the coming of Buxhöwden, who was now approaching Ostrolenka. Two divisions under General von Essen I that had been called up from the Turkish frontier had reached Brest, 116 miles short of Warsaw.

Another bar to success on the Allies' side was the want of unity in the commanders. Bennigsen and Buxhöwden were independent of each other. The *tsar* had sent General Tolstoi to act as his personal representative, and these three officers formed a sort of triumvirate for the direction of the army. The question of a commander-in-chief for the whole had long been in dispute, but in the end the choice fell on old Count Kamenskoi, whom the voice of Russian military and political circles, in Moscow especially, named as the worthiest and most capable adversary to oppose to a Napoleon. Formerly, indeed, in the old Turkish wars, Kamenskoi had been a meritorious commander, but he was now out of date, over seventy years of age, an eccentric old man who was neither physically nor morally qualified for the command of a great army. He was, indeed, well aware of this, and pointed it out with the utmost frankness to the *tsar*, demanding at the same time his recall.

Kamenskoi's first intention—the natural one for any newcomer—was to drive back the French over the Vistula. But his dispositions were little suited to that end. According to these, Bennigsen was to advance to Sochocin, while Buxhöwden divided his army into two equal wings,[23] each of which was to come up on one flank of Bennigsen's, and the left to advance between the Bug and the Narew on Popowo, and so towards Warsaw, which was also the ultimate destination of Essen I. Here, too, dissemination of force is the watchword.

The whole plan was quickly dislocated—before indeed its execu-

---

23. Buxhöwden's army or group consisted of four divisions: 5 Tuchkov, 7 Dokhturov, 8 Essen III, 14 Anrepp (subsequently Kamenskoi).

tion had seriously begun. It was fortunate for the Russians this time that it was so, for Napoleon could have concentrated superior forces against them before the scheme matured. For in fact he anticipated them by forcing the passage of the Ukra near Czarnowo, close to its junction with the Bug.

The Russians at this point had abandoned a wooded island in midstream to the French. The emperor, who had reached the bridge at Okunin between 9 and 10 on the morning of the 23rd, betook himself thither at once, and from the roof of a house reconnoitred the position of the Russians opposite, which was separated from him only by a narrow channel and by the meadows in the angle between the two rivers. The position was a line of low bluffs which formed the third side of the triangle. Field-works had been constructed thereon, but so far as could be seen the force of the defenders was small. It was decided to attack at once, and the construction of a bridge from the right bank of the Ukra to the island was promptly begun. Some of Davout's troops commenced the passage, and by nightfall all was in readiness. The last arm of the river was crossed in the dark, the weak Russian outposts in the meadow-land fell back on their main position, and this in turn, still in the darkness, was carried with a rush by Davout's greatly superior forces, the Russians retreating with serious losses about dawn. The troops defeated were part of Ostermann's division, which was stationed at Nasielsk.

Field-Marshal Kamenskoi's forward movement, as we may well imagine, proceeded but slowly over the bottomless roads; moreover, it was part of the scheme to wait for Buxhöwden to come up. When the news of the engagement at Czarnowo on the 23rd/24th spread the advance came to an entire standstill. The old field-marshal's powers of self-control began to desert him, and he rode to and fro amongst the troops making wild speeches. Bennigsen, although the junior of the three higher commanders, found himself obliged to take the command into his own hands again, and on his own responsibility ordered the retreat to Pultusk. This was successfully accomplished, in spite of ah difficulties, though not without more or less severe rearguard fighting. This time Napoleon's impatience saved his enemies.

The French followed slowly, fighting their way against hunger, privation, and the mire. Of the enemy nothing certain was or could be known, for even the cavalry could not get forward in the knee-deep mud, and the Cossacks, knowing the country and its peculiarities, made good their superiority in reconnaissance and screening duties.

Napoleon reached Nasielsk on the 24th, still in a state of great uncertainty. He considered it possible that he might be attacked by the Russians in great force, and took measures to repel them.[24] On the following day, 25th, he turned north-westward on Novemiasto with Davout's corps, in order to facilitate the crossing of the Ukra by the other columns. Learning that these had already succeeded in passing and that Augereau and Soult were approaching, he turned north towards Ciechanow. Murat, recovered from his attack of fever, overtook the emperor and passed on rapidly to the front with such cavalry as was at hand. He managed to catch up the enemy's marching columns as well, and a fight took place at Lopaczin. Napoleon, coming up to this place, learned that the Russians had retired part on Golymin, part on Ciechanow.

The French advance from the Ukra and Bug now took definite shape. Lannes on the right wing was given Pultusk as his objective. On his left, Davout moved by Strzegocin, and Augereau along the Sonna, and, farthest west, Soult marched by the left bank of the Ukra from Sochocin. To each of these columns part of the I Reserve Cavalry Corps was assigned, but the bulk of the mounted troops under Murat himself hastened on ahead of Augereau. The general direction of the movement was towards the line Ciechanow-Golymin-Pultusk, where the emperor hoped to meet and beat the Russian army. The enemy's centre of gravity he supposed to lie at Ciechanow, upon which point he meant to concentrate the bulk of his own forces. It seemed that heavy masses of the Russians, 20-30,000 men, were thereabouts, and from its position with respect to the road-system Ciechanow was a more likely point of concentration for the Russians than Pultusk. Further, he reckoned upon Bernadotte's striking in on the enemy's right flank, though as news of the right group was lacking this was pure speculation.

Bennigsen's choice of Pultusk was undoubtedly wrong, and the alternative course with which the emperor credited him must be considered as the only logical one. For it was impossible for some of the Russian troops to reach Pultusk, the French already barring the way thither. The march of the Russians by saturated wood and field

---

24. Berthiér was told to write to Soult (Nasielsk, 24th December): "As we are in the midst of the hostile army, which is caught *en flagrant dèlit*, we may be attacked tomorrow by 30-40,000 men. The emperor's intention therefore is that you should march with your whole corps tomorrow at 3 a.m., to come to Nasielsk" (Derrécagaix, *Berthiér*, ii. 190).

tracks was naturally not accomplished without considerable losses in *materiel*; 50 guns and a great deal of baggage stuck fast and had to be abandoned. There was also much confusion, for besides Bennigsen, Kamenskoi also issued orders in his lucid moments. It was only on the morning of the 26th that the old man left the army, after giving a final order that it was to retreat on its own country.

On this day, 26th, Bennigsen stood fast at Pultusk to give time for his scattered columns to come in. The position which he took up, south of the town, was a line of low hills, the left flank resting on the Narew depression, the right on Moszyn. In front, at a mile and a quarter's distance, were the edges of the woods, towards which the ground sloped down gently. In all, Bennigsen appears to have assembled 40,000 to 45,000 men here. On the same day Lannes, coming up from Nasielsk, debouched from the woods into the open, and on Lannes' left from the direction of Strzegocin appeared Gudin's division of Davout's corps, now commanded by General Daultanne.[25] The two units combined numbered about 26,000 combatants.

Lannes resolved to attack. The emperor in writing to him had referred to the "relatively small hostile forces" which were retiring before him. His cavalry likewise reported but few of the enemy, for part of the Russian position—towards Moszyn—was out of sight. He therefore confidently expected victory.

It was in these conditions that the battle of Pultusk took place. After a stubborn contest which lasted until evening, the French were repulsed with not inconsiderable loss. Daultanne reported to Marshal Davout in the night following the battle:

> This has been a bad business. We have failed to capture the Pultusk position, and the troops of Marshal Lannes were unable to hold their own. In order not to put this corps in difficulties, my division was obliged to hold on to its position until 8 p.m., after which it had to retire. I am glad to say that this movement, a difficult matter in the existing conditions, was successfully executed. I have many wounded. The troops fought all day in knee-deep mud, and I am consequently obliged to rest for the moment. The most serious thing is that the ammunition is spent, and it seems practically impossible to get the ammunition wagons up. I shall do my utmost to bring the division to Skaszewo (on Marshal Davout's line of march towards Golym-

---

25. Chief of staff of the corps.

in) tomorrow morning, this unfortunately will compel me to abandon 23 captured guns. It would probably be a good thing to support my retreat with another division.

This was anything but hopeful.

Bennigsen had victoriously held his ground. Nevertheless, at midnight he resumed the retreat. It was in vain that the Prussian Major von Knesebeck, the same who before Magdeburg had counselled a march into the west, and had escaped the Prenzlau capitulation owing to his absence on supply duties, implored him not only to stand fast, but even to pursue the beaten French. Bennigsen was apprehensive of being enveloped on the right flank and forced back upon the Narew, and he had no confidence in Buxhöwden's support, this general indeed having, on the authority of Kamenskoi's order, stood inactive all day at Makow.

Simultaneously with the battle of Pultusk, a sharp engagement was fought at Golymin. The Russians under Prince Galitzin had reached that point from Strzegocin on the evening of the 25th, and had found part of Dokhturov's division (belonging to Buxhöwden's group) in position to support them. On the enemy's side the cavalry and the corps of Augereau came on, both almost entirely destitute of artillery, for to get guns up was a sheer impossibility. In the evening a division of Davout's corps arrived from Strzegocin on the one side, a Russian column under Count Pahlen from Ciechanow on the other. The respective forces in this hot engagement were 27,000 French to 13,000 Russians. The latter, however, possessed a decided superiority in guns, and the short winter's day, the bad weather, and the poor roads were all in favour of the defender.

In such conditions the attacker's columns nearly always start late, and march slowly and painfully. The cavalry reconnaissance breaks down, as even the horses cannot easily get forward; uncertainty prevails as to the enemy, and generally, as in this instance, the artillery, at least the heavier metal, cannot accompany the troops. It is only late in the day that enough reports come in to clear up the situation. Then the troops are deployed for the attack, but far more slowly than in summer and on dry ground. So at last the engagement begins, but before a decision has been achieved the early evening settles down, and the fight is broken off by darkness. We ourselves suffered severely enough from this sort of thing in the Loire campaign of 1870-71, and it must have been far worse in roadless, marshy, and wooded Poland.

Thus, for all their superiority in numbers, it was only at nightfall that the French—at the cost of no small losses—were able to drive out the Russians, who retreated in the night unharmed to Makow.

The emperor had expected serious opposition neither at Pultusk nor at Golymin, but, as we know, at Ciechanow. When Soult arrived at the last-named place he found the birds flown, for Pahlen had marched to Golymin. There were no large forces at or about Ciechanow. In other words, the intended blow in that direction would have been a blow in the air. The reports from Golymin reached Napoleon too late for him to be able to reach the field of action, and he had the mortification of seeing his troops heavily engaged at two different points on the line without himself being able to be present at either. He now assumed that the Russians would fight at Makow. Murat hastened thither, and found plenty of mired guns and vehicles indeed, but no longer any important body of the enemy.

Bernadotte had not come up, and his whereabouts were for the time being unknown. Napoleon had told him that in his movement towards the main army he was to manoeuvre prudently and not to let the enemy commit him too deeply. This had made him cautious, and when, presently, Ney was deflected, his decisions and his movements alike became hesitating. Thus Bernadotte actually got no farther than Mdzewo, and his co-operation proving after all unnecessary he was directed[26] towards Willenberg and Neidenburg on the track of the Prussians. Napoleon himself, who had spent the night of the 26th/27th in the castle of Paluki, went on to Golymin on the 27th to superintend the progress of affairs in person. On the 28th, however, the Russian rearguards were out of reach. The condition of the army was becoming worse and worse, and a cessation of marches and manoeuvres was imperative. Murat wrote to the emperor:

> The want of food broke practically all the restraints of obedience and overrode all feelings of humanity. Sire, it is with pain that I have to bring to your notice the same heartrending picture that probably every marshal has already drawn of the state of affairs in his own command. We find, not merely nothing for man and horse in the villages, but also the villages themselves deserted, all the inhabitants having fled.

---

26. His temporary command of the left wing had ceased with the drawing-in of Ney's corps to the main army. He had now only his own corps and part of the cavalry.—Tr.

The roads were in an appalling state, the bridges in many places destroyed. The marching columns were unable to reach their assigned destinations. No great concentration of forces was possible, for there was no means of feeding a mass. Exhaustion and discontent began to make itself felt in the ranks. For a considerable time things had gone ill with the troops. Hunger was their constant attendant. Their tattered clothing no longer served to protect them against the night's cold, and billets were not to be had. The customary black rye-bread of Poland, which was the only kind now available, suited neither their taste nor their health, and as the mills were for the most part unworkable, it was impossible to grind any better corn. It has been denied, as well as asserted, that the discipline of the army had suffered;[27] but it would have been surprising indeed if indiscipline had not manifested itself, at least to some extent. When the emperor rode past the marching column on the 26th of December, the cry for bread, jestingly translated into Polish by the soldiers, sounded in his ears. At first he took it in good part, but then, as the cry grew louder and louder, he rode up to the grenadier company that was directly in front of him with a stern face and said, also in Polish, "I have none." On another occasion the emperor concealed his dissatisfaction by laughing and singing. "He may well sing, for he has eaten," cried his own Guard grenadiers. Later, the French, it seems, suffered severely from home-sickness too.[28] It is not to be wondered at if December in these strange Bug and Narew lands aroused painful thoughts and memories of *la belle France* and Suabia and Italy.

Nevertheless, the driving-power of Napoleon's personality undoubtedly kept the army up to its work. The soldiers believed in his star and followed him. Baron Percy writes in his *Journal*:

His Majesty marches them every day, which reduces everyone to despair and brings the general misery to a climax. But the emperor has purposes beyond our ken, and we must wait until these are realized before we judge or suffer a complaint to escape us. Never was the French army so unhappy. The soldier, marching always, bivouacking every night, wading up to the ankles in mud the day through, had not an ounce of bread or a drop of brandy, not even time to dry his clothes, and he fell and died from weariness and exhaustion. Many in this condi-

27. Lettow-Vorbeck, iii. 165 ff.
28. *Journal des Campagnes du Baron Percy, chirurgien en chef de la grande armée* (by E. Longin, Paris, 1904).

tion were found in the ditches by the roadside where they had gasped out their lives. A glass of wine or brandy would have saved them. The emperor's heart must have been rent by these things; but he marched steadfastly upon his goal, to fulfil the great destiny that he prepares for Europe. If, unhappily, he were to fail, or to achieve only a half-success, then indeed would the army be dispirited and the voice of discontent uplift itself.

Gradually, however, the cycle of events accomplished itself, in a course too strong for the strongest human will to stay. Psychologically, it is interesting to note how even Napoleon's forceful character little by little began to yield before the inexorable opposition of the country and the season. At last he gave up the hope of fighting his decisive battle before going into winter quarters, and in the latter days his demands on the marshals and their troops came down step by step.

For one thing, the marshals greatly exaggerated their victories over the Russians. Buxhöwden was said to have led 40,000 to 50,000 men in person at Golymin, while the mass which retreated from Pultusk by the right bank of the Narew alone was estimated at 35,000 men. On this showing the main body of the Russian army must have appeared on the field, even though it had fought in detachments and not as a single mass, and this fact helped to bring about the decision to make a halt.

It has been said that Napoleon fell below his former high level of generalship during this part of the campaign and was far inferior to the Napoleon of Jena and Auerstedt, but this is evidently unjust. If we can judge by his numerous orders and proclamations, he was never once overcome by weariness, though this would have been perfectly natural. His ceaseless activity in command seems to have known no abatement. The force of circumstances alone proved mightier than he, and he was too wise to act as did Charles XII of Sweden, who even in such a situation as this persisted in his defiance, and achieved nothing thereby but the ruin of himself and his army.

On 29th December the emperor transferred the army to temporary winter quarters. Bernadotte was to establish himself on the right bank of the Lower Vistula, Ney in the neighbourhood of Soldau, Soult in the area in which he was operating at the time, Davout on the Lower Bug and the Narew, Augereau farther behind him on the Vistula close to his own point of crossing, Lannes on the right bank, the Guard on the left, at Warsaw. Part of the cavalry was to be sent eastwards in front of the army, part to be stationed on the Vistula. There now set in a period of rest in which the troops could receive supplies and recuperate themselves.

But although Napoleon's genius as commander-in-chief shines before us as vividly in these dark days as in his more fortunate campaigns in Thuringia and the Mark, we are struck by another consideration which bears closely on his experiences in Poland. Only now do we realize how efficacious would have been the resistance which he might have had to face there, on the Vistula particularly, and the miserable pusillanimity displayed by the Prussians after the unlucky battles in October, which alone discouraged the continuance of the struggle. At no point on the Vistula had Napoleon met with any serious defence. And yet even the stream itself had given him endless trouble. Its great width, its yielding banks, the floating ice which appeared from time to time, and the lack of bridging materials might well have proved insurmountable obstacles to a weaker will. The bridging equipment carried by the French would hardly have spanned a sixth part of the great river. As the numerous Vistula boats and vessels had been sunk by the enemy, they had to be got out of the ice-cold water and repaired, and this entailed much time and labour, not even suitable tools being available. At Thorn, where the conditions were comparatively favourable, Ney still took a week to build a bridge, and at Warsaw fully 11 days (2nd to 13th December) were consumed, in spite of the stores which were available in the city. At Zakroczyn, Senarmont, the general of artillery who was destined to become famous through the battle of Friedland, superintended the building of the bridge, but he, though hard pressed by Napoleon, found even a fortnight too little for the work, and the greater part of the 7th Corps had to cross in boats. The bridge over the Bug at Okunin took no less than 11 days to build. What might not have happened had the Russians and the Prussians made a serious stand at these points? A very little more luck, and Hohenlohe or Blücher, if not both of them, would have escaped and reappeared as an army in being on the Vistula. But even apart from this, a little energy expended in calling out the forces that were still available and could be obtained from the country would have meant a considerable increase in the means of resistance. It would have been easy to bring up L'Estocq's corps to a strength of 32 battalions instead of 19. Of cavalry and artillery there was no lack. A general who was daring and constant in adversity would have been able to make a glorious, certainly prolonged, and probably in the end successful defence of the river line.

So, indeed, thought Scharnhorst when he reached Danzig. He asserted that the outlook for the national cause was more promising than he himself had believed it to be, and considered that, provided that Napoleon respected Austria's neutrality, the Vistula could be held at least until Prussia and Russia were able to assemble fresh forces of resistance. Every march in advance lengthened the line of operations of the French army and increased the prospect of a successful attack on its flank. Stralsund in the north[29] and Silesia and all its fortresses in the south were still unsubdued. If now Austria were to accede to Prussia's urgent request and openly declare against Napoleon, it was certainly not too optimistic to expect a reversal of the entire military position. "The days of shame and disgrace seemed to be at an end."[30]

The close examination of these circumstances yields a valuable lesson for every commander in evil days. The same natural law which decrees that the force of an attack shall little by little lose its potency, guarantees to the defence even after the greatest disasters the hope of ultimate success. Let him therefore seek his salvation in steadfast endurance.

****

Meantime the Prussian corps had also been in action.

Marshal Ney had, in accordance with Napoleon's orders to Bernadotte, marched south-eastward on Kudsburg, and had only left a somewhat weak flank-guard on the route of Strasburg-Lautenburg that he had originally followed. However, on receiving news therefrom that a Prussian corps of some strength was at Soldau, he turned back in that direction on the 25th of December with the main body of his corps which had marched to Kudsburg. The Prussians had made their arrangements for defence mainly as against an attack from the direction of Lautenburg, considering themselves sufficiently protected on the side of Kudsburg by the broad, marshy depression of the Soldau River. This was traversed only by two embankments, one of them close to the town of Soldau itself, the other near a lodge or outlying building (called Niederhof) south-west of and about a mile and a half from Soldau. Both these embankments were protected by gun epaulments, and in accordance with what looks like sheer custom, on that of Soldau, skirmishers were pushed out to the farther end, where the sand-hills offered a certain amount of cover. The consequence was that the bridges over the Soldau

29. Stralsund then belonged to Sweden, but this Power was also at war with France.—Tr.

30. Lehmann, *Scharnhorst*, i. 475.

River, which was deep and fairly broad, were left intact. It is more or less the story of the Burgthor at Lübeck over again, and one is really staggered by the might of habit. Its result was another mishap exactly the same and just as serious as the first.

After an unsuccessful attempt to cross by Niederhof, the French attacked the Soldau embankment. At the same time, on the Prussian side a battalion told off to the defence of the town was withdrawn and sent to strengthen the right flank, where Diericke's brigade, which lay in that quarter, had taken up a position on the Lautenburg road near Pierlawsken. Thither, too, General L'Estocq himself had ridden out, although in fact no disquieting news whatever had come in from the Lautenburg side and his cavalry had reported the approach of the French from Kudsburg. He had definitely fixed the alarm posts of the troops in case of attack. The troops had occupied them, and he saw no reason to change his mind. After the withdrawal of the battalion from Soldau, General von Diericke sent back the skirmishers of the Rüchel Regiment to replace it, but these too pushed out across the embankment to its south end. After a brief fight they were overpowered and, mingled with the fugitives, the French pressed on across the embankment and up to the entrance of the town. Exactly as had been the case at Lübeck, the artillery did not dare to fire into the mob of friends and foes, but drove away with their pieces. Two guns posted on the embankment fell into the hands of the enemy, along with the town.

On hearing of this, General von Diericke set himself at once to do at least what was urgently needed. The fall of Soldau had broken through the Prussian general's line at its centre, and Diericke faced about towards the town, meaning to cut his way through by force. After a slight artillery preparation, he delivered his assault. Storming into the streets, he actually reached the market-place, where there was a large defensible building held by the French. Beyond this he could not advance, and the French, more expert as they undeniably were in fighting in localities, finally drove back the intruders. In the evening L'Estocq himself came on the scene, and a fresh attempt was made to storm Soldau. In this a battalion under the command of Captain von Grolman[31] of the general staff, working its way round the town, assaulted from the north-east side. But once more it proved impossible to carry the town, and the Prussians retreated on Neidenburg by a northerly detour. Thither, too, retired the detachment stationed at Mlawa, which had been driven out of that place with loss.

---

31. The afterwards famous quartermaster-general of Blücher's army.—Tr.

The loss of Soldau, quite apart from actual mistakes in its defence, is to be attributed to the fatal dissemination of the Prussian forces, for L'Estocq's corps, had it only been promptly assembled, would have been superior to Ney's. This defect was one of those congenital to the Prussian army of the time.

Nevertheless, although the East Prussian campaign was thus initiated by a fresh reverse, it must be admitted not only that the troops fought bravely, but also that the leaders did not lose their heads, as so many of their predecessors had done in Thuringia in the retreat through Saxony and Brandenburg. Ney thus speaks of the Prussian attacks in his report:

> General L'Estocq enraged at finding himself driven out, assembled his officers and made them swear to retake the town in the night. And in fact, between 7 in the evening, and midnight, he led four successive attacks, which were vigorously repulsed although the enemy displayed a courage that bordered on desperation.

General L'Estocq remained halted at Neidenburg for the moment, but receiving on the 27th of December Kamenskoi's orders for a retreat he began to move off in the direction that he himself preferred, *viz.* through East Prussia on Angerburg. General Roquette, who had been sent out north-westward to keep up communication with Graudenz and the Lower Vistula, received an order which is sufficiently remarkable to be reproduced verbatim:

> The retreat is to be according to the enemy's advance. Your connection with the main body will necessarily be lost, as you have a quite different object to attain. This object is, by spreading out a chain of very small detachments, resting your right flank always on the Vistula and extending your left as far as possible, to provide for your own safety and for the covering of East Prussia.

The task, be it observed, was entrusted to a detachment which totalled one battalion and ten squadrons. Comment seems superfluous. Geographical and topographical, or even purely geometrical considerations still figured conspicuously in the Prussian style of war, and the living forces brought into play in respect of number and constitution alike, were considered as of negligible importance.

General L'Estocq entered Angerburg on the 3rd of January 1807.

The Russians, too, had continued their retreat, Bennigsen on the left, Buxhöwden on the right bank of the Narew. Bennigsen had caused the bridge at Ostrolenka to be burned, in order, it appears, to evade a junction with Buxhöwden on the other side of the river, for in that event he would have been subordinated to Buxhöwden, who was the senior officer. It was only when Novogrod was reached that through General von Knorring (who had been sent to the army as *ad latus* to the commander-in-chief) and the Prussian captain von Schöler, a meeting of the two leaders was brought about and a movement of both armies to Johannisburg arranged. This movement was carried out, for the bulk of the forces, by way of Tykocin, where the Narew was spanned by a permanent bridge, and Goniondz. At the last-named place Bennigsen received besides decorations for his victory of Pultusk, the appointment of commander-in-chief. As such he conducted the united forces to Bialla, and Buxhöwden left the front.

General von Essen I, who it will be remembered was approaching from the Turkish theatre of war, took over the direct protection of the Russian frontier against an inroad of the French from Warsaw. Most unfortunately, Bennigsen left Sedmoratzki's division at Goniondz to support him.

CHAPTER 6

From the Vistula to the Alle

On the 1st of January 1807 Napoleon issued his orders for the army to go into standing winter quarters. His intention was to give it a long rest to set it up again, to refit it with all necessaries, and to reinforce it, for he believed that the campaign was for the time being over. When the better season came, then he would give the Allies the crushing blow that adverse conditions had prevented him from delivering in December.

The III Corps (Davout) and IV Corps (Soult) were to stand fast in their positions along the Lower Bug-Narew and on the Orzic; the V (Lannes) was to be between Sierock and Warsaw, the VII (Augereau) between the Ukra and the Vistula. The I Reserve Cavalry Corps (Murat) stood partly on the Omulew, partly on the Vistula about Warsaw. In Warsaw itself the emperor and his Guard were established.

Bernadotte with the I Corps received orders to extend between Osterode and Elbing, to put the rich country of the Lower Vistula under contribution for the benefit of the French army and at the same time to cover it, and to blockade Danzig and Graudenz. Marshal Ney (VI Corps), who was still under his orders, was to quarter his troops to the south of Bernadotte's, about Gilgenburg.[1] The II Reserve Cavalry Corps commanded by Marshal Bessiéres was broken up and its divisions assigned to the two army corps (I, VI) with which they had worked in the previous operations.

The forward edge, or frontier, of these winter quarters was formed by a line along the Passarge and the Omulew, and thence by Ostrolenka on the Narew to Brok on the Bug. The bulk of the army remained concentrated in the emperor's hands about Warsaw, on either side of the Lower Bug; the weak left wing extended as far as the Frische Haff.

---

1. See Map No. 10.

Infantry companies were attached to the cavalry that was in first line in order to lighten the outpost service and also as supports. Independent squadrons went out in front of the outpost line to reconnoitre, and in general all reasonable precautions were observed against surprise. Napoleon ordered the construction of strong bridge-head works at Pultusk, Sierock, Modlin, and Praga, these to be completed by 1st March.

These winter quarters undoubtedly seem to be very widely extended. But the extension was justified by the difficulty of providing quarters for the army in a country that had already been partly exhausted, and it is certain that the emperor expected no irruption on the part of the enemy, who seemed to stand in need of rest fully as much as his own army. In this hypothesis, indeed, he was quite wrong, for the offensive power of the Prussians and Russians had by no means died away as yet. His thoughts and acts were all for the future Russian campaign, for which he made preparations with his customary care and thoroughness. The princes of the Confederation of the Rhine were earnestly enjoined to set on foot or to complete their contingents. On 1st January the emperor decreed the formation of a Polish Division under General Dombrowski out of the 10,000 insurgents assembled at Lowicz; this with some other available troops constituted the newly formed X Corps under Marshal Lefebvre which was told off to the siege of Danzig. A provisional Government was established for Poland, consisting of seven members of the nobility, and Napoleon hoped by means of this council that he would be able to make fuller use of the resources of the land. The rearward communications of the army were carefully organized and guarded as far as the available force permitted. The restoration of the old *enceinte* of Thorn, the inclusion in the defence system there of the neighbouring commanding heights, and the creation of a bridge-head on the left bank of the Vistula promised to give the army a second strong point of support on the great river in addition to Warsaw.

On 7th January there followed fresh and detailed instructions for the quartering of the troops and the administration of the occupied areas, as also for the eventuality of a Russian attack, although indeed this was regarded as improbable. The concentration points for the various corps were: VI Corps, Mlawa; IV, Golymin; III, Pultusk; V, Sierock; VII, Plonsk. Thus the four last-named corps were placed in an irregular rectangle, of which the head was at Pultusk, and the two sides that faced the east were each no more than 12 miles long, while the greatest depth of the cantonment area (to Plock) was some 30 miles. As the cavalry was pushed out to the front for 35 miles or so, the emperor possessed the power in all circumstances of concentrating his great army in advance of the enemy's coming.[2]

Napoleon's dispositions for winter quarter's on this occasion may justly be regarded as a model. They ensured rest and the possibility of recuperation for the army, they screened the investment and siege of the Vistula fortresses, and they permitted the creation of a new and strong base of operations for the coming campaign, the control of a country whose prosperity was still unimpaired, and the utilization of Poland as an asset in the further prosecution of the war.

The emperor had now realized that his operations would necessarily be in districts which could not support his army, and that moreover the vulnerability of his line of supply was increased with every forward step. Before the opening of the next campaign he hoped that the resistance of Danzig and Graudenz—the former place of great importance as a port—would have been overcome, in which case supplies could be brought up the Vistula by water, and he would have been insured against want. The present conditions obliged him to examine very minutely everything that affected supplies and reinforcements for the army—questions that on other occasions the weakness of his opponents had so often permitted him to ignore.

The period of rest was, however, not destined to be a long one. When Marshal Bernadotte received Napoleon's first orders (those of 29th December) for the taking up of closer rest-quarters, he had stood where he was at Mlawa and Chorzellen, in order to support Soult's position on the Orzic, and ordered Marshal Ney to assemble his corps between Neidenburg, Hohenstein, and Gilgenburg. Ney, however, had already advanced farther on the track of L'Estocq, and on the 2nd of January he reached Allenstein, Passenheim, and Ortelsburg, with cavalry as far out as Guttstadt. Then followed the order of 1st January for winter quarters, and Bernadotte warned Ney not to go too far forward and to keep his troops together. Further details, he naturally assumed, could well be left to Ney's own judgment. But this marshal, the "bravest of the brave," lacked the capacity for broad views and correct appreciation of strategical conditions. Contrary to expectation, his cavalry found the country entirely clear of the enemy as far as the environs of Heilsberg, and this induced the marshal to continue in the path upon which he had entered. He shifted his headquarters to

---

2. P. Grenier, *Etude sur 1807. Manoeuvres d'Eylau et de Friedland* (Paris, 1901), p. 45.

Wartenburg, whence on the 6th he issued orders to his troops representing his own views. So far northward did these orders carry them that the most advanced battalions reached Bischofstein and Liebstadt, and the cavalry attained the line of the Alle at Bartenstein. In so doing, apart from other errors, Ney committed that of which, except in this instance, the Prussian army had the monopoly—the error of over-dispersion. The quarters of Ney's command now extended as far to the rear as Ortelsburg and Osterode.[3]

Once Ney had transgressed the allotted bounds, events drove him ever onward. When from Bartenstein he heard that Königsberg was only weakly garrisoned, the idea occurred to him to capture this important place, the second capital of the Prussian monarchy, by a *coup-de-main*, and he immediately took measures to put his idea into execution. Valuable as are the qualities of independence and initiative in a troop-leader, they degenerate into mere wilfulness when, as in this instance, they upset the plans of the higher leading. It must be remarked, too, that the marshal did not even intend to conduct the dangerous enterprise in person, but entrusted it to a flying column under General Colbert, proposing to betake himself to Bartenstein and there await the successful outcome of the venture.

But the venture was not successful. When on the 6th of January the first French horsemen appeared at Bartenstein, the Prussian Court did indeed leave Königsberg and go to Memel, but General L'Estocq was nevertheless ordered to protect the capital. The Prussian corps was, as we know, at Angerburg; its quarters extended behind the Mauer-See, Löwentin-See, and Jagodner-See, and its advanced posts were pushed out in a westerly direction to Nordenburg and Drengfurt. On the south side of Königsberg there was, besides, a small body of cavalry under Major von Borstell, and at Preussisch-Holland was Roquette's detachment, which in pursuance of its extraordinary mission of covering all East Prussia during the first retreat had begun by falling back to Braunsberg, but had afterwards advanced again in obedience to orders from Rüchel.

Brilliant was the prospect that presented itself to L'Estocq of taking revenge on Ney for Soldau and reviving the downcast hopes of the Fatherland by a splendid feat of arms. Ney's troops were scattered over an area of some 50 miles width and the same depth. The Prussians had had several days' rest. The lakes enabled them to assemble

---

3. The area Bischofstein-Liebstadt-Osterode-Ortelsburg gives a front of 30 miles and a depth of 32-35.—Tr.

wholly unperceived, and from this cover they might have dashed out towards Seeburg and Guttstadt with disconcerting swiftness and surprise effect. Their numerous cavalry, well led, must have been successful in catching and destroying a good many of the disconnected French battalions. Unhappily, nothing of the sort took place. In the heart of the old General there was no room for dashing exploits of this sort, and, for another thing, the reports which he possessed as to the enemy were far too incomplete for their dangerous situation to stand clearly revealed, although L'Estocq's strength in cavalry ought to have ensured his being well informed. This want of good reconnoitring on the Prussian side runs through the whole campaign. A small *cossack* detachment which happened to come to Angerburg was placed on the outpost line in the hope that the French would argue the presence of Russians as well as Prussians there. Instead of falling on and beating the enemy, it was sought to mystify and frighten him by petty stratagems of this sort.

On the 8th of January L'Estocq advanced to Drengfurt, but with a portion only of his forces, the remainder staying in their quarters. Consequently, only some small forays were made towards the Guber and the Alle, which gave the junior officers and men opportunity for displaying their quality, but produced no lasting effect whatever. On the 14th the General planned a foray on a larger scale against Schippenbeil, Bartenstein, and Bischofstein, but he gave it up on learning that some of Ney's troops had entered Rossel. This was war after the pattern of the Bavarian Succession[4] and Rhine campaigns.

About this time Bennigsen reached Bialla with his seven divisions.[5] Since he had received his appointment as commander-in-chief he had made up his mind to resume the offensive. He says in his *Memoirs*:

> My intentions were:—to advance, as far as possible unobserved by the enemy, between the chains of lakes in Old Prussia; to drive back the French advance on Königsberg; to regain control of the Vistula, open free and secure communication with Danzig, relieve Graudenz; then to put the army into winter quarters in Old Prussia, to await reinforcements from Russia, and when these came up, to add L'Estocq's whole corps to the garrison of Danzig so as to forbid any approach of the enemy towards the fortress, and to divert him by attacking on the left bank of the Vistula.

4. Called the "Potato War."—Tr.
5. *i.e.* the combined Russian armies, less Sedmoratzki's division.—Tr.

At the same time an order came from the *tsar* to his army[6] requiring them to drive back the enemy over the Vistula.

There is undeniably a touch of boldness in this scheme, and Höpfner[7] declares it thoroughly worthy of a great general. But it has nevertheless one fatal flaw—it presupposes passivity in the enemy and that enemy Napoleon! It ought not to have been forgotten that the Russian general could not expect to obtain the great advantages which he promised himself without a serious conflict with the main body of the French army. This contingency should, in truth, have been the central factor in weighing the problem. But, at least, considerable initial successes were possible. Marshal Ney, oblivious of all danger, was still in his far advanced positions in the region of Bartenstein, the Guber, and the middle Alle, rejoicing that he had exchanged the exhausted Neidenburg and Mlawa country for this relatively well-stocked district.

Bennigsen had the advantage of surprise on his side. No one in the French army had suspected either him or the Prussians of projecting such a move. It is to be recorded in General L'Estocq's honour that he promptly fell in with it. There was, indeed, something unnatural in the idea of beginning to fight again in midwinter. It looks as if the French, and even their emperor, had not quite emancipated themselves from the seductive idea that winter has a right to impose a cessation of military activity. For once priority of invention can be claimed for the Allies.

On 13th January, when Ney had already gone to Bartenstein, he received a letter from Major-General Berthiér, to the effect that the emperor desired no offensive movement to be made during the winter, and that he, the marshal, was to take his place in winter quarters between the corps of Soult and Bernadotte. But even this did not open Ney's eyes. He actually brought up from Willenberg the dragoon division of Grouchy, which had just been placed under his orders, and on the 14th sent a detailed report as to his positions and those of the Prussians, expressing in conclusion the hope that the continued alternation of frost and thaw would restrain the enemy from undertaking any operations, and adding naively that he had no information as to where Bernadotte's and Soult's troops were. He even contemplated peace and an armistice, and at a meeting with General Rüchel on the 17th at Preussisch-Eylau, he succeeded in arranging a suspension of hostilities. Fortunately, however, King Frederick William III refused to ratify this agreement.

6. Leopold von Ranke, *Denkwurdigkeiten des Staatslcanzlers Fürsten von Hardenberg* (Leipzig, 1877), iii. 278.

7. *Krieg 1806-7,* pt. 2, vol. iii. p. 173.

Bennigsen, therefore, unfettered by any valid compact with the enemy, was still in a position to overrun Ney's troops by surprise, if he only acted vigorously and chose the direction of Allenstein, which lent itself best to hindering the foe from escaping southward. And indeed he pushed steadily forward from Bialla without halting or giving his troops even a brief rest. But the march proceeded only slowly, and not westwards by Nikolaiken and Passenheim, but (which was far less effectual) north-west on Rossel and Sensburg. From the 21st of January onwards the Prussians, who meantime had gathered on the Guber about Döonhoffstedt, cooperated on Bennigsen's right by moving on Schippenbeil, Bennigsen sending the Viborg Regiment to reinforce them. Even now Ney was ignorant of what was in store for him, and the emperor's letter of January 7th, which would necessarily have enlightened him, appears not to have reached him. Nevertheless, in the event, his luck was to save him. Bernadotte, who had received this order as well as copies of Ney's correspondence with the major-general, realized with astonishment how little his comrade's doings were in accordance with Napoleon's wishes, and instantly sent off a fresh warning to Ney to come back. This reached Ney on the 17th, just as he was negotiating his armistice.

Your advanced position and your continuance in it after the receipt of orders is not only contrary to the views of His Majesty, but also detrimental to my troops and to the operations entrusted to me.

This at last decided Ney to retreat, although he set about doing so very slowly. At the eleventh hour—on the 20th of January—he began his movement, and the Russians, coming up, found him departing, and were only able to inflict loss on part of his advanced troops.

As the prolongation of the Allies' advance lay in a westerly direction (on Mehlsack and Liebstadt), and Ney's retreat in a southerly one, the marshal was able to extricate his head from the noose, in spite of the extreme peril into which he had put himself. On the 24th he and his corps were once more at Neidenburg without having any serious loss to lament.

Much worse than Ney's might have been the fate of Bernadotte, who meantime had carried out his movement into the Lower Vistula country, and whose left already reached to the shore of the Frische Haff. The opportunity arose for the Allies to recoup themselves for their failure to entrap one French army corps by swiftly falling upon and annihilating another. Bernadotte's three divisions were about Osterode (Rivaud's), Saalfeld (Drouet's), and Preussisch-Holland (Dupont's) respectively, the last-named finding in addition a post at Elbing. Here Marshal Bernadotte received, on the night of the 22nd/23rd January, Ney's report of his retreat and the unexpected offensive of the Russians. Ney himself, however, had failed to appreciate the significance of this offensive, and his communication to Bernadotte bears the clear impress of his under-valuation of the danger that threatened the French left wing. Bernadotte, however, if he lacked Ney's serene daring, far surpassed him in wideness of vision, and he appears to have realized what was impending, for he instantly gave instructions for the southward concentration of his corps on Osterode, in order to get into touch with the *grande armée* and to secure himself from being separated from it. This was by no means easy to accomplish. Dupont's division in particular, which was at Preussisch-Holland and Elbing, and whose vanguard had actually seized Braunsberg and had the Prussian General Roquette in front of it there, must be prepared to make a flank-march in sight of the advancing allied army. Bernadotte himself hastened to Preussisch-Holland on the morning of 24th January, and from the reports which he received there, discovered the full extent of the disaster that threatened him. Hurriedly he wrote to Dupont:

I feel that we have no time to lose in saving ourselves, and I desire you therefore to march off at 4 a.m. tomorrow and to be at Preussisch-Holland by 10 a.m. at the very latest.

The Russians and Prussians in the meantime continued their offensive, but only in a comfortable and leisurely way, although a letter from Ney to the major-general (written from Allenstein on the 22nd), which had fallen into their hands, revealed the enemy's positions, and particularly Bernadotte's isolation. The advance of the small French force above mentioned upon Braunsberg actually diverted the Prussian corps, which was to march on Wormditt, rightwards on Mehlsack, and it was only when the hasty retreat of the French became known and orders were received to make for Hagenau (northwest of Mohrungen) that the corps resumed its original direction towards Saalfeld. The Russians marched by Liebstadt, whence as darkness came on they chased a French post, towards Mohrungen.

In order probably to cover the flank-march of Dupont's division, Bernadotte had rapidly pushed some troops from Preussisch-Holland

and Saalfeld on Mohrungen, and had betaken himself thither in person. On the 25th the Russian advanced guard under General Markov approached from Liebstadt, and the marshal, who showed great decision in such emergencies, did not await; its coming, but rightly advanced to meet it, in order to cover the passage of the troops that had still to come in from Preussisch-Holland. The events showed that this resolute advance was more efficacious than the most brilliant defence at Mohrungen could have been.

General Markov learned from prisoners that Marshal Bernadotte himself was at Mohrungen, and judged therefrom that strong forces of the enemy were in front of him. His judgment seemed to him to be confirmed by the advance of the French, and he therefore halted and awaited their onset at Georgenthal. This position, moreover, he only held until fresh French troops, marching in from Preussisch-Holland and deflected to the battlefield by Marshal Bernadotte, made their appearance on his right flank, whereupon he retired. The main body of the Russian army, of whose movements unfortunately but little is known in detail, must have been at some considerable distance, as otherwise they would undoubtedly have come up to the support of the advanced guard. The Prussian corps likewise did not get to Hagenau, but only as far as Schlodien. Some of its detachments heard the cannon thunder at Mohrungen, but they did not hurry thither, for in those days it was not customary to "march to the sound of the guns." General Roquette, advancing through Braunsberg, joined the main body of L'Estocq's corps on this day.

Thus, in spite of his dangerous situation at the outset, Bernadotte had actually a success to show. But unexpectedly there came the news that Mohrungen itself, in his rear, was occupied by the Russians. This was the fact. The Russian cavalry moving farther south, had pushed out thither one of their detachments, and this had seized the place, which was but weakly held. The small garrison was surprised and captured, and a number of Russian and Prussian prisoners who were in the place, released. When Bernadotte faced about to recapture Mohrungen, the Russian horsemen vanished into the night.

The mishap in Mohrungen did not alter the fact that owing to the indolent march of the Russians and the vagaries of the Prussian corps, Bernadotte had distinctly the best of it. Not only so, but his bold advance against Markov made such an impression upon Bennigsen that he imagined a French offensive in force, and on the 26th concentrated all the troops whom he could reach at Liebstadt. It was only on the evening of this day that he occupied Mohrungen, which meantime the enemy had abandoned.

The French marshal and his corps had got away in safety to Liebemühl. The Allies, indeed, swung in towards the line Liebemühl-Osterode and made arrangements to attack him by envelopment. But there was no engagement, for Bernadotte swiftly evaded the intended envelopment of his left and rear by the Prussian corps, by a night march towards Deutsch-Eylau,[8] whence he continued his retreat upon Lobau. The blockade of Graudenz was given up, and the troops which had been engaged in it (Hesse-Darmstadt contingent and one battalion of Rivaud's division) were drawn in to the main body of the corps.

Like Ney, Bernadotte had escaped to all intents and purposes unharmed, only the rearguard having to fight a few small skirmishes. It cannot be denied that he had acted with great adroitness and resolution. At the same time, his corps was extremely exhausted and was now in urgent need of the rest that he meant to give it at Lobau. The numerical strength of the corps was seriously diminished by its losses on the march; two of his divisions could now muster only 7500 men between them. In a winter campaign such as this, which was not only long drawn out but also had to contend with bad weather and bad roads, the number of effectives melts away like newly fallen snow in springtime.

Marshal Ney, who had advanced again with a large force to Osterode in order to support or disengage Marshal Bernadotte, was informed on the 28th of the course of events, and fell back himself to Gilgenburg.

Thus the French left wing had definitively escaped the disaster that Bennigsen had intended to inflict upon it, and a great effort had been expended to no purpose. The boldness of the commander-in-chief's scheme was not reflected in its execution. The allied army had made its advance not only slowly but also in a northerly direction— that is, in the direction which was least dangerous to the French, and this being so there was no chance of overtaking them unless they on their side acted in the same way. The objects laid down in Bennigsen's memorandum—the protection of Königsberg, the securing

---

8. Deutsch-Eylau must be distinguished from Preussisch-Eylau; the former lies about 18 miles W.S.W. of Osterode, the latter far to the north, 25 miles short of Königsberg. Preussisch-Eylau is the scene of the battle presently to be described, to which indeed the German original always gives its prefix of "Pr." It must be remembered that Prussia proper was outside the limits of Germany until 1866, hence the distinction.—Tr.

of communications with Danzig, the relief of Graudenz—were all indeed attained, but the favourable opportunity of dealing a heavy blow to two isolated army corps of the enemy, and so reducing the preponderance on the French side to an equilibrium, was let slip unused. But above all there was lacking the guarantee of security for what had been gained, which only a decisive blow against the French main army could give. So far from this, the gains themselves were actually neutralized in part by the moral effect of the "slap in the face" at Mohrungen. Thus we learn from Bennigsen's experience, that it is not merely, nor even principally, high resolves and bold schemes that constitute generalship, but first and foremost well-directed energy of execution.

For sixteen days the Russians had been un-restingly on the march, and now they too stood in most urgent need of rest. For this Bennigsen proposed to allow three days at least, which it was expected would also give time for the supply-wagons that had been left behind to reach the front. The commander-in-chief meant to remain on the line Saalfeld-Guttstadt, but his troops in pursuit of the retreating enemy pushed on to Deutsch-Eylau, Osterode, and Allenstein, and their reconnoitring patrols still farther to the south.

The Prussians were permitted by Bennigsen to continue their advance towards Marienwerder and Graudenz, and they eagerly seized the opportunity of doing more than the bare minimum laid down in army orders. Another Russian regiment, that of Kaluga, was sent to reinforce them.

But there was another more important reinforcement than this. Since 18th January, Colonel von Scharnhorst had been attached to L'Estocq's headquarters. Unfortunately, his position and the influence that he was officially entitled to exercise were only too limited. Frederick would probably have promoted him Major-General and Lieutenant-General in rapid succession, and then proceeded to put him, junior of his rank as he was, at the head of the whole corps, just as he did with Seydlitz and the cavalry at Rossbach. Frederick William III was not to be moved to take such extraordinary measures even at the most critical moment.

He had sighed over the dearth of good generals in his army before the war began, and the experience of these three months demonstrated only too sadly what good reason he had to do so. But his unwillingness to give offence or act contrary to tradition kept him from having recourse to the obvious expedient of retiring the greybeards who were good for nothing, and promoting in their place the workmanlike staff officers of whom he had a goodly number.[9]

On his arrival at Wehlau, where he joined the court, Scharnhorst had been received with the utmost graciousness by Frederick William and Queen Luise, and was delighted to find that "they were no longer weighed down by despondency." He was doomed all the same to long and weary waiting at Memel before he could obtain the desired permission to join the field-force. He was assigned to General L'Estocq, who, as the king himself said, was beginning to show the infirmities of old age, and whom he was to "assist in every way," a difficult enough task in any case, but peculiarly so here, as Scharnhorst found himself placed in strange conditions in which he was at first unable to find any suitable scope for his activities. Youthful recollections—it is almost always these that have the firmest hold—took L'Estocq back to the days of the Seven Years War, in the latter part of which he had been an *aide-de-camp* of Zieten. After that, during the expedition of the Duke of Brunswick into Holland (1787), he and his hussars had won easy fame by the capture of an old armed ship.[10] The pure product of regimental duty, he shared to the full the old regimental officer's prejudice against everything labelled "general staff." And, to be fair, the record of the war hitherto had not been such as to reflect any credit upon the staff officer, who for the last few decades had made himself the somewhat arrogant professor of new and scientific methods of war, but in the conduct of an army had come to utter shipwreck. L'Estocq had hitherto reposed complete confidence in his personal staff, all "practical" men, and above all in his senior *aide-de-camp*, Captain von Saint-Paul, who was an intelligent and ambitious officer with a relatively brilliant record behind him,[11] and moreover derived support from his relations with Colonel von Kleist, the reporting *aide-de-camp general* to the king. It was only human nature for this confidential person to regard Scharnhorst as an interloper, and inexcusable though

9. Max Lehmann, *Scharnhorst*, i. 479.
10. See the author's *Rossbach and Jena*, p. 418.
11. Hildebrand, *Die Schlacht bei Pr. Eylau*, p. 22. Saint-Paul was born in 1768 in Nordenburg, had reached the rank of *Rittmeister* at the age of twenty-seven, and in 1807, at the age of thirty-nine, was promoted major. He was therefore a specially favoured officer, and was regarded as possessing exceptional qualifications, and it was impossible that he should readily accept Scharnhorst's authority. He died in 1813, as commander of a regiment, at the age of forty-five.

it may seem, it is to some extent comprehensible that he should have attempted to combat Scharnhorst's influence with the old General. It must be remembered that Scharnhorst's great services during the retreat on Lübeck were practically unknown to his new comrades, and he would naturally be thought of primarily as the Chief of Staff who had failed to avert the great disaster of Auerstedt and was not likely to do any better here. Under such conditions, it is easy to see how much of the effect of his ability and comprehensive judgment was necessarily lost. Yet in spite of all this, the influence of Scharnhorst's strong and earnest spirit soon made itself increasingly perceptible in the leading of the Prussian corps.

Successful cavalry skirmishes preluded its further operations. In Marienwerder a French general was carried off with two other officers and 30 men, and on the night of the 28th/29th another general was surprised at Bialechowo, north-east of Graudenz. On the 29th General L'Estocq advanced as far as Rosenberg, on the 30th and 31st to Freistadt, his advanced guards even to Lessen and Schwarzenau. Communication with Graudenz was reopened. The Prussians were encouraged by news that readied them of Napoleon's returning to Berlin, prostrated by nervous fever, and of the bridges over the Vistula at Thorn, reconstructed by the French, having been swept away by floating ice.[12] General L'Estocq proposed to continue his operations.

****

The Allies were destined to be cheated of their own ulterior desires just as they had but now cheated the French of their illusions. The Russians obtained little of the long rest in quarters that they had expected, and the Prussians' offensive was never realized. Napoleon, so far from being sick of a nervous fever or being worn out by his previous fatigues, was displaying the most astounding activity in Warsaw. He followed with the minutest attention every movement of his various corps, and busied himself unceasingly with providing for their wants and preparing for the spring campaign, for the work of reconstituting and refitting the army was still very far from completed. Politically, too, there was much to be done. Negotiations with Austria went on vigorously, Napoleon desiring a definite settlement with that power as regards the eastern question, which touched his interests very nearly. To Marmont, who commanded the French forces in Dalmatia, went the welcome news that Turkey had,

---

12. This in fact happened on the 23rd of January.

on 30th December 1806, declared war on Russia. The imagination of the world-conqueror swept over land and sea to the distant Indus. We are reminded of the plans that stirred his soul in the days when he was marching from Egypt into Syria.[13] Marmont was instructed to support the Turkish *pashas* of Bosnia and Bulgaria in every way, with officers, supplies, and necessities. In case the Porte asked for an auxiliary corps, the emperor was willing to send him with 25,000 men to Widin where, in combination with 60,000 Turks, he would be able to compel Russia to dispatch a second army to the Danube and so facilitate the emperor's own operations.

With Prussia, too, negotiations went on incessantly, his object being to induce her, either in concert with Russia to make peace in terms advantageous to France, or separately to enter into an alliance with him. At Posen the emperor had addressed these threatening words to General von Zastrow: "If the Russians are beaten and the king has not already separated himself from them, there will no longer be a King of Prussia." Now, finding himself confronted by renewed resistance on the part of the Prussians, he repeated this menace. On the 29th of January Talleyrand wrote to Zastrow:

> I must not conceal it from your Excellency that in the event of the non-acceptance of an alliance His Imperial Majesty will, to obtain his object, take measures to exclude the house of Brandenburg from the country for ever.[14]

When, on the 18th of January, the emperor received from Barten-stein Ney's report of his forward movement, his views and his projects, he caused the Marshal to be informed by Major-General Berthiér that he needed neither advice nor plans of campaign.

> You must be sensible, *monsieur le marechal*, of the fact that iso-lated undertakings are detrimental to the general plan of opera-tions and might involve a whole army in difficulties.

When, on the following day, Ney's unauthorized negotiations for an armistice became known, the major-general was instructed to in-form him that the emperor's plans were fixed, that he, Ney, was not now employed independently as he had been before Magdeburg, but

---

13. Yorck von Wartenburg, *Napoleon als Feldherr*, i. 148. "He proclaimed to the peoples of the East that he would capture Constantinople and overthrow the Turk-ish empire. A new empire was through him to come into being, and he imagined himself returning to Paris by way of Vienna, victorious."
14. Lettow-Vorbeck, *Krieg 1806-7*, iv. 50.

had his defined place in the line of army corps, and that it was not permitted to him to conclude an armistice on his own account. To this was added the admonition:

> His Majesty's commands are that in future your army corps is to march in mass and not disconnectedly (*décousu*), as you handled it in your late movement. The Emperor orders you to occupy the cantonments which have been assigned to you. Do so, however, gradually.

On the 20th of January the emperor learned, further, that the Russian General Essen's corps, 24,000 strong, was stationed between Lomsha, Nur, and Bryansk. Next there came information, vague at first but soon clearer, of the Russian army's continued presence in Old Prussia, though it was not until 23rd January that anything was known of its renewed advance. Soult was the first to notify this.[15] On the 23rd Davout sent in word that the Russians were beginning to harass his outposts, and on the same day Ney wrote to Berthiér from Hohenstein:

> It is asserted that the enemy has stripped a great part of his left wing, between Ostrolenka, Johannisburg, and Nikolaiken, entirely bare of troops in order to advance by Rastenburg in the direction of the Passarge.

The darkness began little by little to lift. The Russians were certainly moving. But their plans were still an unsolved riddle, and it is instructive to cast a glance into the workshop of Napoleon's mind in the days which followed.

At first the emperor comforted himself with the idea that he had to do with nothing more than the consequences of Ney's ill-considered advance. Nevertheless, as a prudent general he prepared for emergencies by giving orders that in case the news of a Russian advance was verified, Soult was to concentrate his corps at Golymin and to inform Augereau at once. The bridging work at Sierock and Pultusk was to be hurried on.

By 25th January Napoleon had admitted the possibility that the indices that were forthcoming pointed to a general offensive of the Russians. Augereau was to collect all his troops on the right bank of the Vistula and to place himself in readiness behind Soult. Outlying divisions were drawn in closer to the army.[16] Next day (26th), how-

---

15. Ney's report of the 22nd did not reach the emperor.
16. Oudinot from Kalisch to Posen, Espagne from Posen to Lowicz.

ever, the emperor again suffered himself to be quieted by the idea that the enemy, like himself, must be desirous of staying in his winter quarters, and that he would certainly settle down in them as soon as he had succeeded in scaring Ney into retreat. Nevertheless, he ordered more advanced points of assembly for some of the corps, so as to support the exposed corps of Ney and Bernadotte more closely in case operations were resumed. Soult was to occupy Willenberg strongly.

On the 27th Napoleon's view of the situation was completely changed. What was the piece of information that actually decided him cannot now be established with certainty. A report from Bernadotte, written on the evening of 24th January, after the marshal had betaken himself to Mohrungen, came in to Napoleon's headquarters. Its general tenor was similar to that of the warning call sent by Bernadotte to General Dupont on that day, and may well have had a disturbing ring. Ney, too, had sent in this message to the major-general:

Trustworthy information derived from traders agrees with the stories of deserters and prisoners in stating that there is a considerable mass of Russian troops assembled at this moment between Mühlhausen and Preussisch-Eylau and that the united army under the command of General Bennigsen is 80,000 strong.[17]

The instant that his convictions had taken shape, the emperor resolved to break up from winter quarters and to answer the enemy's offensive with a heavy and annihilating counter-attack. From this point his generalship is masterly. We might well call it the lion's awakening but for the fact that Napoleon was already on the alert. This time he was resolved not to return to rest until he had destroyed the Russians. In quick succession his orders shot forth.

The same evening (27th) he told Murat to march on Willenberg, there with Soult's corps and all the reserve cavalry within reach to form the advanced guard of the *grande armée*. The rest of the reserve cavalry was to assemble at Mlawa, whither also Augereau was to come with his whole corps. Davout was to concentrate about Pultusk. The emperor's general scheme was to assemble the bulk of the army about Willenberg, and thence, preceded by the advanced guard, to advance against the left flank of the enemy.

Special instructions were issued for the eventuality of the enemy's moving on the Lower Vistula. Bernadotte was in this case to retire on Thorn, where Lefebvre's newly formed 10th Corps was to be ready

---

17. Pierre Grenier, *Etude sur 1807. Manoeuvres d'Eylau et de Friedland,* p. 48.

to support him. It appears that Napoleon laid particular stress upon the maintenance of Thorn. Warsaw was too far away. He required a nearer point of passage on the Vistula on which to base his operations. Ney, although placed next to Bernadotte, was not to support him, but to cover the concentration of the *grande armée;* Murat to assemble the reserve cavalry at Mlawa at once and to form the advanced guard in conjunction with Ney's VI Corps. Thereafter the *grande armée* was to wheel to the left and fall upon the exposed flank of the Allies as they moved towards the Vistula.[18]

Lannes' V Corps was given a special mission. It was to hold the Russian corps of Essen I in check in the angle between the Bug and the Narew. The Emperor's plans even went so far as to provide for the eventuality of the enemy's crossing the Lower Vistula.

On the 28th, after receiving information that the enemy had not continued their pursuit of Bernadotte in the direction of Thorn, the emperor conceived the plan of "breaking into the enemy's midst and flinging back to right and left such portions of his army as had not effected their retreat in time." The offensive by Willenberg is now the emperor's watchword. On the 1st of February he intended to place himself at the head of his army there, and to drive it like a wedge into the enemy. No less than 29 dispatches written by him on this day (28th January) are preserved, and form a good specimen of the work of commanding an army at a moment of crisis.

On the evening of the 31st of January, in readiness to move off next day, Murat was to be with his cavalry in advance of Willenberg, Soult at Neidenburg and Janow, the Guard at Chorzellen. The axis of the general movement of the *grande armée* was to be the road Chorzellen-Willenberg-Ortelsburg. If the enemy was found to be more to the west, the emperor meant to deprive him of his communications with the home country and his line of retreat, by anticipating him on the right bank of the Alle and confronting him at one of the passages of that river.

It is interesting to observe, moreover, how far the emperor's mind ranged in meditating the future course of operations. To General Clarke, lately appointed governor of Berlin, Napoleon caused the following to be sent:[19]

As a corps of the enemy may be cut off and thrown back on the Lower Vistula or even farther, I have desired you to send troops to

---

18. P. Grenier, *Etude sur 1807,* pp. 50-1.
19. He had previously been governor of Erfurt.

Stettin, to watch events closely and to keep Marshal Mortier[20] informed. You will then be in a position not only to prevent the enemy from crossing the Oder, but also to stop him and delay his march so as to enable the corps sent after him in pursuit to overtake him.[21]

One is tempted to accuse the emperor here of making plans too far ahead, an error which indeed entraps many a commander who is gifted with all too rich an imagination. At the same time it must be especially observed that Napoleon refrained from giving any detailed orders, his intention being simply to set out clearly certain possibilities of the future for the benefit of all concerned. No one was to allow events to take him unawares.

His own view was still that the Allies would retire as soon as he launched his attack, and thereafter he intended to follow them up with all his forces, even Bernadotte closing in from the extreme left so as to ensure the concerted action of the whole army under his single control.

On 30th January he left Warsaw. In passing through Pultusk he gave Marshal Lannes further particulars of the task that he was to perform. In the first instance Lannes was to advance threateningly in the direction of Nur, in order to divert attention from the main army's offensive. Later, he was to secure the right bank of the Narew from the mouth of the Omulew to Sierock, above all maintaining his hold on this last place; and he was also to cover the interval between Sierock and the Austrian frontier. In this he could use the bridge-heads of Sierock and Pultusk as pivots for his operations, but in case of need his line of communications was to be by Modlin and not by Praga (Warsaw). In this, once more, was manifested the emperor's intention of making Thorn, and not Warsaw, his main bridge-head and point of passage on the Vistula.

As it turned out, Lannes fell ill immediately afterwards. Savary replaced him, and the projected advance was given up. On his journey to the front Napoleon, to his great satisfaction, was able to convince himself that comprehensive arrangements had been made for the supply of the troops, especially as regards bread, and he still further developed his supply instructions by organizing a general system of refilling. A large mobile park was to be brought up, the vehicles of which were to be loaded with bread and brandy and sent up to headquarters,

---

20. Mortier, it will be remembered, was with the VIII Corps in Mecklenburg and Hither Pomerania.
21. P. Grenier, *Etude sur 1807*, p. 53.

returning when empty to Warsaw to refill with fresh supplies. Polish country carts were collected for the same purpose. As soon as the army had advanced more than seven days' marches, only biscuit was to be sent up to the front.[22]

Daru, the intendant-general of the army, received detailed instructions for the collection and forwarding of great quantities of supplies, which bear witness to the extreme care and far-sightedness of the emperor. It is true that in the end the arrangements he had made broke down, but this is practically bound to happen when, as here, an army enters and traverses without halt or check a land of evil roads, in which even the miserable country carts find it impossible to follow the troops.

On January 31, the eve of the new campaign—destined to be brief and sanguinary—on East Prussian soil, the various parts of the army were thus distributed (Map No. 11):—In front, Murat and Soult near Willenberg, the cavalry pushed out to about Ortelsburg;[23] to the right rear, Davout at Myszyniec; to the left, Ney at Gilgenburg; farther back, the Guard at Chorzellen, and Augereau at Ciechanow and Mlawa. Bernadotte, who was as well provided with cavalry[24] as Murat, lay out to the west towards Neumark, whither he went on the 31st, in order to protect Thorn more effectually. A glance at the map shows the magnitude of the danger that at this moment menaced the left flank of the Russians. True to his principles, the emperor meant in the next few days to throw himself across his enemy's rearward communications, in order that the battle, when it came, should mean not merely defeat but annihilation to the Allies. In a letter from Berthier to Bernadotte we read:

I need not tell you, Monsieur le Marechal, that the emperor's intention is to cut off the enemy.

Napoleon himself, reaching Willenberg on this same day (31st), at once sent orders to Murat and Soult to march on to Passenheim, and to Ney to close in to a point half-way between Gilgenburg and Allenstein. Bernadotte was to conform by coming in to Gilgenburg, where he was to cover the rearward communications of the army; he was to march at night in order to prevent the enemy's knowing of his

---

22. Lettow-Vorbeck, iv. 47.

23. Murat had with him the cavalry divisions of Lasalle, Milhaud, and Grouchy.

24. Bernadotte had at his disposal the cavalry divisions of Klein, Hautpoul, and La Houssaye.

movement; if this was impracticable, he was to continue to draw back slowly in the direction of Thorn, and as soon as the enemy ceased to press him, but not before, was to resume the advance vigorously.

To the troops Napoleon addressed an inspiring proclamation:

> Soldiers! In the midst of winter as at the beginning of autumn, beyond the Vistula as beyond the Danube, on the banks of the Niemen as on those of the Saale, ever are you of the *grande armée*. I shall direct your movements, you will do all that honour commands, and if they dare to stand up before you, few of them shall escape.

Just as long ago he had pointed out the prosperous plains of Italy to the hungry soldiers of the Republic, so now he wished his army comfortable quarters for the rest of the winter "in the fair land of Old Prussia."[25]

The movements of the French army did not pass entirely unnoticed by the Allies' headquarters. The Cossacks did excellent work. Bennigsen certainly found out on the 30th that the French were massing at Mlawa and Neidenburg. In consequence he moved four of his divisions towards Allenstein, and informed General L'Estocq, who sent Scharnhorst to him. But the commander-in-chief did not attach any special importance to these events. He thought L'Estocq was strong enough by himself to threaten Thorn. Sednioratzki's division at Goniondz received orders to advance upon Pissa and threaten the right flank of the French army. He flattered himself that the enemy thus attacked from all sides would withdraw in affright behind the Vistula, without hazarding a general engagement.

But he was to be saved, and by one of those amazing accidents that so often play the major part in war, by "His sacred majesty Chance," as Frederick called it. The letter mentioned above as having been sent to Bernadotte by the French headquarters at Willenberg on the 31st fell into the hands of the cossacks.[26] On the evening of 1st February it lay

---

25. Lettow-Vorbeck, iv. 53. The proclamation was issued on the 30th, before the departure of the emperor from Warsaw.

26. It may be permissible to point out that what was luck to Bennigsen was scarcely ill-luck to the French, but rather the penalty of negligence. Only one copy of the dispatch was sent, and that not by a representative of the staff but by a young officer, fresh from France, who had just been posted to a regiment in Bernadotte's corps and had reported himself at headquarters for instructions as to how to join it. See F. L. Petre, *Napoleon's Campaign in Poland* (available in a Leonaur edition), and authorities there referred to, for a detailed account of the messages interchanged between Berthiér and Bernadotte.—Tr.

before Bennigsen at Mohrungen, and the Russian general was able to form an accurate idea of the surprise that the emperor was about to give him. At once he ordered the whole army to concentrate about Allenstein. The greater part of the army was already on its way thither. Prince Bagration, who with the advanced guard had followed up Bernadotte by Lobau, and L'Estocq's corps were also able to close up on the others.[27] The Russian general asserts that his idea was to fall back to Wartenburg on the main Königsberg road, where he would have regained his line of communications, which thereafter he would have run no risk of losing. But there is no document in support of this, and it is doubtful whether it was not later that the idea occurred to him.

For the actual concentration Bennigsen had selected a position, near Jonkendorf or Jonkowo, north-west of Allenstein, formed by a considerable range of hills, and having in front of it a belt of watermeadows about 1½ miles wide and intersected by ditches. This belt was formerly the bed of a lake, and even today it is in parts marshy and difficult to cross. According to the old ideas which attributed the highest value to frontal obstacles, the position was one of exceptional strength. Unfortunately, the enemy was under no sort of obligation to attack it. It blocked not one of the French lines of advance, for the more important roads northward passed, and pass today, right and left of it.

Prince Gallizin, who with considerable forces was already at Allenstein, was at once ordered to move into the position of Jonkendorf, leaving only a rearguard to cover the withdrawal of an advanced force under Prince Dolgoruki, which was expected from Passenheim. This measure was thoroughly justifiable, assuming that Bennigsen intended to accept the decisive battle on the Jonkendorf line; and incidentally it tells heavily against his assertion that he really meant at the time to fall back on Wartenburg, for one does not withdraw troops from the place to which it is one's immediate intention to march them.

---

27. L'Estocq was at Freistadt, 43 miles away.

CHAPTER 7

The Campaign in Old Prussia

The campaign which now began, and culminated in the battle of Eylau, is one of the sternest of the century. The horrors that it brought with it, the efforts that it exacted from man and beast, surpassed anything that this war had hitherto seen, and indeed anything that the French army had experienced in all their previous campaigns in Europe.

On the 1st of February, Passenheim, after a brief fight, fell into the power of the advanced guard of the *grande armée* (three cavalry divisions and the IV Corps (Soult), under Murat).

The cavalry at once pushed forward on Mensguth and Bischofsburg, and also on Wartenburg and Allenstein.

Davout assembled his corps with the intention of marching to Ortelsburg next day, but the emperor's orders required him to leave behind detachments to secure the right flank of the army. Napoleon was more careful of his rearward communications than he had ever before been, as he felt himself unusually dependent upon them. "The force of circumstances has compelled me to return to the magazine system," he wrote to Daru. Ney, Augereau, and the Guard began their movement upon Allenstein.

The emperor's view was that the main army of the enemy, before which Bernadotte had retired, would now be turning back and would seek to place itself in safety by retiring through Allenstein or Guttstadt. In that event the Allies were bound to run right into his arms. He had in mind, however, the alternative possibility that they would throw themselves upon Thorn, as ten years before Wurmser had thrown himself into Mantua, and he warned Marshal Lefebvre. Of Bernadotte there was no news whatever, impatiently as Napoleon expected it. Indeed, even in the other corps the circulation of orders and reports was far from being as rapid as it had been in previous campaigns, and in consequence Napoleon adopted an expedient which the Germans afterwards employed with success in 1870-1, *viz.*, that of detaching officers of his own staff to the various commands to send in information with the least possible delay. For his notions of the enemy's position he was thrown back upon hypotheses and calculations of probabilities derived from an appreciation of the conditions. Thus the war moved freely in its native atmosphere of uncertainty, and the emperor's decisions are in consequence doubly instructive.

On the 2nd of February we see both armies moving towards Jonkendorf, the Russians from the north and north-west, the French from the south and south-east, without either knowing much about the other's doings. In these conditions fighting alone as a rule dissipates the mist. And so it was in this case. Murat and Soult encountered the Russian rearguard under Dolgoruki and Barclay at Allenstein and attacked it. The deep-cut, romantic valley of the Alle gave the defender the opportunity for a stout resistance. The French marshals cautiously held their hand, for they estimated their opponents at 25,000 and had at present no strong support behind them. Fighting went on until nightfall, and then the Russians, whose strength had been about one-half of that attributed to them by the other side, drew off to Göttkendorf in the direction of their main body. Allenstein was occupied by the French, who pushed on cavalry for some distance beyond the place.

The emperor's assumption was that Bennigsen with the bulk of his forces was at Mohrungen[1] and would move thence on Guttstadt.

> Everything goes to show that the enemy is seeking to concentrate at Guttstadt. It is impossible to suppose that he will allow his left flank to be enveloped.

It was at once decided to anticipate him there, to which end the main portion of the *grande armée* was to advance down the right bank, and Ney by the left bank of the Alle. It was supposed that Bernadotte would arrive by way of Osterode, thereby fulfilling the double object of becoming available for the decisive battle and of securing the communications with Thorn, upon which place the emperor intended henceforward to base himself. *"Changer de ligne d'opération est une opération de génie"*[2]

---

1. "The information that we have succeeded in obtaining is that General Bennigsen is at Mohrungen "(P. Grenier, p. 57).

2. Letter to the king of Spain, 22nd September 1808 (P. Grenier, *Etude sur 1807,* p. 58).

Early on the 3rd, Napoleon was at Allenstein in person, and the ideas he had formed underwent a complete transformation. The Russians were not marching in disconnected fractions on Guttstadt, but, as he was able to assure himself, in position before him near Göttkendorf, between the Alle and the Okull-See. He at once determined to attack. But it would be necessary to wait for Ney, for with Murat's cavalry and Soult's corps alone nothing decisive could be undertaken. As soon as Ney should come up he was to form the left flank of the attack, west of Allenstein; in the centre, Murat with his cavalry and one of Soult's infantry divisions was to advance through the town; while on the right Soult with his two still available divisions was to work away to the right by Diwitten and envelop Bennigsen's left. The Guard and Augereau were to form the reserve.[3]

But the emperor waited in vain for Ney's coming, and after no more than a front-to-front cannonade in the neighbourhood of Göttkendorf, the Russians retired to their main position at Jonkendorf (Jonkowo). In the evening the two armies faced one another separated only by a deep-cut, bushy-banked rivulet, but contented themselves with an exchange of cannon-shots.

Soult meantime had carried out his movement through Diwitten, and in his search for a passage over the Alle he had encountered the Russians at Bergfriede. Bennigsen had early realized the danger to his left and the importance of the passage, and as early as 14th January, when advancing from Seeburg, he had posted there the 14th Division under General Count Kamenskoi, with which there were three Prussian heavy batteries attached to the Russian army and commanded by Major Huguenin.

The details of the interesting and important combat which followed, like so much else that took place in these days, are unfortunately but little known. Four Russian battalions seem to have had the special mission of guarding the defile and the bridge of the Alle. One was pushed out across the 200-yard embankment that traversed the marshy river valley at right angles, to occupy the village of Bergfriede. The Prussian custom that had wrought such evil at Lübeck and at Soldau seems to have been in vogue in the Russian army also. On the heights of the western bank stood the three Prussian batteries whose guns commanded the approaches to the bridge, but to right and left of them the high ground seems to have been entirely unoccupied.

About 3 p.m. the artillery of Leval's French division came into ac-

3. Map No. 12.

125

tion against the Prussian batteries, and began also to sweep the defile of Bergfriede with enfilade fire.[4] Then the village and the bridge were attacked by infantry wading the Alle[5] below Bergfriede, while another column went away with the object of seizing the unoccupied heights beyond, and thus opening the defile to the assailants from the rear. Both attempts failed. The French indeed penetrated Bergfriede, but were hurled back by the Prussian artillery fire and the stout resistance of the Russian infantry, and the turning movement was likewise unsuccessful at the outset. A renewed attempt at envelopment secured the evacuation of the village, the garrison of which was thrown back to the left bank. But a sheet of case-shot from the guns of the defence prevented the assailants from following up.

The French, however, came on again in greater force, and finally forced their way over the bridge. A Russian counter-attack with the bayonet led to hand-to-hand fighting on the bridge and the embankment, in which the French were once more repulsed. In the heat of the pursuit a Russian company actually forced its way over the bridge, only to be repelled in turn. Ultimately the French appear to have succeeded in getting possession of the hollows on the left bank and by a fresh enveloping attack to have dislodged the enemy with considerable loss.[6] Then night fell, and the French found themselves in possession of the passage.

The Russians indeed assert that this remained in their hands, but from what followed it seems more probable that the French claim is justified. Later, Guyot's cavalry brigade of Soult's corps pushed on to Guttstadt, where it found and seized Russian baggage-trains, magazines, and hospitals.

If we take a bird's-eye view of the relative positions of both armies on the evening of 3rd February, we observe a remarkable likeness to the situation of the 13th of October 1806 on the Saale. In the one case as in the other the defender is actually outflanked on his left while expecting attack from another quarter than that whence it really threatens. Put the Alle in place of the Saale, substitute for the combat of Bergfriede Tauentzien's engagement in the Landgrafenberg at Jena, put Guttstadt in place of Naumburg, and

---

4. This account is based upon Höpfner, *Krieg 1806-7*, pt. 2, vol. iii. pp. 199 ff.

5. *Durchwaten*. Sir Robert Wilson's narrative puts it rather differently: "The Alle was frozen, but impassable on account of the snow that rested on its bed."—Tr.

6. According to French accounts, the Russians lost 1100 men and 6 guns. The French admit a loss of 300 dead and wounded only, including 26 officers, but this estimate is exceedingly improbable, under the circumstances of the fight.

the parallel is evident. Just as Brunswick four months ago, so now Bennigsen was on the point of losing his rearward communications ere the battle had begun.

The full import of all this is, firstly, that Napoleon in each case so directed his advance that the battle, if he won it, would necessarily result in overwhelming disaster to the enemy, and secondly, that he managed to attain his objects without halving any clear and complete idea of the enemy's position or grouping. In the whole mass of conditions and circumstances he instinctively derived the essentials, and with a prophet's vision foresaw things as they would turn out. From so high a standpoint and with so comprehensive an outlook, his judgment was incorrect only in minor details. In each of the two instances, although envelopment played the decisive part, his first and principal object was to make certain of the victory itself; thus in the present case he took care that Soult should allow Davout's approaching corps to come entirely into line "without losing anything in turning movements."[7]

Napoleon thought the long-desired battle was within his reach, and in the bivouac of Göttkendorf, whither he had moved his headquarters, he expanded his orders in view of it. Davout was to move by Spiegelberg, place himself on Soult's right, and take his part in the decisive attack upon the Russian left flank. Bernadotte alone would be unable to arrive in time. The emperor had now learned that he had fallen back as far as Strasburg, and that the order sent to him on 31st January had fallen into the enemy's hands.

But the decisive battle was not to take place after all. Bennigsen had let slip the precious opportunity of attacking the emperor in the morning, and now, realizing the danger that began to threaten him, he evaded it by marching away in the night. L'Estocq had not yet rejoined, and the appearance of large French forces at Bergfriede and of Guyot's cavalry at Guttstadt must have made the Russian commander-in-chief anxious as to his line of retreat. At Guttstadt as at Naumburg the mere appearance of the French produced exaggerated and alarmist reports.

In the darkness the Russians drew off northward to Wolfsdorf. Bennigsen's immediate object was to recover the Königsberg road, and for that Guttstadt would have been a more suitable choice. It would seem that it was solicitude for the still absent L'Estocq that led him to select Wolfsdorf instead.

****

---

7. Lettow-Vorbeck, iv. 68.

We return now to the Prussian corps at Freistadt. On 2nd February it had received from Bennigsen the news that Napoleon was on the move and was expected to be at Willenberg on the 1st of February. According to Scharnhorst's report, General L'Estocq would not at first accept the idea of an immediate retreat, thinking that the enemy's main army was in front of him on the Vistula, but it seems that the convincing counsels of his adviser soon caused him to change his mind, and in fact the corps drew back on the same day (2nd February) to Deutsch-Eylau.

Unfortunately, Scharnhorst had gone to the army headquarters and was not on the spot to prevent relatively large detachments being once more made from the corps. The mixed columns of Generals Roquette and Esebeck and the little cavalry detachment of Major von Borstell,[8] in all 4 battalions, 10 squadrons, and a horse battery, were told to advance from the Marienwerder district, where they were at the time, to the southward first of all, so as to "screen" L'Estocq's withdrawal. Presently this hazardous order was cancelled, but the troops were not at the same time brought in, being ordered instead to continue to cover the Lower Vistula valley and so remaining outside the decisive events of the days that followed.

On 3rd February (Map No. 12) L'Estocq reached the neighbourhood of Osterode, and there he received Bennigsen's order to retire on Jonkendorf. In order to avoid contact with the enemy, the movement was made by a northerly detour, which so far deferred his junction with the main army that his co-operation in battle on the 4th could no longer be thought of. Receiving further information as to the commander-in-chief's plans for retreat, the Prussians continued to move northward during the days following. It is evident, however, that L'Estocq did not realize the full extent of the danger; had he done so, he would have made more vigorous efforts than he did.

During the night of the 3rd/4th and on the 4th (Map No. 13) the Russian army marched steadily on by narrow snow-covered ways. The movement was very slow, and when morning came on the 4th the Russian rearguard had not yet left the abandoned position. Napoleon indeed deployed the French forces to attack it, and on their left (Ney) there was sharp fighting. But the deception could not endure for long. Napoleon's keen vision soon discovered that his hopes were cheated again and that the enemy was escaping him. In doing so, Bennigsen was more successful than Brunswick—but then

8. Lettow-Vorbeck, iv. 58, 70.

the Duke would have arranged his "retrograde movement" in several successive echelons, whereas Bennigsen drew off with all his forces in a single body.

Not but that there was lamentable confusion in the Russian army. If checks on the march forced the rearguard to stop, the supports given to it were taken from any higher unit that happened to be close at hand, and the divisions were thoroughly mixed up in consequence. While the guns thundered in rear the marching columns progressed slowly, now halting, now moving on a little. The nature of the East Prussian roads in those days will be described later. They undoubtedly contributed a great deal to the difficulty of the movement. It is indeed wonderful that dissolution was not complete. But the Russian soldier of a hundred years ago displayed just the same traditional stoicism and capacity for passive endurance as the Russian soldier of today showed in the retreats of the Manchurian War.

On the morning after, the rearguard reached and rested awhile at Warlack, near Wolfsdorf. At this place Bennigsen and the main body had stayed on the 4th, but learning that the French were working round their left flank from Guttstadt, they had moved back again in the night, although the pressure in front was not very severe and the fighting on this day had only been slight.

The French too were tired. Napoleon reached Schlitt with the main body of his army on the 4th, Soult alone somewhat farther out towards Ankendorf.

The Prussian corps had not advanced far either (having in part missed the road assigned to it), and indeed the outpost brigades stood shivering at their place of assembly, Alt-Ramten, until 7 p.m. before they received orders to march to their positions on the Upper Passarge. The main body and the reserve reached their appointed destinations, Mohrungen and Seubersdorf, very late, portions of them indeed during the night. A rearguard remained out to the south of Mohrungen. But more serious was the fact that the crossing of the Passarge at Deppen—which the reserve was to have occupied, pushing its outposts over to the right bank—was already in the hands of the French.

When the newspapers today report a steeplechase by our officers, when a troop in pink gallops across the fields, following the swift hounds over fence, hedge, and ditch, we often hear unpleasant remarks about this aristocratic form of sport. And when a bad fall puts an end to some young life, bitter is the outcry against youth's bravado. People are only too ready to overlook the supreme value which these equestrian feats possess for war purposes and the splendid results they may produce in the hour of need. A good officer may often, by a rapid and dangerous ride, save many more lives in war than are sacrificed over a period of many years to this exhilarating sport. It is the indispensable preparation for efficiency in war-time.

During the campaign on the Loire, when Prince Frederick Charles had to send a most urgent message to the 6th Cavalry Division, which was far ahead to the southward, one of his orderly officers (Count Hermann von Arnim-Boitzenburg) accomplished the ride from Orleans to Vierzon and back, a distance of no less than 103 miles, in a single day. Now here, on the 4th of February 1807, the distance that separated Thyrau, L'Estocq's last headquarters, from the place of assembly of the outpost brigades at Alt-Ramten was only one-sixth as great, *viz.* 17 miles, and yet the bearer of the orders was on the way from the evening of the 3rd, or at any rate the night of the 3rd/4th, until 7 p.m. on the 4th. The grave consequences that this belatedness might have, quite apart from the hardships it imposed on the troops, was presently demonstrated by one of the saddest episodes of the campaign, the disaster to the outpost brigades at Waltersdorf on the 5th. Had these reached the Passarge earlier, while it was yet daylight, they would have necessarily suspected something of the danger that threatened them and would have moved off earlier next morning.

It is possible that the galloper was detained by the badness and obscurity of the tracks and by the snow, but what is certain is that he would have been able to do more had he been assisted by previous training and urged on by the knowledge of the importance of his mission.[9] Let no one imagine that such feats as the Orleans-Vierzon ride, when need suddenly demands them, can be accomplished without long and serious training. Success, and least of all a success of this sort, is not to be obtained by an extempore effort. Experience, which alone demonstrates its possibility, is indispensable for its achievement. Without the firm conviction that his task is feasible, any man must fail, for he begins by losing heart. The body and the soul moreover must be steeled to meet such an extraordinary strain, and this steeling is the product of practice, and practice only.

There was indeed no lack in those days of men who showed themselves stout horsemen and would face a difficult ride over obstacles

9. Nothing is known as to whether he met with an accident. In war such important messages should always be conveyed in duplicate by two officers.

without fear. Of the officers of the Gensdarmes Regiment a French ambassador reported that they were the most daring riders in the world. What was lacking was well-considered, systematic training and trial, and also exercises deliberately planned with the object of intensifying the sense of responsibility in such missions, and of branding a merely moderate achievement as a grave default.

May the habit of rapid long-distance riding, that we have now acquired, never die out, but become more and more settled as years go by; for, all modern inventions notwithstanding, we can never dispense with horsemen who can cover 90 miles and more between morning and evening. A good man in the saddle is now and always the surest means of communication between commander and troops in the field.

On the morning of 5th February, just at the moment when L'Estocq at Mohrungen heard of the delay to his outpost brigades, there came word that Bennigsen was continuing his retreat in the general direction of Landsberg. The Prussian corps was requested to follow the movement of the Russian right wing, keeping at a distance of only 2 miles, and moving in the general direction of Mehlsack-Zinten. What then? Between the Russians and the Prussians on the Passarge stood the French.

Moreover, having in mind the great initial distances to be covered, General L'Estocq had put back the hour of assembly for the march of the 5th. The situation was doubly serious, therefore, and yet it would not have been wise at this stage to issue fresh orders, as these would only have led to additional confusion. It would indeed have been feasible to draw the main body and the reserve closer together about Waltersdorf, where they could have waited for the incoming of the outpost brigades without the French being given an opportunity to crush any fraction of the army. But this wait would have once more prejudiced its junction with the Russians.

The most exposed faction was naturally the outpost brigades which were on the left bank of the Passarge, at least 6 miles south of the Deppen crossing, already occupied by the enemy. Nothing was done to enable them to extricate themselves; cavalry from the main body was indeed ordered to watch or to occupy the passages of the Passarge immediately below this point, but that was of no help to the troops threatened. It was at Deppen itself that they were in danger of being cut off, and unhappily the danger was soon to become fact.

While the main body and the reserve marched away to Liebstadt—where there were already French cavalry to be driven out—the weak outpost brigades were coming up from the south. It was noon when they approached Waltersdorf, and they found their way already barred. Napoleon at Schlitt had received information that a hostile column was approaching on the left bank of the Passarge and had rightly guessed it to be the Prussians. Marshal Ney was at once ordered to advance with his corps and the dragoon brigade of Lasalle, by Deppen on Liebstadt, in order to separate them from the Russians. While marching on Liebstadt the marshal found himself suddenly attacked on his Left flank. His assailants were the two Prussian outpost brigades of Büllow and Maltzahn and their supports, which were coming in by way of Bergling to the rendezvous at Waltersdorf. The force consisted in all of 5½ battalions, 10 squadrons, and a horse artillery battery under the grey-haired General von Klüchzner. It speaks well for the troops that they attacked the enemy unhesitatingly,—such is the conduct of all brave troops when they find their way to a rendezvous barred,—but the outcome was grievous.

Marshal Ney, leaving Lasalle's cavalry still facing Liebstadt, turned back, and his great superiority of force soon told upon the few thousand Prussians, who were driven back south-westward on Reichau. They attempted there to effect their junction with the main body by a detour round the south end of the Nariensee. But by ill-fortune the village street of Willenau, which they had to traverse in doing so, was found to be blocked up with baggage. They did their best, indeed, to extricate themselves by working on slantwise through gardens and courtyards, but meantime the pursuers had received the valuable reinforcement of Klein's cavalry division, which overtook the retreating troops and took many prisoners, the battery included. The pursuit continued almost to Mohrungen. The losses were heavy, and they fell upon the best troops;[10] but even more serious was the fact that this column too, one-third of what was left of L'Estocq's corps, was now driven off, and could take no part in the coming decision. The wreck of the outpost brigades, in fact, ignorant of General L'Estocq's halt, marched away for safety to Preussisch-Holland, whence they meant to rejoin L'Estocq by a further detour through Braunsberg.

The main body, after a march that, wearisome in itself, was made still slower by the heavy 12-pounder batteries, had reached the neighbourhood of Wusen and Schlodien, its billeting area extending thence half-way to Mehlsack. Anxiously General L'Estocq waited at his head-

10. Thirty-five officers, 1098 men, including 33 officers and 856 men prisoners. The latter were set free by cossacks at Willenberg on the 12th.

quarters at Schlodien for the outpost brigades, but no news of them came. And yet, if only he had called in the detachments of Esebeck and Roquette in good time, these would have met the remnant of the outpost brigades and brought it with them, with the result that 5000 more Prussians would have been available to attack on the day of Eylau.

For the next day's march the ground between Langwalde and Packhausen was chosen as the rendezvous.

Marshal Ney, who had for the moment lost sight of L'Estocq's column, believed that at Waltersdorf and Liebstadt he had won a considerable victory over the whole of the Prussian force and driven it westward. He estimated its number at 8000.

The Russians had effected their night-march from Wolfsdorf under the protection of strong rearguards. These, under Generals Baggovut and Markov, fell back from Warlack on Wolfsdorf, but there for three whole hours offered the most vigorous resistance to Murat and Soult, after which the retreat continued by Arnsdorf and Freimarkt to Drewenz, where Bennigsen called a halt, leaving the rearguard at Frauendorf. An attempt of Murat to outflank and isolate the latter by a movement by Open was checked by a brilliant attack of the Russian cavalry.

Napoleon had soon seen that his opponent had given up the idea of retreating by Guttstadt and was falling back northward by Arnsdorf. The advanced guard of the *grande armée* was sent in that direction. On the right, Davout approaching from Wartenburg was directed on and beyond Guttstadt, in readiness at any time to outflank the Russian left. Augereau and the Guard followed directly. Ney,[11] after his expedition on the left bank of the Passarge, was ordered, if the Prussians tried to effect their junction with Bennigsen by going still farther northward, to close in to the army again, for the emperor desired to have all his forces in hand for his blow against the enemy's main body. He himself went to Arnsdorf. The cavalry brigade of Marulaz pushed on to the right front and actually reached Heilsberg, but was driven out again by a Russian flank-guard.

Bennigsen, in spite of the fact that it was not now possible for him to be overtaken on the Königsberg road, for the third time decided, on the evening of 5th February, at Drewenz, to make a night-march to Landsberg. Thus it befell that on the 6th of February the French once more found the birds flown. It was said that the Russians were

---

11. Ney had, as we know, received at Schlitt the emperor's order to drive away the Prussians who were moving on the left of the Passarge.

concentrating at Landsberg, and the order went forth to all the corps of the *grande armée* to march on that point, Davout alone keeping away towards Heilsberg (Map No. 14a).

Then came Ney's report of the fight at Waltersdorf, and opportunity beckoned to the emperor to destroy utterly the last remnant of Prussia's military power. Marshal Ney was ordered to press the Prussians farther still, and drive them into Bernadotte's arms.[12]

For the first time Napoleon gave expression to his dissatisfaction at the paucity of news sent in by the latter. He assumed him to be advancing on Osterode, and told him "to manoeuvre so as to complete the ruin of the Prussians and to make them prisoners."

Thus two whole corps of the *grande armée* were told off at the same moment to hunt down this small Prussian force. On many occasions during this campaign we can discern the bitter personal hatred that Napoleon bore to Prussia, beaten down and almost helpless as she was. Later expressions might lead us to suppose that his hatred was based on a premonition that the momentarily shattered kingdom of Frederick the Great would in the future become his bitterest and most dangerous enemy. This, however, is not very probable in the then conditions. Prussia was, in fact, crushed so thoroughly that no one believed in her speedy resurrection. It would, however, be an explanation acceptable both to psychology and to common sense to say that the emperor felt a certain secret anger that for the past ten years he had hesitated, perhaps actually feared, to make war upon the Prussian monarchy. Now that it had been proved to be so far weaker than he had imagined, he saw his error, and his anger thereat rose until it expressed itself in a fierce longing for the total ruin of the foe he had once thought so formidable. *Humanum est odisse quem laeseris!* And in this longing the political advantages that he expected from Prussia's complete disappearance confirmed him.

The 6th of February witnessed two more combats. Davout advancing down the Alle by both banks had to drive the Russians out of Heilsberg by main force, and the centre of the *grande armée* marching by the direct road encountered a vigorous resistance at Hof, south of Landsberg. Bennigsen had posted General Barclay there with a rearguard of 5000 men in order to give the main army a start

---

12. "Napoleon, receiving from Ney a report to the effect that lie had not completely crushed L'Estocq's column, ordered him to finish off the Prussians, by moving on Wormditt to cut off their retreat while Bernadotte took them in rear" (P. Grenier, *Etude sur 1807,* p. 02).

and to prevent it from being entangled in a general engagement. Only at nightfall did the French succeed in driving back their stubborn opponent on Landsberg.[13]

So severe was the fighting at Hof that Napoleon seriously thought that there would be a battle at Landsberg, and directed the concentration of his army towards that place.

The attempt to drive off the Prussians on the 6th was unsuccessful. Ney believed them to be retreating upon Preussisch-Holland, in the direction of which place the outpost brigades had withdrawn. Starting late and moving slowly, he and his troops followed the general advance of the army, aiming at Wormditt, whence he could either draw in to take part in a battle against the Russians, or hunt down the Prussians should they emerge again. Consequently L'Estocq on this day was neither pressed nor even disturbed, and, in order to give his troops a little relief, made only a short march to Engelswalde. The day was more or less a rest-day.

Once more, on the morning of the 7th of February, Napoleon found his expectations unfulfilled. The mass of the Russian army had again used the hours of darkness to evade the decision, and this fourth night-march had taken Bennigsen back to Preussisch-Eylau.[14] The emperor had to change his dispositions yet again. Marshal Davout, who was already approaching Landsberg with his corps, was placed upon the Bartenstein road, as usual with the idea of turning the Russians' eastern flank and cutting off their communication with their own country. The obstinacy with which the emperor clung to this idea is astonishing. On the other wing Ney was now directed upon Kreuzburg, and received a fresh task, that of barring the Königsberg road to the Russians. The Prussians were to be left to Marshal Bernadotte, who was informed that L'Estocq was beaten and in retreat.[15] The centre of the *grande armée* advanced towards Eylau.

****

---

13. The total loss of the Russians in the fight at Hof (also spelt Hoff and Hoofe) are given by Höpfner as not less than 5 guns, 2 colours, and about 2000 men.

14. Henceforward the prefix "Pr." will be omitted.—Tr.

15. "Napoleon, thinking that L'Estocq, cut off, had doubled back, ordered Ney to move on Kreuzburg in readiness to cut off the retreat of the Russians on Königsberg after the battle" (P. Grenier, *Etude sur 1807*, p. 62). The phrase "after the battle" sounds improbable. If Napoleon at the moment of giving this order believed that he had a battle in front of him he would not have omitted to call in Ney, just as he called in Davout, to take part in it.

The retreat of the Russians, carelessly and improvidently arranged, had, on this day, as previously, been carried out with the usual clumsiness. When morning came the rearguard was still at Landsberg, and it had to fight incessantly as it drew back through the wooded and undulating country beyond. Not until it reached Eylau did it find a support to fall back upon. There, however, was Bennigsen, who had at last resolved to stand firm, to risk the battle, and to await the course of events.

At first, indeed, it had been his intention to fall back still farther, to Allenburg, where his communications with the Niemen and Russia could no longer be endangered, and to hand over the defence of Königsberg to the Prussians. Presently, however, he changed his mind, and stood fast at Eylau. The motives that induced the change it is now impossible to establish with certainty, but they can be guessed fairly accurately from the attendant circumstances.

The condition of the Russian army on its arrival at Eylau must have been extremely alarming. Since the retreat from Jonkendorf it had been incessantly on the move, having been obliged to spend its nights marching and its days in repulsing the pursuing enemy. There can be but few instances in the annals of war of so large an army's making four consecutive and uninterrupted night-marches. The rearguard would stand freezing in the cold snow-covered fields, usually without fire or food, until morning, when it was allowed to follow the retreating column. The means of sustenance afforded by the comparatively thinly populated country were utterly inadequate for the needs of an army traversing it in closely concentrated masses, and the height of distress was reached. In addition the troops were greatly fatigued by the narrow, winding, snowed-up roads, and the staff arrangements were bad.

We insert at this point, in spite of the fact that it has already been published, the thrilling description of a Russian officer of German descent who went through this campaign. It was written while the facts were still fresh in his memory, a rare thing in war. To the young officer without war experience it presents an unvarnished picture of the state of things that may, indeed must, occur in the absence of experience in the care of troops; a picture which will haunt his memory and sustain him in untiring and unfailing attention to duty, should he ever be called upon to take part in the higher leading; one, too, which will convince him of the value of those fatiguing peace-manoeuvres against which very likely he murmurs in secret.

We have just arrived.[16] This is the first moment I have had since leaving Jonkendorf in which to bring my diary up to date. I am so numbed, mentally and physically, by hunger, cold, and exertion, that I hardly have the strength or the desire left to write this down. No army could suffer more than ours has done in these few days. It is no exaggerated calculation to say that for every mile between Jonkendorf and this place the army has lost 1000 men who have not come within sight of the enemy. And the rearguard! What terrible losses it has suffered in those perpetual fights! The way they go about things is incredible and quite irresponsible. Our generals seem to vie with one another in a methodical undoing of the army. The disorder and confusion passes human conception. Bennigsen drives ahead in his carriage as usual, and the divisional generals follow their commander's example. General staff officers and column guides are seldom in their appointed places, consequently it often happens that all detachments of the army are marched off at the same moment and all try to take the same road. This results in the last divisions having to stand half a day or night in the sun with empty stomachs and wet feet. We left many dead and many sick men behind us on the road in this way. It takes a patient, healthy Russian to stand all this. We have survived so far through being constantly on the move and by the cold weather, but the consequences will be terrible. Often during a night-march through a wood or a defile the troops would be obliged to go in single file past some trifling object which blocked the way, *because no one gave the order to remove the obstacle.* What would I not have given to have slept out on the snow for a few hours during these marches, but even that might not be. We had hardly taken 20 to 30 paces before the order came: 'Halt!' Then the weary soldier would sink instinctively to the ground, only to get up in a few minutes and do as many more paces. This would go on for hours, whole nights indeed, until at last we came within sight of some broken-down powder-wagon which had caused the block. Mounted, dismounted, we tried each way in turn; but it was too cold for the one, and we had no strength left for the other.

The poor soldiers glide about like ghosts. You see them

16. At Eylau, 7th February 1807, 2 p.m.

137

asleep on the march with their heads resting on their neighbours. I myself arrived half asleep and half awake, and the whole retreat seems more a dream than reality.

The patience which our soldiers display in this business is truly commendable, and better than any philosophy. To one who has served in other armies this sort of thing is doubly grievous, because he knows by experience that it could be and ought to be different. Is there any precedent for reducing an army like ours to such a condition! In our regiment (the Azov), which has not seen the enemy and was complete when it marched across the frontier, the companies are reduced to 26 or 30 men apiece. The grenadier battalion scarcely musters 300 men, and the other two are even weaker. Not all the regiments have lost so many, it is true, as they had fewer recruits. Most of those that we have left behind are in fact recruits and hard bargains. One could almost credit Bennigsen with the desire to retreat still farther, did the state of the army permit it. As, however, it is so weakened and exhausted as to render a forced march on these same lines practically impossible, he has at last decided to do what he ought to have done long ago—*to fight!*

The French advanced guard dogs our army mercilessly day and night, and is at this moment driving the main body out of Eylau before our eyes. We have barely saved our heavy artillery. We marched off at Landsberg towards evening, and have been the whole night and all today on the road. The French rested at Landsberg, but they will not fail to overhaul us here all the same, because their march is better ordered and they know what they are driving at. The army is in battle array, and tomorrow will be the decisive day. Tonight will be terrible. *It is frantically cold and we have no fire.*[17]

We can imagine with what anxiety the commander-in-chief must have glanced down the ranks of his approaching columns, asking himself, perhaps, whether it were still at all possible to continue the march, or whether he must accept battle even at the risk of defeat. In the crit-

17. Unfortunately Lettow-Vorbeck, who first published this description, was not allowed to name the author, and after his death all efforts to trace the writer, whose remarkable powers of observation excited hopes of the existence of many other contributions of equal value to the history of the war, remained unsuccessful. (See Hildebrand, *Die Schlacht bei Preussisch-Eylau,* p. 5.) It is hoped that the publication of this may perhaps even now be instrumental in bringing the precious manuscript to light.

ical situations of war there always comes a moment when choice must be made between two impending catastrophes, and it seems preferable to choose possible destruction in battle because it is the more honourable solution. The day of Eylau teaches afresh that a strong resolve, even in such desperate circumstances, always contains the germ of a potential change for the better.

Then strike in boldly, never fear,
For God is with us everywhere;
And hopes half-hoped and deeds half-done
Nor Heaven nor Freedom ever won.

Other factors, too, operated in favour of standing fast. Had Bennigsen marched on towards Allenburg, all chance of drawing in L'Estocq would *ipso facto* have been forfeited. This eventuality he undoubtedly regarded as a very serious one, for before it lost its detachments the Prussian corps had been 25½ battalions. 55 squadrons, and 8 batteries strong, and Bennigsen could not at the time have known how large were the gaps made by the penchant of the higher leading for dispersion. Moreover, Königsberg, the second capital of Prussia, an important town of 50,000 inhabitants even then, and the largest in the kingdom after Berlin and Breslau,[18] the only city in the theatre of war whose resources could be of real use to an army, would almost certainly be lost. It is true that it possessed a bastioned *enceinte*, but this was a mere earth rampart, and the perimeter was almost as great as today, and this made defence difficult. Losing this town meant losing at the same time all connection with the sea, a situation which was bound to make a most unfavourable impression politically. In fact, the campaign begun with such high hopes in the middle of January would have ended, without a decisive blow having been struck, in a tame and pitiful conclusion.

Tactical considerations also urged the acceptance of battle. The country that the army had traversed after leaving Landsberg was undulating and wooded, and its hills were of some elevation, the ensemble therefore presenting little opportunity for the movement and deployment of large masses of troops. At Eylau the ground was more open and offered a better field of view than any yet met with in the whole march. To the north-east of the little town were low hills with gentle slopes. Lakes, water-meadows, and marshes were frozen hard and thus

---

18. The garrison is not included. Warsaw is left out, as it only belonged to Prussia for a few years.

made passable. All this was in favour of the Russian mass-tactics, and Bennigsen's resolve to accept battle cannot but be approved.

There is, lastly, one more point that must not be overlooked, as it is of importance for the understanding of the battle. There is an idea generally prevalent that Eylau was then the point at which the great army routes to Königsberg on the one hand, to Friedland-Allenburg-Wehlau-River Niemen on the other, separated, and that it was necessary at this point to make a definite choice of direction. Although this idea is suggested by the lie of the road-network and the position of the *chaussées* as they are today, it dominated the earlier historians as well. Lettow-Vorbeck[19] speaks of the Russian army's covering the routes leading to their own country, while L'Estocq's Prussian corps, called in to the right flank, was to cover the Königsberg road. Höpfner remarks that Eylau was the *extreme* point at which it was undoubtedly open to Bennigsen to choose whether, in case of further retreat, he would give up Königsberg or his shortest communication with Russia, adding that:

> The strategic position of Eylau quite as much as the suitability of the ground decided the Russian general in favour of accepting battle there.[20]

Even modern plans of the battle conform to the general idea. Nevertheless, it is quite erroneous. In those days the great army route from Warsaw to Königsberg passed not by Eylau, but from Bartenstein by the Rohrmühle, Melohnkeim, Lampasch, and Romitten to Mühlhausen, leaving Eylau well on its left.[21] At Lampasch the other great highway branches off to Domnau-Friedland-Allenburg.

The road from Landsberg by Eylau and Schmoditten to Mühlhausen, in the general line of which the modern *chaussee* lies, was then only a narrow connecting lane between village and village, and was enclosed by a double row of trees. On account of the so-called "statutory-labour," or *corvée,* which they were obliged to perform for

---

19. *Op. cit.* iv. 100.

20. *Op. cit.* iii. 220.

21. In Lettow's plan the old military road can be traced at the Rohrmühle south of Melohnkeim, at Lampasch farther up, and again north of that. The representation of the road Landsberg-Eylau, Schmoditten-Königsberg is based, in this battle-plan also, on the old idea; for the road is shown as a wide post-road or highway, which is certainly not in keeping with its character at that period. The standard reference map in dealing with the network of road is Schrötter's of 1804, the best topographical map of East Prussia at the time, and that which in all probability the generals used.

the nobility, the East Prussian peasantry of those days took care to have very small and light carts, and the roads were correspondingly narrow. An overturned vehicle, a fallen horse, an obstacle of any kind whatever, however trifling, could cause a prolonged stoppage of the kind that our Russian eye-witness so graphically describes. A gun on the ground could absolutely prevent movement until some trees had been cut down on one side or the other to make room. It was a very easy matter for the side that had the highway at its disposal to overtake its opponents who were toiling through the country lanes. The lane, or rather successive lanes from Landsberg, by Eylau, at last joined the Warsaw-Königsberg highway at Mulhausen.

This fact, which is also of some importance in connection with the course of the battle,[22] puts a new complexion upon Bennigsen's resolution to stand fast at Eylau. There, as he actually stood, he had still the free choice of the line of retreat. The village of Lampasch, near which the two main routes diverged, lay well behind the centre of his position and was thus completely protected. On the assumption that Eylau was, what it was not, the actual parting of the ways, it would be quite proper to blame Bennigsen, as he has been blamed, for having already passed the decisive point, which lay in front of his line and had to be given up at the very outset of the battle. Had this been the case, one of his reasons for standing fast would have been baseless, and the halt by so much less justifiable than it really was.

****

On the 7th of February, as on the other days, the Russian rear-guard (under Prince Bagration) had frequently to halt in order to repel Murat's insistent cavalry, for the army was marching in a single long column and still made very slow progress. During the day the prince sent back to army headquarters to ask for a support of cavalry. Bennigsen consented, and at once five cavalry regiments that had not yet moved into the battle position, as well as some infantry, turned to the front and moved forward, meeting the rearguard near Grünhöfchen. Finally, as time was still needed to enable the main column to traverse Eylau and form up in the assigned order of battle beyond, Bagration had once more to halt and to make a prolonged stand quite close to Eylau itself, his actual position being on the low

22. So far as I am aware, the credit of having called attention to the contrast between the old and the new positions of the highways is due to Pfarrer Dr. J. Hildebrand of Schmoditten, who has made careful researches and written a short essay on the subject. (See his *Schlacht bei Pr. Eylau am 7. und 8. Februar*, p. 21.)

hills between the Tenknitter See and. The Waschkeiter See, where besides the lakes there was also a peat-bog (Torf-Bruch).

It was 2 p.m. when the French from Landsberg appeared before this advanced position at Grünhöfchen. Their condition, too, was pitiable, as we can tell from the evidence of a first-rate witness, Baron Percy, surgeon-in-chief of the *grande armée,* who had followed Napoleon through Passenheim and Allenstein.

> The fire and the smoke of the bivouac," he tells us, "made the soldier dry, brown, unrecognizable. His eyes are bloodshot and his clothes filthy and burnt. He is shrunken, piteous, half-dreaming. Often he startles one with the curses and imprecations that despair and impatience wring from him.[23]

One advantage the French certainly had: they were superior to their opponents in the art of living on the country. Percy expresses his astonishment at the number of the heads and skins of slaughtered animals that he met with, and he calculates that every soldier must have consumed 4 lb. of meat daily. On the other hand, bread was entirely wanting.

> Never was there such a spectacle of desolation as that which the poor little town of Passenheim presented. In the streets everything is wrecked and thrown aside. Never has there been such a riot of vandalism.

The roads were covered with the corpses of men and horses. Innumerable fragments of equipment and broken fittings of wagons lay everywhere around. The frost made itself bitterly felt. "What a climate, what cold, what a country!" Thick woods were traversed in which ordinarily an efficient guide would have been essential, but now an endless chain of stragglers and broken-down vehicles marked the path of the army's march. The farther north, the worse became the state of affairs. The battlefield of Hof made a frightful impression. "Never have so many corpses lain on so small a space;" everywhere the white fields were flecked with blood, though the falling snow was beginning to cover up the bodies. Especially thick lay the dead where a little group of pines had afforded a point of support for the defenders. The top of one hill revealed a dreadful sight, a hundred corpses lying in groups. Horses, still living but utterly exhausted, stood on the track, soon to sink from hunger on the hill of the dead. No sooner was one field of battle traversed than another came in sight.

---

23. E. Longin, *Journal des Campagnes du Baron Percy,* 151 ff.

What must have been the aspect of the troops, particularly of the mounted troops in these conditions, may easily be imagined. The horses were for the most part mere skeletons, which dragged along under their riders at a walk, but were quite incapable of trotting.

Even on the emperor himself the winter campaign in Poland and the Eylau campaign had a peculiarly lasting impression, and even after both were well over, in March 1807, he complained indignantly that his officers had never had their clothes off for two months and that he himself had not been able to take off his boots for fourteen days.

In snow and mud, without wine and spirits, without bread, we lived on potatoes and meat, made long marches and counter-marches without the simplest comforts.

CHAPTER 8

The Battle of Eylau

(7th-8th February 1807)

Such were the circumstances in which was fought the two days' battle of Eylau. Although the campaign was one of the most important and most sanguinary in the records of the nineteenth century, yet the information that we possess about its course is so self-contradictory that it is not possible today to give an accurate reconstruction of a good many of its details. Conformably to its purpose, the present work deals with the conflict of the French and the Russians in its broad outlines only, and with the doings of the Prussian corps, and its intervention at the decisive moment, in greater detail. Prince Bagration had posted the strong rearguard under his command on the not inconsiderable hills which lie south-west of the Torf-Bruch and close to the Tenknitter See. A Jäger regiment in skirmishing order covered the front. Behind the Torf-Bruch, on a front extending from the Langer See, near the north end of the Waschkeiter See, to the quasi-suburb of Eylau called Freiheit, was deployed the Russian 8th Division with strong bodies of cavalry on each flank.

Against this position the French advanced guard from Grünhofchen came on very vigorously. At first it was repulsed, and Russian cavalry crossing the hard-frozen surface of the Tenknitter See flung themselves upon the left flank of the attack, broke up an infantry regiment engaged in it, and captured an eagle. Then, however, the attack was renewed and both flanks threatened with envelopment, in which Augereau's corps apparently took part as well as Soult's. For a time the Russians resisted this attack too, but presently by Bennigsen's orders they fell back to Eylau, Barclay holding the town itself to cover their withdrawal. The rearguard was then broken up, part of it being sent to the right flank, part to Serpallen on the left of the main position.

The first act of the drama, stern and bloody, was over, and now there began the second—the fight for the town.

This, it seems, took place contrary to Napoleon's intentions. To Augereau, when that marshal joined him on the field, he said:

> It has been proposed to me to carry Eylau this evening, but in the first place I am no friend of night-attacks, and in the second place I do not want to drive my centre too much until Davout and Ney, my right and left wings, have come in. I mean therefore to wait on this plateau, which, crowned with guns, affords an excellent position for the infantry. Then when Ney and Davout have come into line, we will all advance upon the enemy together.[1]

If this report be just, it is at the same time valuable as showing that Ney was meant to act against the Russians and not against the Prussians.

The Russians had not had time thoroughly to organize and pre-pare the defence of Eylau. On the extreme right, near the bailiff's house—a group of strong old buildings where the road to the suburb Freiheit emerges—there seems to have been no more than a cavalry detachment. It was there that the French first effected an entrance, and thence, in the face of an obstinate resistance, they forced their way into the street that leads to the market-place. At the same time the assailants gradually pressed in by the road from Landsberg and the Landsberg-Strasse within the town.

At the other, or south-east end of Eylau there stands on a hill a church which in 1807 was surrounded by solid walls. Against this the French formed up their columns of attack on the north part of the Langer See, and it was carried after heavy fighting at about 5 p.m. But in and around Eylau market-place the Russians offered a stern resistance. The fighting grew more and more murderous. Cannon engaged cannon with a street's width between,[2] or drove through narrow streets over the bodies of dead and wounded men. Little by little the French, more experienced house-fighters as they were, made their advantage felt. The Russian losses mounted up. General

---

1. Schlichtling, *Taktische und Strategische Grundsäatze der Gegenwart,* pt. iii. 7.

2. A French gun at the upper end of the Landsberg-Strasse where it enters the market-place fought a Russian gun that was placed in a gateway to its right front. Here the inn Zum Deutschen Hause now stands. The distance from muzzle to muzzle was little more than 50 paces.

Barclay's right hand was shattered, many of the higher leaders were killed or wounded, and Prince Bagration (who was still in command) began to evacuate Eylau.

At this moment Bennigsen suddenly appeared at the exit of the town with the Russian 4th Division, which he had brought up in three columns from the reserve of the main line. This was launched to the attack, and by 6 p.m. Eylau was once more in the hands of the Russians. But half an hour later it was deliberately evacuated by Bennigsen's express orders. This almost unaccountable decision Bennigsen himself, in his *Memoirs*, explains[3] by saying that he had wished to attract the French towards the strongest part of the position, which was that lying behind the town. This explanation, it need hardly be said, will not bear investigation, and in all probability Bennigsen's order was the outcome of one of those sudden impulses that so often storm into the heart of a commander in a fierce fight such as this, and which defy analysis.

The French moreover, for their part, assert that they *re-captured* Eylau. Be this as it may, the town was certainly in their hands during the night. The emperor established his headquarters in a merchant's house in the Landsberg-Strasse—a fine and at that time a comfortably furnished house, but now vulgarized by alterations and improvements—which was able to accommodate the secretaries and the general staff as well. Next morning, as was ever his habit, he rose very early to reconnoitre the enemy's lines.

****

On the 8th of February 1807, a Sunday, dawned the real day of battle. Of the *grande armée* the following units were in position or immediately at hand: Murat with his four four-regiment cavalry divisions (Milhaud, Klein, Hautpoul, and Grouchy) of the reserve; Soult's corps; Augereau's corps; the Guard. Marshal Davout was to have advanced along the Bartenstein road to within four miles from Eylau.[4] Communication between this corps and the main army had been opened on the evening of the 7th, an officer from the major-general having appeared at Perscheln to exchange news with Davout's divisional commander, Morand.[5] On the other flank Ney, heading for

---

3. Höpfner, *Krieg 1806-7*, iii. 225.
4. "Une lieue et demie," *Opérations du IIIe Corps*, p. 158.
5. Hildebrand, *op. cit.* p. 18.

Kreuzburg, had reached Orschen and Eichen. Thus only Bernadotte and his 15,000 men[6] were so far absent that it was impossible to bring them in. Uncertain as to the emperor's intentions, he had stood fast at Strasburg until 4th February, and he only began his advance next day, reaching Lobau on the 5th and Osterode on the 6th, and thence following the track of the main army towards Landsberg. Nothing therefore was to be expected of him in the way of co-operation for some days to come.

The deployment of the French army for battle is indicated on the plan.[7] The front ran along the Bartenstein track to Eylau and thence leftward on a line whose prolongation would fall just clear of the south-east corner of Althof. On the extreme right flank near Zehsen was Milhaud's cavalry division, next on Milhaud's left in front of Rothenen was Saint Hilaire's division of Soult's corps, from which Augereau's corps continued the line to near Eylau church. In rear were the three cavalry divisions of Klein, Hautpoul, and Grouchy, the last named on the ice of the Langer See. In reserve, under cover of the west slope of the churchyard hill, stood the Guard, with its cavalry, like Grouchy's, on the Langer See. In Eylau itself and to the left of it, near the Schneidemühle, was Soult with his two remaining divisions, whose line was prolonged leftwards over the open ground between Freiheit and the Walkmühle, by the cavalry brigades of Durosnel, Guyot, and Colbert, detached respectively from the VII, IV, and VI Corps and placed there. In advance of the front, along the Bartenstein track, and on the churchyard hill and at the Schneidemühle, north of Eylau, stood long lines of guns, the most important of these being that on the heights, where now stands the memorial commemorating the battle.

The Russians had brought together all their divisions for the battle (2nd, 3rd, 4th, 5th, 7th, 8th, and 14th). Their method of marching in densely concentrated masses had at any rate this advantage to set against the sufferings that it had brought upon the troops, that (apart from the Prussian corps) not one of the larger units was missing on the day of battle. But, on the other hand, the divisions were much mixed up. We have already seen how during the fighting of the 7th, the rearguard was reinforced by the units that happened to be at hand at the moment, irrespective of the higher organizations

---

6. The cavalry divisions of Klein and Hautpoul which had originally been with Bernadotte had returned to the main army as early as 4th February.

7. Map No. 15.

to which they belonged. Bennigsen had formed his light troops into special detachments under Bagovut and Barclay. In the line of battle itself the divisions were absolutely indistinguishable, for the army was formed after the old fashion, in single phalanx of several lines. The right wing, very strong in cavalry, had on the 7th extended as far as Schloditten; on the 8th, however, it reached no farther than the Walkmühle, as Bennigsen withdrew troops from the front to the reserve and adopted a shorter line. The first line extended from the Walkmühle, bending back a little towards Klein-Sausgarten, along the low ridge which terminates in the so-called Kreege-Berg. The regiments had each two battalions deployed in line, and the third in column at a short distance behind. A second line was also formed. The left flank like the right was secured by large forces of cavalry. The 4th, 7th, and 14th Divisions were drawn up in masses in support, and with the rest of the available cavalry and a large force of artillery formed the reserve. Numerous guns were distributed along the front for its better protection, including three considerable masses—one of 40 position guns and 20 light guns[8] on the right wing, a second of 70 position guns in front of the centre, and the third of 40 guns in front of the left. An independent advanced echelon was formed on the left by the light troops at Serpallen, on this day commanded by Bagovut alone.

A glance at the battle-plan tells us that it was here that the weak point in the position lay, for this extreme left wing in its advanced situation presented its flank full in the direction of Bartenstein, whence it was to be expected that Davout's corps would come. It should have been placed as a *rearward* echelon at Klein-Sausgarten, or better still at Melohnkeim, when it would have formed a strong reserve to prevent the envelopment and rolling up of the army. Such might well have been the role of Sedmoratzki's absent division, which here on the battlefield would have played an important and decisive part, instead of uselessly remaining behind to support Essen's far distant corps.

The accounts that are given of the strength of the respective armies are unsatisfactory. They are based upon calculations which in their turn rest upon figures which are known for the days before or the days after the battle; some of these are very doubtful. But we shall not be far wrong if we assume that the two sides were approximately

---

8. In this line of guns there were also the three Prussian batteries of Major Huguenin, to which was added later a fourth under Major Brockhausen.

equal—70,000 to 75,000, including the respective commands of Ney and L'Estocq which came up on the evening of the 8th.[9]

Ten or twelve hundred yards only parted the two opposing hosts. The night of the 7th/8th February was severe, and the temperature fell to 5° and even 1° Fahrenheit. The French indeed were able to find some shelter in Eylau and the adjacent villages, consuming their resources without mercy and leaving desolation in their wake. Far worse was the situation of the Russians on the bare hills north-east of the town. The senseless order that no fires were to be lighted must of itself have made their sufferings worse than the enemy's. In such an order as this we recognize once more the might of accepted dogmas. It is of course important, generally speaking, that one's position should not be betrayed to the enemy, but in this case it was already known to them and the rule did not apply. The Russian 4th Division, withdrawing from Eylau after its counter-stroke, was obliged to stand fast in the darkness, close to Eylau, to prevent the enemy's advancing, and contact was never for a moment lost.

Even if Bennigsen had intended to march away in the night for the fifth time in succession, numerous watch-fires would have aided him rather than the reverse. But no purpose whatever was served by keeping the poor frozen troops without fires when it had been decided to accept battle. That very decision made it important to give the troops a good night's rest by a warm fire and the best procurable fare. Many a

---

9. Hofpner (iii. 227) puts the combatant strength of the Russians at no more than 58,000, to which there were added 5000 Prussians, while he gives the French 80,000. Lettow (iv. 101), on the other hand, calculates the Allies' strength to have been 82,500, and the entire total of the French, including even the regiments of Ney's command which did not arrive until after dark, 75,300 at most. His estimate is based, as regards the Russians, on the reports of the Prussian General von Chlebowski, who was present with Bennigsen's headquarters. These reports give 48,000 as the strength of the Russians on the 13th, and 53,000 on the 18th, to which must be added the losses at Eylau. This would give the seven Russian divisions present an average strength of 12,000, which, when we take into account the prolonged marching of December and January and the previous rearguard fighting, seems a very high figure. The events of the retreat from Jonkendorf in particular tell against it. The number of men who died or were left behind therein must have been very great. In the calm following the battle many a man reappears in the ranks who was previously missing, and as a rule the figures mount up rapidly in consequence. The estimate is probably closer to the truth as regards the French side, though these too seem to be a little high. Berthiér says that the emperor had considerably superior forces in front of him, and was only able to assemble at the decisive point 54,000 men out of the 300,000 whom he had in Germany (Derrécagaix, *Le Maréchal Berthiér*, vol. ii. pp. 200, 202).

disaster has resulted from the unreasonable application of an inherited maxim of war, and the consequences must not be ignored or underestimated in the present case. It speaks volumes for the discipline of the Russian army that in spite of their necessity—the necessity that is said to know no law—the order was actually obeyed. Next morning the hedges and fences (in those days numerous) still stood intact to bear witness to their self-restraint, and the accounts of those eyewitnesses who are said to have seen from Eylau church-tower the fires of innumerable Russian bivouacs are the product either of untruthfulness or of hallucination.[10]

The drama of 8th February was opened in the grey of early morning by a heavy fire from the Russian guns against Soult's position, and especially Eylau town itself, where for a while it caused great confusion. The French army rushed to arms and moved into its assigned positions. Napoleon placed himself at the church. He is said to have climbed the wooden stairs[11] that in those days led up, on the outside of the north wall, to the gallery, which afforded a wide view; but he must have changed now and then to a position on one of the flat rises near the Bartenstein road.

His guns at once took up the challenge of the Russians, and a heavy general cannonade occupied the morning hours.[12]

The emperor, as usual, intended to attack. From the events that followed, it is easy to see that the strategic envelopment of the Russian left flank that he had so persistently sought to bring about, was meant to develop during the battle into a tactical envelopment which should sever the Russians completely and finally from their communications with their own country. He imagined a great left-wheel of his whole right wing and centre, with Eylau and Soult's corps as the pivot.

Thus it was that the whole left wing of the French battle-line stood at the halt throughout the long day of conflict, and that on this side the battle turned into what was to all intents and purposes mutual observation, with continuous but heavy cannonading, varied only by a few more vigorous episodes, such as the brief forward dash of a Rus-

---

10. Hildebrand, *op. cit.* p. 10.

11. Now replaced by a buttress which has been built on.

12. The batteries suffered less in this than the troops that stood behind them. In the artillery of the French Guard only two officers fell, whereas the Guard infantry standing in reserve behind the church hill lost some 400 men. In five artillery regiments, taking the casualties of both days together, only 5 officers were killed and 9 wounded (Hildebrand, *op. cit.* 12).

sian Jäger regiment out of the line of battle,[13] and a Russian cavalry charge, which, however, in the deep snow degenerated into a slow walk and was repulsed by the carbines of the French left wing cavalry. Directly afterwards the Cossacks tried to outflank the latter, but they too were driven off.[14]

The actual effect of all this artillery fire, here, there, and everywhere, it is difficult to estimate. The thick cloud of smoke that settled down between the combatants must have diminished their losses. It appears that the Prussian batteries distinguished themselves by the accuracy of their fire.

In the emperor's projected left-wheel the decisive part fell to Marshal Davout, who was to come in from the Bartenstein road and cooperate in the general onslaught upon the Russian left wing.

The 3rd Corps, on the day of Eylau, consisted of the same regiments as on the day of Auerstedt, though their numerical strength was very different. "Infinitely reduced by the losses it had suffered in this battle (Auerstedt) and by the combats and marches that had subsequently taken place,"[15] the corps now numbered only 15,000 men. In the advance from the Heilsberg and Landsberg district the 2nd Division (General Friant) was in front, and on the night of the 7th/8th it was encamped between Perguschen and Beisleiden. The 1st Division (Morand) was at Zohlen, the 3rd (Gudin) at Bartenstein.[16] The cavalry brigade (Marulaz) belonging to the corps, which had accompanied the advanced guard of the *grande armée* in its movement upon Eylau, had returned to Davout's headquarters at Beisleiden at nightfall.

There in the night the marshal received the emperor's orders to move off before daybreak on the 8th of February, to join the army at Eylau and attack the Russians' left flank. Accordingly the divisions paraded early, and moved off before it was light, Marulaz's cavalry brigade in advance, and Friant's division behind it, straight on Serpallen. Morand followed through Perguschen, and Gudin from Bartenstein

---

13. This attack was directed against the Walkmühle, which was held by Soult's outposts, and which the Russians captured.

14. Six cavalry regiments under General Markov appear to have been placed on the extreme right flank of the Russians, between the Walkmühle and Schloditten; these are not shown on (Lettow's) plan.

15. *Operations du IIIe Corps,* p. 159.

16. As Friant certainly arrived very early before Serpallen, his account is not improbably correct. Morand's division passed through Perguschen as early as 6.30 a.m., but Friant was in front of him, and pushed directly upon Serpallen. The distance between Perguschen and Serpallen is only 2½ miles.

was already *en route* for Eylau at 3 a.m. Marshal Davout also opened up communication with Saint Hilaire's division.[17]

Before daylight Friant encountered Cossacks in front of Serpallen, whom he drove away. He then formed the division for attack, placing Marulaz's cavalry to cover his right flank, and moved on the village, which was carried at daybreak.[18] The resistance of the Russians was trifling, and Bagovut had soon retreated to Klein-Sausgarten.

The sound of the guns at Serpallen may very likely have been inaudible at Eylau. The phenomenon described below in connection with the entry into line of L'Estocq's Prussians shows that the roar of battle on this occasion was in general heard only at short distances. It may well have been, therefore, that the emperor's ear detected no sound of the combat that was already in progress on his right wing. But as soon as the snowstorm which fell during the battle gave place to clear weather, Davout's attack must have been seen. This is the simplest explanation of why the emperor between 8 and 9 a.m. gave his much criticized order for the advance of Augereau's corps and Saint Hilaire's division. Neither his growing impatience at Davout's absence nor the fact that he had noticed a gap in the Russian line and resolved to break through it, can be produced as a reason, for neither argument will bear examination. The battle was in its first stages and the time to be impatient was not yet. It was likewise premature to attempt to break through the front, for it is absurd to suppose that Napoleon at this precise moment suddenly abandoned the working principle which he had consistently followed from Willenberg onwards—envelopment of the Russian left flank—in order to profit by a moment's doubtful opportunity.

On the contrary, his resolution is in entire harmony with the general principles of the conduct of a battle. Davout's enveloping attack was just opening. But no envelopment is successful unless at the same time the enemy is vigorously tackled in front. This Napoleon knew better than any man before or since. If he did not do so, the Russians would be given time to strengthen their left flank from the centre, fling back Davout by superior numbers, and so deprive the assailant of the promise of coming victory. Further evidence is afforded by the

17. Right of the emperor's line at Eylau.—Tr.
18. Another account says that this took place between 8 and 9 a.m. The account here followed is that of Davout's report, which, although it is only a broad outline, is nevertheless in general very plain and lucid (*Operations du IIIe Corps*, Paris, 1896, p. 158 ff.). We have also made use in part of the latest Russian publications in the *Voyeniy Svornik*.

58th Bulletin of the *grande armée*, which states that Augereau's advance had been designed to distract the enemy's attention and prevent him from turning his full force upon Davout. The critic, so far from having cause for amazement, can only regard the conclusion as a logical one. Those who are unable to see events as one connected whole may well condemn the assault, prematurely delivered and bloodily repulsed as it was. But success is not always the best criterion of the soundness of the original scheme.

Augereau and Saint Hilaire moved forward. The great and oft-told tragedy of Eylau was at hand.

Saint Hilaire, whose artillery was already engaged with that of the Russian left wing, inclined more and more towards Davout's battle-field, and his division took part in the enveloping attack. Augereau aimed full at the Russian centre. Here was the harmony between frontal and flank attacks that is so rarely realized in execution.

On the day of Eylau Augereau was ill, and had desired to be relieved of the responsibility of leadership. Nevertheless, at the first cannon-shot he appeared amongst the troops conveyed on a sledge, and at the last moment he mounted his horse. Both his divisions (Heudelet and Desjardins) had already suffered sensible losses in their position on the Bartenstein road to the left of the churchyard, two general officers having fallen there. The order to advance was regarded by the troops as a deliverance. They moved forward in two columns upon the enemy's centre. Their artillery was to have accompanied them, but did not do so, being, it is said, "held up by an obstacle,"—probably, however, because the horses could drag the guns no farther through the deep snow. Instead, it returned to the heights above the Bartenstein road.

Soon, not only these batteries but those of the Guard that were in line with them as well had to cease fire as their own advancing infantry came between the gun-muzzles and the enemy. An icy north wind and a dense snowstorm drove full in, the faces of the French, so that it was impossible to see for a distance of twenty paces. The original direction was lost. The regiments on the right wing pushed in front of those that were marching on their left, and the attacking columns crowded together, closer, deeper, more helpless every moment. At last, blinded with snow, they stumbled upon Russian infantry, which slipping away to the right and left cleared the front of the hitherto invisible great battery of the Russian centre.

At this critical moment the snowstorm ceased. Dense sheets of case-shot, fired at 80 paces distance, swept the approaching French masses. The wings of the infantry firing line swung inwards and embraced them in a semicircle of fire. The French indeed strove to deploy for fire-action, but their muskets repeatedly missed fire, for the snow as it melted on their clothes had damped the primings. More and more deadly became the fire as the Russian line of battle took it up to the right and left, In spite of all, Augereau's corps broke through the line of the defending guns. But its fate was now sealed. From its concealment behind the heights the Russian cavalry sprang out and flung itself upon the now exhausted attackers. The longest resistance was that of a square of the 14th Regiment of the line on the right flank of the attack, but in the end this was completely destroyed by infantry fire and case-shot.

In twenty minutes Augereau's corps had been annihilated. As an independent unit it disappeared from the army list. The corps commander and both the divisional commanders were disabled. Mere remnants drifted back to Eylau.

The snow having ceased, it was in the full view of the emperor and his staff that this awful scene was enacted. Napoleon himself was in danger. The Russian counter-stroke penetrated almost to the church-yard hill, and drew from the emperor more than once the half-wondering, half-angry exclamation, "*Quelle audace!* "Marshal Bessiéres sent for the horses, and a cry went up, "Save the emperor!" But the assailants came up spent and breathless, and the French cavalry hurrying up on the flank, struck them in rear and dispersed them.

Meanwhile, by the emperor's orders, Murat's cavalry with the Horse Grenadiers and the Chasseurs a Cheval had filled up the gap in the line of battle and advanced to deliver a counter-stroke. The infantry of the Guard Napoleon kept firmly in his own hands.

In all 18 cavalry regiments were put in. But we must not imagine them as regiments with the full ranks and complete organization that we associate with our own—for such a force indeed there would have been neither deploying nor manoeuvring room. The squadrons had shrunk to handfuls, which now rode closely locked into the turmoil to rescue the broken corps and check the oncoming Russians. A series of French cavalry charges followed. But these attacks were not of the sort that we are wont to see at our army manoeuvres, for the horses were incapable of such exertions. There can have been no question of anything more than a short advance at the trot and a feeble gallop. The deep snow, too, was an obstacle to movement. The Guard cavalry was in a better condition than the rest, and the two Guard regiments which figured in this general attack took a more effective part.[19] Small groups broke through the Russian line, and individual survivors of these groups regained Eylau by roundabout ways. In the end friend and foe fell apart, and the position in general remained practically the same as it had been at the beginning, except that the French seemed to have advanced beyond the line of the Bartenstein road.

The issue of the day now depended wholly on the progress made by Davout and Saint Hilaire.

An important factor in this was the using-up of the Russian reserves. In the chaotic turmoil of conflict created by Augereau's advance, Bennigsen had put both the 4th and the 7th Divisions into the fighting line. The 14th,[20] too, was no longer in hand, having already moved off to strengthen the left wing. It had covered the retirement of Bagovut's detachment, and thereafter had established itself, along with the latter, between Klein-Sausgarten and the Kreege-Berg, in touch with Ostermann's 2nd Division, which formed the left of the main line.

The French frontal attack was thus far from being a complete failure. The situation indeed reminds us of that brought about by the attack of the Prussian Guard Corps on the 18th of August 1870 (Saint Privat). This too is denounced as premature—by those who forget that it caused the enemy to gather there the forces of his right wing and so to weaken his defence at Roncourt, which facilitated the enveloping movement of the Saxon corps and so actually made possible the decision at nightfall.

After the capture of Serpallen Davout's attack developed on a large scale. Friant's division, with the corps cavalry brigade (Marulaz) and also Milhaud's cavalry division, was on the right, and on the left Morand's division, which came up by Mollwitten, advanced upon the Klein-Sausgarten-Kreege-Berg line held by Bagovut and Kamenskoi, while farther to the left Saint Hilaire's division, drawing away from the main army, engaged Ostermann and the Russian 2nd Division.

The conflict that followed was severe and swung to and fro. On the extreme right General Friant was at first successful in capturing Klein-Sausgarten. But he was unable to hold it. The Russians assumed the of-

---

19. The French casualty returns show for these two regiments alone 5 officers killed and 30 officers wounded, while the eight regiments of Milhaud's and Hautpoul's divisions together lost only 8 officers killed and 33 wounded (Hildebrand, *op. cit.* p. 17).

20. Commanded by Kamenskoi (not, of course, the former commander-in-chief, but a junior of the name). General Anrepp had been killed at the combat of Mohrungen, 25th January. Tr.

fensive in turn, supported by cavalry in force, and although the counter-stroke was repulsed the advance of the assailants came to a standstill.

On Friant's left (divisions of Morand and Saint Hilaire) similar scenes were enacted. Here too the Russians repeatedly counter-attacked, but were always driven back and in again. Morand's report thus describes a general counter-stroke that was delivered from the Kreege-Berg:

It was about 1 p.m. when the hostile infantry, with which we had been engaged for five hours past, came down from their hills and threw themselves upon us with the bayonet. We rushed forward to meet them and threw them back as far as their artillery, which we captured. Eighteen guns fell into our hands, we were masters of the heights that command the Königsberg road, and a great number of the enemy who were not able to escape became our prisoners.[21]

Davout, too, gives a vivid description of the scene, which was evidently unusually impressive.

The Russian army was only two hundred paces off; it was coming on headlong with bayonets at the charge, and with thirty guns supporting it. They came within half-pistol-shot. . . ."[22]

With the storming of the Kreege-Berg the die would be cast, as far as this flank was concerned. The advancing Russians had been mastered and driven back, and their artillery on the Kreege-Berg itself had been overrun. The French had but to re-form and hold their ground, and the issue on this side of the battlefield would be definitively in their favour.

Morand's statement that the Kreege-Berg commands the Königsberg road sounds strange when one refers to the battle-plans, but it is quite correct. What he undoubtedly refers to is the *old* highway, which anyone standing on the Kreege-Berg and looking eastward towards the Rohrmuhle and Melohnkeim sees for the first time lying below him.[23]

The victors were, however, not long permitted to enjoy their prize. While they were still re-forming, in the midst of a snowstorm, a mass of Russian cavalry suddenly emerged from under cover of the hill. A

21. *Operations du IIIe Corps,* annexes, p. 286.

22. *Operations du IIIe Corps,* p. 164.

23. Morand's report is in this regard very clear and significant. When, in fact, shortly afterwards the divisions of Friant and Gudin advanced at and east of Klein-Sausgarten to give him air, he says: "However, the enemy having been *vigorously attacked on the Königsberg road,* we retook the heights."

battalion of Saint Hilaire's command which was supporting the left flank of Morand's division was flung back upon it. The division itself was driven back towards Serpallen, while Saint Hilaire retreated to the Bartenstein road, whither Klein's cavalry division was hurriedly sent to his assistance from the main army.[24]

The envelopment was thus on the point of breaking down when the situation on the extreme right underwent a change. The impulse seems to have been given by the arrival of Gudin's division on the field. Friant's division, with Gudin's support, was at last successful in definitively capturing Klein-Sausgarten and in driving the Russians there back on Auklappen. The two divisions thus came in rear of the Kreege-Berg position, which the gallant defenders were now obliged finally to evacuate. Morand's and part of Saint Hilaire's divisions occupied the Kreege-Berg for the second time, and held it fast for the rest of the day. Guns were brought up, and began to sweep the Russian lines effectively.

Although—in consequence of the great disaster to Augereau—Napoleon had called back Saint Hilaire's division more to the left to act as a strong link between the army and its enveloping wing, the unwearied Davout did not rest content with the success he had achieved. He advanced the whole division of Gudin to a hill between Klein-Sausgarten and Auklappen (presumably the north end of the Kreege-Berg) and there rallied all of his corps that was still in condition to fight. Thus he stood, victorious, full in rear of the Russian centre. Bennigsen's army began to dissolve. The beaten Russian troops streamed back through Auklappen, with Davout's renewed attack at their heels. The farm was captured, after a fluctuating contest, by the French. It was the same at the birch-wood (Birken-Wäldchen) adjacent, whither part of the Russian left had retired. There was now no stopping the attack. Even Kutschitten was eventually taken by the French, and the battle was, for the time being, decided.

The Russians had lost. Crowded together in an acute angle of which the point was the front of Eylau and the branches lay along the tracks to Lampasch and to Schmoditten, they were in no condition to resist much longer. Already the interior of the angle was filled with wounded and demoralized men. The line of retreat to Domnau, Allenburg, and the home country was severed. In the direction of Königsberg the Schmoditten lane was still open; for Ney, whom Napoleon had called up to close it, was still afar. But this narrow track

---

24. This Russian attack was delivered by General Korff with 20 squadrons.

was utterly insufficient for the whole army, and the troops retiring thereon could be headed off by the French right wing, moving on Mühlhausen by the easier highway.

One weakness lay in the situation of the French. Davout's enveloping wing had extended too far to the right and was strong nowhere. A well-timed and well-aimed blow could break it, and by one of the remarkable coincidences of history, the very troops that had at Auerstedt inflicted the heaviest blow upon Prussia were now, after an uninterrupted career of victory, to suffer in turn no less severely at the hands of the little Prussian corps.

****

General L'Estocq's march from Engelswalde to Rossitten on 7th February had proved extraordinarily fatiguing. The distance covered, measured from the rendezvous to the head of the main column, was it is true little more than 18 miles, and by counting in the detours which the outposts and certain other detachments had to make, as also the marches to and from quarters, it still did not amount to more than, probably, 24, or in one or two cases 27 miles. But only those who have a knowledge of the district traversed in these marches can have an accurate notion of what they signified. To this day the narrow lanes between the villages go up and down, in and out, winding round obstacles, and becoming in bad weather bottomless. If a frost sets in such as that which reigned during those February days in 1807, the greasy soil, cut up by deep ruts, freezes into brick-hard, pointed ridges. It is impossible to ride except at a foot's pace, and equally difficult for infantry. At one of our manoeuvres with heavy artillery in the summer of 1902 our troops made acquaintance with the nature of the roads in that same region after a spell of rainy weather, and the day's work done by the powerful horses which drew the howitzers is said to have been the most exhausting they had ever achieved. In the winter of 1903-4 they had a chance of seeing what frozen roads were like on very similar soil in the neighbourhood of Friedland and Allenburg. One squadron marching there had to lead the horses 13½ miles along the high road. Small wonder, then, that L'Estocq's troops were again very late in reaching their quarters at Hussehnen and Rossitten on the evening of 7th February. There were many who did not arrive until late in the night, and General von Plotz and the reserve were as late as 4 or 5 a.m. (Map No. 14a.).

To bring home to ourselves the state of the troops we must remember that they had marched between 85 and 90 miles, not counting detours, since the afternoon of 2nd February under much the same conditions. For the greater part the marches had developed into night-marches. Unfortunately, the old-established formality still prevailed of marshalling the whole of the troops at the beginning of a march and withholding from them any information about their quarters until the end, when the main column had reached the appointed goal. Thus they were often left waiting in the snow-covered fields, without fire or provisions, until they could move on to the scene of their short night's rest. They had by that time most of them received greatcoats, but on the whole they were wretchedly clad and more wretchedly nourished. The continued retreat, the news which reached them at Hussehnen of the unlucky fight at Waltersdorf, and the glimpse into a future of unrelieved gloom and uncertainty were bound to exercise the most depressing effect upon their spirits. Only the splendid will-power of both officers and men can account for the unfailing and uncomplaining readiness with which these brave troops faced each new exertion.

General von L'Estocq had, in accordance with Bennigsen's instructions, driven with Scharnhorst by way of Kanditten to Orschen. There he found his progress blocked by the French, and was informed that the Russians had already retreated towards Eylau, and that he would not be able to get through to that place. He therefore resolved to give up the meeting and continue his drive by Bornehnen to Hussehnen, the new headquarters, sending back in his stead Lieutenant Kurssel, who had come to him from Bennigsen's headquarters on the 6th.

The assembly had already been ordered for 6 a.m. at Hussehnen, when in the night of the 7th/8th, at 3.30 a.m., Lieutenant Kurssel arrived there, bringing Bennigsen's order to close in towards Althof to join the right wing of the Russian army.

The battle of Eylau had commenced. That its issue would perhaps definitely decide the fate of the Prussian kingdom was clear. "We are playing for high stakes," wrote Scharnhorst to a friend at that moment. He did not by any means disguise from himself that the prospects were not particularly favourable, but he never faltered for one instant. The necessary orders for the change in the direction of the march were immediately given, and were all carried out during the night.

The baggage-trains, which on the day before they had resolved to abandon to the enemy if the worst came to the worst, were to assemble at Bomben on the 8th and take refuge beyond the Frisching by way of Glauthienen. The Chlebowski Battalion and a squadron of the Wagenfeld Cuirassiers received orders to turn off towards Mühlhausen to secure the crossing over the Beisleide and the junction of the track through Eylau from Landsberg with the great high road Bartenstein-Königsberg. Colonel von Maltzahn and the remainder of the outpost brigade which had escaped from the fight at Waltersdorf and was on its way to rejoin the corps by way of Preussisch-Holland and Braunsberg, received the order to cover the Kreuzburg-Königsberg road behind the Frisching, while General von Esebeck was to take post with his dragoons, the (Russian) Kaluga Regiment, and half a horse battery at Wittenberg south of Königsberg, to form a reserve for the defence of the Frisching. The heavy batteries were sent off straightway[25] from their several quarters to the Russians at Althof, where, as we know, there were already other Prussian batteries under Major Huguenin.

The framing and issue of these orders must have required the whole time until the column was formed up for the march. The tired troops assembled very gradually at Hussehnen, and it was probably about 8 o'clock when, at the approach of the rearguard under General von Prittwitz, the column as a whole began to move. General von Plotz sent word that he was obliged to give his men a little rest and would follow as soon as possible.[26]

This involuntary delay, in the event, nearly proved fatal, and certainly influenced the fortunes of the day in no small degree.

The line of march chosen by L'Estocq and Scharnhorst led from Hussehnen through Wackern, skirted the northern edge of the Eylau forest (commonly called Stablack), touched the south end of the village of Schlauthienen, and continued thence by Domtau and Gorken.[27] The column moved in the following order: Vanguard: 50 Towarczys[28] and 40 Auer Dragoons. Main body of advanced guard: 9 squadrons Auer Dragoons[29] and Bredow's horse-battery. Main body in 3 small divisions: first that of General von Auer (10 squadrons Towarczys, half-battery horse artillery (Decker), 3 battalions of the

---

25. One of the two batteries collapsed on the way and did not arrive on the field for the battle.

26. General von Plotz had under him two infantry regiments (von Plotz and von Ruits). Their recruiting areas being in Poland, they were consequently very weak at this time. He had also a grenadier battalion (Braun), apparently the grenadier battalion von Massow as well, and finally 1½ horse-batteries.

27. Map No. 14b.

28. Polish lancers.—Tr.

29. One squadron of this regiment was told off as baggage guard.

Russian Viborg Regiment); then the 2nd, under General von Rembow (2 battalions of the Schoening Infantry Regiment, Schlieffen Grenadier Battalion); and lastly, the 1st Division, under General von Diericke (Fabecky[30] Grenadier Battalion, 2 battalions Rüchel Regiment, 5 squadrons Baczko Dragoons, 4 squadrons Wagenfeld Cuirassiers, and half-battery horse artillery (Rentzel)). Farther back was the rearguard under General von Prittwitz (Stutterheim Fusilier Battalion, 5 squadrons Prittwitz Hussars, and half-battery horse artillery (Sowinski). The units marched in the order named. The intervals between advanced guard and main body and between main body and rearguard were only small.

This march was the prelude to one of the most memorable days in the military history of our country, and one of the most instructive in modern warfare. It was probably obvious to every officer, or at least to the greater number, that the future of Prussia hung in the balance. It is this fact which explains the uniform willingness and punctuality in execution and the close, firm cohesion of this little band—the last representatives of the brilliant Old-Prussian army to appear as a corps on the field of battle.

To make the course of the fighting march which now commenced intelligible, we must first describe the nature of the terrain more accurately than is done on the maps, which, although they make it appear hilly and wooded, still give but an incomplete notion of its actual appearance. It is far less easy to take in at sight than it looks. Considerable hills with steep inclines, small chains, and knolls follow one another confusedly. The lie of the ridges is destitute of any system. The outlines of the woods are many of them ill-defined, being blurred by excrescences of scrub and scattered groups of trees. The streams are mostly bordered by bushes, and villages and farmhouses—especially those in the valleys—surrounded by thick trees. The roads are narrow, and frequently, as has been mentioned above, they wind round the angles of the hillsides and circumvent the marshy meadows. A marching column, even though it may have been spied for a moment by the enemy's scouts, can easily disappear from sight again. Only from Graventhien onward does the country become more open and easy of survey, while near Eylau it rises to flat-topped hills, and with broad gentle down-slopes beyond. The country surrounding the little town was therefore probably easy to overlook.

---

30. The family name von Fabeck was then still spelt thus.

Deep snow covered the ground on the day of the battle, hindering the movement of all arms, and of cavalry in particular. Brooks and meadows were frozen. Only a few particularly muddy, boggy places were left, which would not have supported horses and riders. Some of the little mountain streams running out in a northerly direction from the Stablack were probably still open and without a covering of ice in spite of the sharp frost, and this may account for the check which Ney's advanced guard suffered on the evening of 8th February at the Drangsitten bridge over the Pasmar. When I examined the battlefield on 21st December 1906, I found the brook still open in spite of a temperature of 7° to 5° Fahrenheit, most probably because of the steep gradient of its course. On the day of the battle the cold had become considerably modified after the bitter night that had preceded it. There was a temperature of 25° to 23° Fahrenheit, but it had been far colder on the clays before. Taken all in all, the terrain of Eylau must be accounted perfectly passable for the whole of the troops during the fight. Nevertheless, ground which has been ploughed for the first time and then frozen over is no trifling obstacle to a quick advance. As soon as the vanguard of the Prussian column emerged from the angle of the wood between Wackern and Schlauthienen, it suddenly discovered eight or ten of the enemy's horsemen on a hill to the right, just east of the road Bornehnen-Schlauthienen. General L'Estocq thereupon ordered the advanced guard to trot through Wackern. The order, however, was executed but slowly, for the troopers instead of trotting led their horses through—on account, it is said, of the cold, though the state of the road is a more likely cause, for no one is forced to dismount by nine or ten degrees of frost. The first half-regiment (5 squadrons Auer Dragoons) crossed through the wood, advanced towards the hill on which the enemy had been seen, then, as more French cavalry came in sight, wheeled to the right into line.

It was Ney's advanced guard which was deploying. It had marched from Orschen through Bornehnen in the direction of Kreuzburg. The marshal had, as we know, been instructed to proceed towards Kreuzburg to gain ground on the Russians' left flank, and also, if possible, to separate the Prussian corps from the main army.

The strip of ground to the south of Schlauthienen that is free of woods is peculiarly narrow and difficult to take in by eye, and the French can hardly have realized what was in front of them. Thanks to this, General L'Estocq gained time, under cover of the first half of the

Auer Dragoons, for the second half of the regiment and a horse-battery, as well as the 10 squadrons of the Towarczys of the main body, to hurry forward past the angle of the wood and through Schlauthienen.

The fourteen or fifteen united squadrons with the battery, deployed behind Schlauthienen (very probably on the windmill north-east of the little village) in order by their artillery fire to prevent the enemy from blocking the place by their gun fire. Simultaneously L'Estocq pushed out 2 companies of the Schoening Infantry Regiment and 3 companies of the Viborg to the right front, into the edge of the wood near the Bornehnen track. They had only a limited field of fire, but were nevertheless able to command the approach to Schlauthienen with their fire.

The enemy too brought forward some artillery on the hills. An artillery duel began across the Schlauthienen hollow. But the sight of the impressive mass of cavalry on the far side and the graze of cannon-balls on the near side of the village, together with the proximity of the 1st half-regiment of Auer Dragoons, made the French stop short. The Prussian march column could now pursue its way through Schlauthienen, and General L'Estocq, seeing this, called in the 1st half-regiment Auer Dragoons and Bredow's horse-battery again.

Suddenly there came the roar of guns from the rear. The head of another of the enemy's columns (probably Ney's left flank-guard) had appeared farther west on the track leading from Skerwitten. This gravely imperilled the march of the tail of the Prussian main column through Wackern. General von Prittwitz, who was close behind with the rearguard, realized this, and sent off the leading company of his fusilier battalion (Stutterheim) under Captain von Krauseneck (the future Field-Marshal and Chief of the General Staff) to occupy a wood which at that time lay between Hussehnen and Wackern and, it appears, had a slight command over the track on its north side. The wood has vanished, and the only trace of its existence today is a patch of bushes. Captain von Krauseneck and his brave fusiliers held up the enemy with their fire long enough to allow the Baczko Dragoons and the Wagenfeld Cuirassiers[31] to pass quickly through Wackern. But he was soon so violently attacked that he had to fall back towards Wackern.

But meantime the enemy, like their comrades farther east, brought up their artillery to fire into the Prussians as they filed past. Wackern was taken by the French before the rearguard had marched through.

---

31. The rear units of the main body.—Tr.

Colonel von Stutterheim nevertheless flung himself on the village with the leading company of his fusiliers, drove off the enemy with the bayonet, and joined Krauseneck's company on the far side. Both subsequently reached the main column. The French now passed right and left of Wackern, proceeding northward. General von Prittwitz, finding his way blocked, attempted to force it by his horse artillery fire, but in vain. He was therefore obliged to turn off with his remaining troops[32] in the direction of Kreuzburg. But the determined attitude of the fusiliers and the appearance of Prittwitz's comparatively numerous cavalry so far pinned the enemy to the spot that they lost sight of the retiring Prussian main column and molested their march no more. Its passage through Schlauthienen was thus rendered possible, though it appears to have been accompanied by constant fighting.[33] The road by Domtau and Gorken was now impassable. Instead of attempting to force an opening, L'Estocq and his counsellor Scharnhorst resolved to turn off northwards towards Pompicken. The decision was correct and its consequences momentous. A junction with the main army on the battlefield was the one thing urgent on that day—it was there, and not here at Schlauthienen, that the decision lay. They resolved accordingly to reach the safety of the hills at Waldkeim, and thence to march on Eylau by Graventhien. While the two companies of the Schoening and the three companies of the Viborg Regiments, valiantly defending themselves against the pursuing French, successfully rejoined the marching column, the Pabecky Grenadier Battalion occupied the southern edge of Pompicken village, to ensure the passage for the others. This time it was the Wagenfeld Cuirassiers and a horse-battery who deployed on the neighbouring heights. A fresh fight ensued. The enemy attacked with infantry and artillery from the direction of Schlauthienen, which they had meantime occupied, but were repulsed. They then approached the west entrance of Pompicken from Wackern, but the two fusilier companies of Stutterheim and two guns from the half-battery Rentzel offered a gallant resistance, and succeeded in beating them off.

The attention of the enemy was meantime more and more attracted by the rearguard, which finally absorbed it to the exclusion of all else. Prittwitz had now been joined by General von Plotz who came up from Bomben, and the two together fought so skilfully the whole day

---

32. The 2 remaining companies of the Stutterheim Fusilier Battalion, 5 squadrons of the Prittwitz Hussars, and half a horse-battery (Sovinski).

33. There may have been a snowstorm in progress here, during Augereau's attack on the Russian centre, which would help to hide the march of the Prussian column.

through with their inferior forces that Ney, apparently taking them for the whole of L'Estocq's corps, followed them towards Kreuzburg.

Meanwhile L'Estocq continued his march in the direction of Drangsitten, past Waldkeim and Leissen and through Graventhien. On the right of his road, as the map shows, lay boggy patches of meadow which have since, it appears, been made passable. To the south of this low ground, French detachments marched for some time parallel with the Prussians. Several times did they attempt to cross it, but each time infantry or cavalry was rapidly thrown off to the right of the marching column and repulsed them. The fusiliers, too, after vacating Pompicken, were followed as they retired by French detachments, and some skirmishing occurred. Unfortunately no details of these small and yet instructive fights have been preserved. Neither can a reliable account be given of the movements of the troops who fell back on Kreuzburg, owing to the lack of internal evidence. But what we do know is the brilliant finale, L'Estocq's safe arrival on the battlefield of Eylau after a dangerous flank march. Höpfner[34] says:

> The General's tactics are a model of the way in which a flank march in the face of a near and powerful adversary should be conducted.

The artillery fire at Eylau became visible between Graventhien and Drangsitten.[35] The flash of every discharge was seen, but no report was heard although the distance was so small.[36] The pace was accelerated. The Schlieffen Grenadier Battalion stayed behind on the Pasmar bridge at Drangsitten to check the enemy again, in case they should try to follow up too soon. The battalion was joined by the two fusilier companies coming from Pompicken. L'Estocq's column was thus deprived of another 1½ battalions, and now consisted of only 8 battalions, 28 squadrons, and 2 horse-batteries—probably not more than 6000 men in all. Althof (Map No. 15) was reached at 1 p.m.

There the corps was met by Russian officers who came to ask for supports, while giving a good account of the state of things on the field. General L'Estocq refused, for he had no desire still further to split

---

34. *Der Krieg von 1806 und 1807*, ii. vol. 3, p. 236.

35. Höpfner speaks of the "hills" between these two places; these hills, however, do not exist. The terrain is flat, rising very gently 10 feet or so, and sloping as gradually down to the Pasmar brook.

36. This curious natural phenomenon was similarly observed at the manoeuvres of the 3rd Army Corps, 1876, and markedly, too, at the corps manoeuvres of the 1st Army Corps in 1902.

up his seriously reduced forces. One of the Prussian officers attached to the Russian headquarters now brought an order to march towards the *left wing* and wrest from the enemy the advantage they had gained. But it still remained to choose between several possible points of attack.

> Scharnhorst's unerring vision selected the one which promised the most brilliant result. It had not escaped him as he viewed the battlefield from the hill at Althof, that Davout in his efforts to overreach the Russian wing had pushed out very far with his own. Scharnhorst's attack therefore was aimed at the enemy's flank, at Kutschitten.

So says Max Lehmann in his famous Life of Scharnhorst. But in fact the terrain at Althof itself is perfectly flat,[37] and offers no point of vantage from which any such view could be obtained, while the most considerable rise in the ground near the lane between Althof and Schmoditten only affords a glimpse of the roofs at Kutschitten. Part of the battlefield is hidden by the village of Schloditten. Auklappen is just visible on the hill, but not very distinctly.[38] It can hardly have been possible, therefore, to distinguish the several positions of friend and foe in that quarter. The whole of the Russian right wing and the French left, stretching from the Walkmühle to the hills north-east of Eylau on the road to Lampasch, are all that can have been seen, though these at least would be visible in some detail. At any rate, L'Estocq and Scharnhorst perceived that no serious danger threatened their allies in that wing. A stream of fugitives from Kutschitten and Auklappen had already begun to pour down the flat slopes towards Schmoditten. The march was therefore continued in that direction, after the corps, which had hitherto marched in a single column, had been split up into three. But although the correct decision was thus suggested by circumstances, it is not on that account any the less creditable.[39]

The centre column traversed the village of Schmoditten itself, the

---

37. From the highest point down to the Pasmar River there is a gradual descent of about 15 feet. The church-tower at Schmoditten indeed affords a complete bird's-eye view of the battlefield, but it is not stated that any officer of L'Estocq's staff ascended it.
38. The high trees in the park, some of which probably existed at that time, define the position of this manor-house. Nothing else could have been distinguished, as the author found when he visited the battlefield at the same hour on a clear winter's day.
39. The regimental history of the Rüchel Infantry Regiment (now the Grenadier Regiment Kronprinz) also states that General L'Estocq on arriving at Schloditten (a mistake for Schmoditten) recognized the dangerous situation at Kutschitten. It would certainly have been impossible for him to do so earlier.

other two skirting it on the north and south respectively, all three marching on Kutschitten, now straight before them and on slightly higher ground. Just after the little brook beyond Schmoditten had been crossed, French skirmishers were espied on the hills of Auklappen and Kutschitten. Larger bodies could also be seen at Kutschitten, and it was evident that the village was occupied. L'Estocq deployed his troops for the attack. The Rüchel Regiment drew away leftwards and aimed at the north end of the village; the Russian Viborg Regiment formed the centre, and the Schoening Regiment the right wing. Then came in second line the Fabecky Grenadier Battalion, and close at hand the Auer and Baczko Dragoons and the Wagenfeld Cuirassiers.

What regiments they were, too, with their splendid record of attested worth! There was hardly a cavalry battle in King Frederick's wars at which the Auer and Baczko Dragoons had not been present. As for the infantry regiment Rüchel, it had helped to drive the Swedes out of Pomerania and Prussia, the Turks out of Hungary, the French out of the Rhineland, Italy, and Flanders, and had poured out its blood in rivers during the Silesian wars. When the leader of the corps,[40] with his knowledge of history, led these troops into battle on that day he must have felt that the thousands and tens of thousands of heroes who had built up Prussia's greatness were at his side to help and to bless in all their victorious strength. And was it not, too, the iron marshal whom they opposed, he who had reaped at Auerstedt the fruit which laxity and want of judgment had sown in the camp of the Fatherland? He should learn that day what the Prussians were still able to achieve under a leader worthy of the name.[41]

The Towarczys worked away farther to the left than the Rüchel Regiment, turning Kutschitten by the north. They were joined by a band of some 200 cossacks. The artillery, after traversing a thicket (now only recognizable by its undergrowth), had commenced the attack by opening fire from a gentle rise on the Schmoditten-Kutschitten track at a range of about 550 yards. The Russians who were streaming past in retreat received orders from L'Estocq to join in his advance. But the only result was that they continued their retreat on Schmoditten grouped in larger bodies than before.

While the Schoening Regiment, leaving Kutschitten to its left, ad-

---

40. Meaning, of course, Scharnhorst.
41. Max Lehmann, *Scharnhorst*, i. pp. 488, 489.

vanced against the French skirmishers on the hills between Kutschitten and Auklappen, the other two regiments (Viborg on the right, Rüchel on the left) flung themselves straight upon Kutschitten. The enemy rushed out to meet them from the exit of the village, but were immediately driven in again.[42] Lieutenant von Schachtmeyer with part of the skirmishers of the Rüchel Regiment pushed in from the left (*i.e.* from the north side of the village), while Colonel von Hamilton with the regiment itself, in columns, stormed the northern part of the west edge, and the Russian Regiment Viborg captured the south side with loud hurrahs. The garrison consisted of the French 51st Regiment of Morand's division, 4 companies of the 108th Regiment of Friant's division (Davout's corps).

The combat appears to have been very sharp. The *Journal of Operations* of the French III Corps reproaches the garrison with having shown far too much *témérité* in defending themselves against an enemy who was in such superior force. Kutschitten took fire, but the village was then, as today, built in a straggling fashion (the original outline appears to have been preserved), and the victors were therefore able to press forward and through it in spite of the buildings which stood in flames. The defenders attempted to make a renewed stand immediately south of the village. But they were routed here also, and at the same moment, by the Towarczys and the Cossacks, who it will be remembered had made a circuit round the north side of the village and now suddenly and unexpectedly appeared in rear of the French.

The ground sloping gradually from Kutschitten towards Lampasch screened the movements of the allied cavalry from observation. The light cavalry brigade of Marulaz, which up till then had covered Davout's extreme right wing, seems to have withdrawn; neither did Milhaud's cavalry division, which was near at hand, come to the assistance of their hard-pressed comrades. The official report,[43] indeed, says that the inaction of the cavalry was due to the unfavourable character of the ground, but we may justly suspect the validity of this excuse, for, as we know, the ground was frozen and deeply-covered with snow. There are, besides, no ditches or stream-beds of any importance south of Kutschitten. A more obvious explanation would be that the French cavalry horses were not capable of anything faster than a walk after their previous exertions and privations.[44]

The result was that the gallant defenders of Kutschitten, deserted

---

42. *Geschichte des Grenadier-Regiments Kronprinz (früher v. Rüchel).*
43. *Opirations du IIIe Corps, 1806-7,* p. 168.
44. Hildebrand, *Die Schlacht bei Pr. Eylau,* p. 26.

by their comrades, were surrounded and almost annihilated.[45] An eagle was captured[46] and three lost Russian guns recovered. The chief part of the honour of recapturing Kutschitten falls to Colonel von Hamilton. L'Estocq alludes to his regiment (in his report to the king) as "the brave Rüchel Regiment," and adds: "This regiment renewed its ancient fame by its brilliant action."

After the capture of Kutschitten L'Estocq's whole corps marched with the greatest rapidity to the small birch-wood (Birken-Wäldchen) which lay to the south. (It has now disappeared, but its position and extent are marked by single trees and groups of trees and by a light thicket at the southern end near to Klein-Sausgarten.) The right wing was formed by the Schoening Regiment; on its left was the Fabecky Grenadier Battalion, which had been brought up into first line; behind these was the Russian Viborg Regiment; and the left wing consisted of the Rüchel Regiment. In second line came in order from right to left the Wagenfeld Cuirassiers, the Auer Dragoons, and the Baczko Dragoons. As before, the Towarczys and Cossacks protected the left flank, reaching out farther towards Melohnkeim and heading for Klein-Sausgarten, when the advance was made on the Birch Wood.

The ground south of Kutschitten not only lies higher than the surrounding country, but also is absolutely flat, without any gentle declivity, until the plateau breaks into a sharp down-slope[47] close above the brook which, flowing from Auklappen towards Lampasch, outlines the wood's northern edge. Thus, in the last decisive contest about to be fought, the French were in low ground and could only be perceived by the attackers, who approached along the high ground, when close at hand. We will take the description from Höpfner's admirable work.

In the glow of the setting sun, with bands playing, the infantry advanced in perfect order towards the birch copse below. A fierce cannonade was in progress on both sides, but not a musket-shot was fired. The skirmishers who were holding the edge of the copse were overthrown, and our troops pushed their way in up to within 50 paces of the battalions[48] that stood in

---

45. *Ils furent enveloppés et éprouvèerent une grande perte (Operations du III⁰ Corps,* p. 168).
46. And presented to Queen Luise on her birthday, 10th March *(Geschicte des Grenadier-Regiments Kronprinz).*
47. 1 in 15 to 1 in 12, according to the contours in the original (Lettow) map.—Tr.
48. Höpfner adds at this point, "of Friant's division." But as a matter of fact they belonged to Gudin's division, as is evident from the Journal of the III French Corps (p. 168).

columns inside the wood, while the Rüchel Regiment passing along the right-hand side of the wood fell upon the enemy's right flank. At very close quarters—the history of the Rüchel Regiment says at short musket-shot—there was now a fierce musketry and case-shot fire, which lasted about half an hour, and in which the French in their dense masses suffered severely. ...After heavy losses the French gave way, were pursued with the bayonet, and completely expelled from the wood.

It was the 12th French Regiment that had stood in the Birch Wood. It subsequently joined the 1st Battalion of the 25th Regiment behind (*"sur la droite à la sortie des bois"* probably, therefore, towards the Kreege-Berg), and rallied, with the remainder of Gudin's and Friant's divisions, for a new effort of resistance.

At the same time Auklappen was recovered by the Russians, and here too the retiring movement of the French made itself evident. Marshal Davout came up himself in all haste to put a stop to the general retreat. He collected all the available artillery on the Kreege-Berg and hurried through the ranks of his corps crying to them that they must perish with honour.

The brave will die covered with glory, and only cowards will make acquaintance with the wastes of Siberia.[49]

There was still half an hour of daylight after the capture of the Birch Wood, but this short space of time did not, probably, suffice to reorganize the troops and develop a third effective attack, besides which the enemy's powerful artillery on the Kreege-Berg would first have had to be beaten down. Darkness set in, therefore, without further action. L'Estocq's troops, splendid as had been their goodwill on this great day, showed signs of weariness after their fighting march of twelve to fourteen hours. Besides which the Russian General Kamenskoi, who had come over from Auklappen, refused most deliberately to assist in a renewal of the attack.[50]

The French contend, it is true, that they held Auklappen up to and after nightfall: "*Ce fut dans cette position entre Auklappen et Lampasch que*

49. *Operations du IIIe Corps*, p. 168.

50. The Russian account in the January number of the *Voyenniy Svornik* of 1907 says the exact contrary. If, however, we bear in mind the state in which Count Kamenskoi's troops must have been after the previous long and fierce fight, we are inclined to think that the Prussian version is the correct one. The *Russhiy Invalid*, Nos. 21, 22 (1907), says nothing of any desire on Kamenskoi's part to attack.

le III Corps passa tranquillement la nuit. " But this contention is obviously erroneous, for the Birch Wood not only lay exactly in the middle of the line named, but also stretched well beyond it southwards. On the other hand, the Kreege-Berg and the flat hills to the west remained in the hands of the victor of Auerstedt.

The Russian General von Knorring came up to L'Estocq, congratulated him on his great success, and announced that he had made arrangements throughout the Russian lines to form in columns of attack. But the attack itself did not take place. It was not to be commenced without the consent of the commander-in-chief, and at the time Bennigsen could not be found.

He is said to have ridden to meet L'Estocq's corps and to have lost his way, but this suggestion is inexplicable. The space between Kutschitten, Eylau, and Schmoditten into which the Russian army was crowded before the last favourable turn of fortune, can today be viewed as a whole, and was almost equally easy to overlook at that time. The only features which existed then and have now disappeared are small thickets, and these were mostly on low ground beside the ditches and the stream-beds. L'Estocq's column approaching in close and regular order must have been visible everywhere. Towards evening, according to the Russian account, Bennigsen was with the left wing, and gave General Ostermann orders to prepare to attack. Presently, however, he altered the order again, resolved to advance with the right wing, and rode thither accordingly. But he did not in the end carry out his plan. However this may be, at any rate the favourable moment was allowed to pass unused.

Meanwhile, about 7.30, Ney and his corps appeared on the battlefield. The officer whom the emperor had dispatched with the order to come on to the field, making a wide detour for security, had ridden through Landsberg and Orschen. He was close upon Kreuzburg when he came up with Marshal Ney, who had probably realized that he had no longer L'Estocq's whole corps in front of him, as he had supposed, but only detached fragments of it. He now altered the direction of his troops and led them along the same road which L'Estocq had used, passing through Pompicken and Graventhien. In front of the corps, Bellair's brigade and a light cavalry brigade of Lasalle's division were again in front—these were the same troops which had moved upon Schlauthienen in the morning, some of whose detachments had remained in observation of L'Estocq's movements. At the Drangsitten bridge they were checked by Stutterheim's fusilier companies, and the broken bridge had to be repaired. This done, they continued their march, the Prussian fusiliers retiring before them through Schmoditten to the grange called Sollseyn. It was after eight o'clock and completely dark when the French deployed in the direction of Althof. The Schlieffen Grenadier Battalion was still posted there, but, after a short struggle, threatened with envelopment by the enemy's superior numbers, they retired in square in the direction of Kutschitten, passing between Schloditten and Schmoditten. At 9 p.m. they joined the troops in the Birch Wood and took their rest.

The French followed them through Althof and approached Schloditten, which was crowded with the wounded and only garrisoned by weak Russian detachments. Schloditten was taken after yet another slight engagement, but the Russian and Prussian batteries prevented any further advance by firing case-shot into the darkness. Up till now the Russian right wing had maintained unshaken its original position, supported by its powerful artillery. Now, however, late in the evening as it was, serious danger threatened it, and Bennigsen promptly decided to recover Schloditten. A few regiments of the 3rd Division were dispatched to that place, and the village was regained. The French retired on Althof, where the mass of Ney's corps had meantime assembled, and the rest of the night was spent there. Thus was the battle restored on this wing also. At 10 p.m. all fighting ceased entirely, and innumerable watch-fires, besides the burning villages, began to light up the white snow-covered fields.

The five days' fighting, the two days' struggle at Eylau itself, the consecutive night-marches through the snow, sharp frost, hunger, and every sort of fatigue and anxiety had terribly affected the Russian army. We have already seen in what condition they arrived at Eylau. They fought in spite of it with unbending bravery, but there came a time when nature asserted her rights. The dissolution of which General L'Estocq had seen such clear evidence on his arrival beyond Schmoditten, must have been even greater during the night. There were many unwounded men who left the field with the wounded, as will always be the case in any battle of long duration. Many others left the ranks, driven by hunger into the surrounding villages. Regiments and battalions had shrunk to insignificant handfuls, one of the divisions (General von Ostermann's) numbering only 2710 men under arms.

General Bennigsen heard with alarm the reports which came in from different parts of the field. He certainly cannot have had more than 30,000 men under his control at the moment. His actual losses amounted to nearly 25,000. But in the opposite camp the French were in similar plight. They had undergone fearful losses, as for instance in the destruction of Augereau's corps, and moreover, being less habituated to the conditions of the country and the severity of the season than the Russians, they suffered more keenly from both these causes. In spite of everything, therefore, it was still within General Bennigsen's power to choose whether he would go or stay. Not that the choice was easy. Fate, on the evening of the battle of Eylau, set before him one of the most difficult questions that ever taxed the insight and character of a commander. But it is the general who first admits the battle to be hopeless who loses it.

Involuntarily our thoughts turn to the evening of Vionville. Things looked worse for us then than for the Russians on 8th February 1807. The Prussian losses on 16th August 1870 had been comparable to, if not actually as heavy as, theirs. But the superiority of the French was very great, almost two to one; whereas at Eylau, according to recent calculations, it was nonexistent. The troops were equally exhausted on both occasions. Men and horses were utterly worn out after ten or eleven hours of fighting. On 16th August not a company squadron or battery cooked a meal. The lack of water after a very hot day was keenly felt on the plateau upon which the Prussians found themselves. Even during the fight, the ammunition had given out both for infantry and artillery.

There, too, numerous bodies of troops, scattered by hunger and thirst, were lost in the darkness. Supervision and control being, under the new conditions of warfare, less effectual than at Eylau, the dissolution was greater. The many wounded needed as many pairs of hands to shelter and nurse them. Search was made in the dark for lost leaders. Nowhere were there any bodies in close order. The only large groups of men were those gathered round a few sutler's carts which in spite of all obstacles had reached the battlefield. The long artillery line in the Prussian centre was deserted except for a few sentries who stood loyally by their trusty guns. There was hope, indeed, of considerable reinforcements the following day, but they could not arrive much before noon. Only the IX Corps, or as much of it as had not already been used up in the fighting, was available in the early morning, while all appearances pointed to the fact that the French must still have a considerable force fresh and ready to engage, which might attack at daybreak.

In such moments a commander cannot depend upon calculations by numbers. To come to a decision he has to trust his own insight, his experience, his professional knowledge, and that unaccountable power of presentiment that is so often vouchsafed to greatness. According to the strength of his nature will this decision be cast. Prince Frederick Charles had a strong soldierly spirit. He never for a moment lost confidence in the ultimate victory, not even during the critical phase of the battle in which the defeated Prussian left wing poured back past Mars-la-Tour into Tronville after the sanguinary repulse of their attack on Greyfère Farm. As the sun sank against the horizon and anxiety as to the result of the battle was writ large on the faces of the observers, he turned round and calmed them with the simple words: "Another half-hour in this position and it will be a regular victory."

All of us who were there, as we rode off, on that pitch-dark night, down the steep road to Gorze, were uplifted by the consciousness that we had seen a truly great man at his work that day.

Bennigsen was no Frederick Charles. He had neither his strength of character nor his high sense of responsibility. Some among his entourage were for standing fast, in particular Generals Knorring, Steinheil, and Ostermann. The Prussian staff, too, as we know, wished to continue the battle. But Bennigsen shrank from the great resolution and decided on a retreat, choosing, to make matters worse, the direction of Königsberg. This meant the abandonment of direct communication with Russia, and the grave danger of being forced away and completely enveloped by the enemy, should their strength be still equal to such an undertaking. As against Napoleon, who could generally make impossibilities possible, the direction chosen was doubly dangerous.

The Prussian corps was to form the rearguard, but when the order arrived to that effect Scharnhorst immediately resolved not to obey it. His anguish over the desertion of the battlefield and the decision against renewing the attack the next morning was profound. He wrote to Kleist, the king's *aide-de-camp* general, on 9th February from Friedland:

It is a great misfortune that the battle was not renewed on the following morning. The troops were extremely fatigued, it is true, but after all the enemy was in similar plight.[51]

But he refused under any circumstances to agree to the Russians

51. Quoted in Lehmann's *Life of Scharnhorst,* i. p. 490, note 4.

cutting themselves off from the roads that could bring them supplies and reinforcements. The bad impression which this abandonment would have made in Russia, at court, and in the army (where Bennigsen had to cope with no little enmity and jealousy), would necessarily have been a serious matter, and its results could hardly be estimated.

Thus did the Prussian generals come to the second great decision of that day, the decision to retire along the Domnau road in the direction of Friedland and Wehlau. It was somewhere about midnight (at 2 a.m. according to Höpfner) when the corps marched off from the battlefield. It was difficult to find the way in the darkness. In the deserted villages no one could be discovered who could have undertaken to act as guide on the snow-covered roads. At last two grenadiers were discovered who were natives of that region, and with these two seated on a gun in front the column was set in motion. They marched as far as Domnau, and then on to Friedland the same day, 9th February, unmolested by the enemy, who probably would have credited anything sooner than the retreat of the victor.

The communications with Russia remained open. For the second time the Russian army had been saved.[52]

****

Napoleon's hopes were cruelly disappointed by the result of the great battle of the 8th. The fight which, since the middle of December, he had so ardently desired had been fought, but how sadly the course it had taken must have belied his expectations! "Never had the *grande armée* encountered such opposition."[53] The huge enveloping attack of the French right wing and centre that was to have mastered the whole field of battle, had won nothing more than the Kreege-Berg and Klein-Sausgarten, and even this much at the cost of terrible losses. The Russians were still in possession of their natural line of communications, the attempts to force them off it, to pin them against the Haff or the coast—to *destroy* them—had failed signally.

In Davout's corps and Saint Hilaire's division, on whom the brunt of the battle had fallen, the ranks were terribly thinned. By their own admission they were reduced to one-third of their former strength. Augereau's corps as an organized battle-unit had ceased to exist, while Soult's corps had suffered heavily in the struggle for Eylau on the 7th. The names and numbers of regiments, brigades, and divisions were all

---

52. Lehmann, *Scharnhorst,* pp. 491–2.
53. Derrécagaix, *Le Marechal Berthiér,* ii. p. 201.

that remained to distinguish the worn-out cavalry. Many of the horses had collapsed from sheer exhaustion during the attacks on the Russian centre. It was utterly impossible to go on. Here again, as in Poland, natural conditions triumphed over human exertions.

Apart from the Guards, the three light cavalry brigades of the left wing and Ney's corps which had just come in were the only units in a condition to move. These fresh troops might have sufficed to overthrow the enemy; but the outcome was doubtful, while if they too were destroyed a great catastrophe was inevitable, for Bernadotte could not be counted upon before the 11th or 12th, when he would probably have been too late to avert the disaster.

There was dissatisfaction amongst the marshals with the course things were taking.[54] In the army discipline had gravely deteriorated. Numbers of unwounded men deserted the battlefield on the pretext of escorting the wounded, while others had absented themselves from the fight altogether. On the 9th of February Marshal Davout was forced to take drastic measures against the skulkers.[55]

Hunger, too, drove many from the ranks, and in the general search for food in the neighbourhood the men even forgot their own wounded. The little town of Eylau, which had been devastated and sacked from roof to cellar, was of course crowded out. Spectre-like figures of soldiers could be seen slinking about the streets in search of eatables. During the battle many had faced certain death in the storm of bullets for the sake of a handful of potatoes or a bowl of soup. The horses which fell were roasted at the bivouac fire and greedily devoured. Again, as in Poland, the emperor heard the cry for bread arise in the ranks.

Worse still, marauders sprang up in great numbers, and spread even to the left bank of the Vistula. Not even their own officers felt themselves safe from these men. Baron Percy, the chief surgeon of the *grande armée,* and his assistants had their horses, all their personal belongings, swords and even hats stolen during the battle, while engaged in their arduous task. Marbot, too, relates how, lying wounded

---

54. *"Les maréchaux, qui avaient déjà été témoins de la répugnance des troupes a franchir la Vistule, au mois de décembre, partageaient ces pensées* (on all the difficulties surmounted) *sans toutefois s'y arrêter. Mais elles leur revinrent plus d'une fois à l'esprit, cinq ans plus tard, lorsque la période des grands revers commença dans les mêmes contrées. Pour le moment, ces impressions donnèrent lieu à divers mécontentements."* (Derrécagaix, *Le Marechal Berthiér,* ii. p. 202).
55. Two gunners, for instance, who had slunk off and only returned to their corps after the battle, were made to receive a *savate,* a sort of bastinado, on the grave of their dead comrades.

in the middle of the battle, he was robbed of all his clothes by a soldier of the train. The body of a general[56] who died of his wounds at Worienen was pulled out of the grave in the expectation, probably, of finding it dressed in his gold-laced uniform. Coffins were also broken open and plundered at the village of Schmoditten. Everywhere the marauding spirit broke out.

These phenomena are easier to comprehend when we bear in mind that, despite the emperor's comprehensive instructions, communication with the base was practically cut off. Every unit, every soldier indeed, was confronted with the necessity of providing for himself, and this without money. For no money was forthcoming. The corps who had fought at Eylau had, since 1st January 1806, received four months' pay only, and that was in October and November at Berlin. A small sum on account followed in January 1807. The emperor stated that he did not wish his soldiers to spend their money while they were abroad, but in reality he was no doubt driven to these harsh measures by considerations of internal policy. He had found the finances of the country in a hopeless condition after the Republican regime of paper *assignats*, and his popularity as a ruler rested not a little on the fact that he had restored order in that department. He prudently desired, therefore, to avoid making any heavy demands on France, lest he should forfeit the sympathy that he commanded in France and wished to keep intact for the new dynasty to be founded. War was to support the warrior, the army to be paid by enforced contributions abroad. But these had so far been scanty. The funds in the military chest of the *grande armée,* which had previously been in very low water, touched 5,300,000 *francs* (£212,000) in January 1807, but of what use was this insignificant sum in face of the enormous demand?[57]

The soldiers still followed his star readily and were manageable enough on the field of battle. But the constitution of the army founded largely on victories and the carving out of fortunes began to show its weakness. The Russian cannonade at Eylau on the morning of the 8th had aroused a veritable panic in the place. A similar effect was created when the wounded Marshal Augereau drove through the town with a large escort at one o'clock in the afternoon, the trampling of their horses' hoofs being mistaken for the oncoming of the enemy's cavalry.[58] Not only had the emperor become more and more contemptuous of

---

56. Dahlmann, an Alsatian, called *D'Allemagne* in the French reports.
57. Details in von Lettow, vol. iii. p. 162 *et seq.,* and in Hildebrand, p. 39 *et seq.*
58. *Journal des Campagnes du Baron Percy,* p. 163.

the masses who served him as material, but the same feeling had taken possession of his marshals, who had been promoted, step by step, with astounding rapidity, and had become great men while still young. In most corps interior economy was neglected, and the structure of the army was becoming loosened in any case. It is beyond doubt that the chaos at Eylau in the evening was extraordinary and that the frenzy of the fight had unnerved the French troops, hardened as they were. The battlefield must have presented a terrible sight.

One cannot turn one's eyes in any direction without seeing twenty or fifty corpses together; it is an appalling butchery![59]

On the evening of Eylau the *grande armée* was completely exhausted, and incapable of making a fresh effort.[60]

The emperor could not fail to realize that the result of the whole campaign must appear to the army as both imperfect and bought at a ruinous price. He had stumbled upon absolutely unsuspected difficulties, "and his fortune had seemed for a moment to wane." The spoilt children of victory had counted on a brilliant and complete finale to the second campaign of the war, and the general impression of disappointment was inevitable.

Napoleon spent the night of February 8th/9th in the house of a brick-maker near the Landsberg road, and not far from the farm of Grünhöfchen (the little thatched buildings of which were, about the middle of last century, erroneously pointed out as Napoleon's headquarters). The bivouacs of his Guard encircled him.

Portions of Davout's corps had fallen back still farther, some regiments, it is said, traversing Perscheln, where General Friant had taken up his quarters for the night. French troops also passed through other places in falling back on the night of the 9th.

It is not known whether the emperor actually gave an order to retreat. Judging by his character it is improbable, although he was evidently far from feeling confident of success. But there is evidence that the question was *considered*. He wrote to Duroc, a little before 4 a.m.:

We had a most sanguinary battle at Eylau yesterday. The battlefield remains in our possession, but although the losses are heavy on both sides, I feel mine more on account of the distance. . . . It will soon become necessary to shift headquarters

---

59. *Journal des Campagnes du Baron Percy,* p. 165.
60. Pierre Grenier, *Etude sur 1807,* p. 65.

back to Thorn.... for it is possible that I may go to the left bank of the Vistula, where we should be in quiet winter quarters, safe from the incursions of cossacks and swarms of light troops.

When arms were not sufficient to achieve his ends he enlisted diplomacy. He had heard that Tsar Alexander wished to know on what basis France would negotiate, and instructed Talleyrand to say, in a diplomatic note addressed to Prussia, that he would agree to open negotiations, and proposed Memel as the place of meeting. But there is a considerable gulf between these preparations and a definite order to retreat.

Baron Percy, the surgeon-in-chief, who had established himself in another hut near, relates that the emperor sent for him at 6 a.m. on the 9th to inquire the number of wounded. He was lying fully dressed on a mattress which was spread out on the floor of a miserable room. Without rising, he asked for details and news of persons. "His expression was grave and calm." Percy reported that 4000 wounded had already been attended to. The high figure and his complaint of want of means impressed the emperor. "*Quelle organisation—quelle barbarie!*" he cried, and went on to discuss the future organization of the medical service.

St. Chamans, Soult's *aide-de-camp*, found the emperor still in the same position when he brought the news of the Russian retreat, which Davout also claims to have reported. Thanks to the darkness, the enemy had got away unnoticed.

Even the sequel of victory was of a kind to which the army was unaccustomed. The enemy had escaped, and his traces had to be sought for on all sides.[61]

The emperor sprang up on hearing the good news. His face, we are told, became suddenly radiant, while the dejection which had been stamped on his features a moment before vanished. We can easily believe it, as everything had been at stake for him and he could now see at least deliverance from a situation as critical as any he had ever known.

He made his arrangements at once. Soult was to stand fast, Murat to pursue with the whole of the cavalry. Pursuit was, however, ineffective, as the horses were no longer equal to the task.

In accordance with his habit, Napoleon went over the battlefield, where a thrilling picture must have met his eyes. The heaped-up dead of the 14th Regiment attracted his particular attention and wrung

61. Derrécagaix, *Le Marechal Berthier*, ii. p. 203.

from him words of gratitude for the mass of brave men lying before him on the field. There had been great losses among the officers, particularly those of high rank.[62] As for the troops, gloomy indeed must have been their feelings. Their *"Vive L'Empereur!"* was not so impetuous as usual, and cries of *"Vive la paix!"* were heard amongst them.

Napoleon's knowledge of human nature warned him that the army could not for the moment endure the strain of a further great effort, although the *decisive* victory, which he had intended to bring about before settling into winter quarters, still eluded him. He contented himself, therefore, with staying in the neighbourhood of the battlefield until the 16th, and although Bernadotte was approaching, nothing serious was undertaken. He then took the army back into winter quarters behind the Passarge and the Upper Alle, whither the Allies slowly followed.

That, notwithstanding all this, he deliberately posed as a conqueror and sought to make the world believe that he had won a great victory, cannot be regarded as a crime on his part. It was calculated to further his object, and it was therefore justified. He must have felt keenly the falling off in strength which was now evident in his own army, the inevitable result of any strategical offensive in so extended a theatre of war. He recognized, too, with astonishment, the difficulties which an army has to overcome when, after no matter how glorious a triumph over its first opponent, it is confronted by a second who is still fresh, and sees itself forced to begin all over again. His keen glance showed him that the swing of his offensive had reached a dead-point at which a comparatively slight blow might absolutely reverse it. The political complications that would follow such a reversal were of incalculable gravity. The unwelcome truth—that the army was weary of war—had at all costs to be hidden from his avowed as from his secret enemies, and this being so his boasting, overdone as it was, did as much good to himself, his army, and his country as honourable candour would have done harm.

******

The question as to what would have happened had Bennigsen held out is difficult to answer. Was Scharnhorst's agitated appeal against the

---

62. Three generals were killed outright, while five more died of their wounds within a few days, among them Hautpoul, who, with Dahlmann, lies buried in the park at Worienen near Eylau. The total was 275 killed, 660 wounded officers. For purposes of comparison we may mention: Vionville, 16th August 1870, total loss of officers, 236 killed outright or dying of their wounds, 470 wounded; St. Privat, 18th August 1870, 328 killed, etc., and 571 wounded.

retreat justified or not? No definite answer is possible at this time of day. There are almost as many arguments for as against it. The Russian right wing might have held Ney off on 9th February, L'Estocq's corps have amplified its success. It is possible that Napoleon might really have been induced to retire, had he found the enemy drawn up in front of him again the next morning. On the other hand, he might have put in the Guard to reinforce Ney's fresh troops and changed Bennigsen's voluntary retreat into an enforced one.

It may, in short, be said that a greater than Bennigsen would have been justified in holding out, but that no blame attaches to him for not doing so.

A complete turn of fortune was, at that point in the sanguinary war, undoubtedly an imminent possibility. No straining of the facts, no arbitrary assumptions are required to convince one of this. Four months had passed since the double battle of Jena and Auerstedt, precisely the length of time taken by the French Republic in 1870 to set up an army hundreds of thousands strong and employ it to fight great battles. It may have been impossible for Prussia to do anything of the sort in 1806, since the soul of the nation, the administrative system, the level of culture, and the communications were not adequate to the effort, but that she might have done far more than she did is undeniable. Great results would have been obtained by abolishing all exemptions from service, and by levying all men fit to serve in the provinces still controlled by the Government. Even without accepting so low a standard of equipment and training as that with which Napoleon contented himself, a fresh corps of 40,000 to 50,000 men might have been got together. The regimental depots of Brandenburg, Pomerania, and West Prussia had escaped across the Vistula, bringing with them the greater part of their stores. Arms might easily have been procured from England, had an agreement with this power been promptly arranged. There was no lack of horses in East Prussia. In short, neither want of men nor want of material can be brought forward as an excuse for the absence of any serious effort to rise up in arms.

Energy was lacking on the part of the Government, the will to make a great effort was wanting on the part of an ease-loving generation, and with them alone lies the blame. According to Friedrich von der Marwitz's estimate,[63] an army of 37,000 men might have been put in the field, without counting the garrisons of Danzig and Graudenz, and that this was a reasonable possibility in 1807 is demonstrated by

---

63. *Aus dem Nachlasse F. von der Marwitz,* i. 222 (Berlin, 1852).

what was done in East Prussia six years later. A corps such as this would have altered the course of the winter campaign and completely turned the scale at Eylau. We might, indeed, make a more modest assumption and yet arrive at the same conclusion.

Even with such lukewarm preparations as were actually made, there were in January some 11,000 infantry and 8000 cavalry ready to be employed. Had these been called out, as the situation so imperatively demanded, they would have sufficed to chain victory to the standards of the Allies. These troops might have been assembled at and around Königsberg, have reached Gross-Lauth and Mühlhausen by a short march on the 7th, and, reinforced by the numerous unnecessary small detachments that had been sent out, arrived on the battlefield in good time on the 8th. With the superiority thus obtained, an overpowering victory would have been absolutely certain.

But, instead of this, the new infantry battalions had, from a number of quite secondary considerations, been transferred as early as the middle of December from the capital of the province to the far side of the Memel. The squadrons which had been assembled at Gumbinnen and Insterburg had been likewise made to take cover behind the same river. They had in their ranks a large number of long-service men and were, as far as can be seen, perfectly fit for action. It is hard to resist the temptation of imagining this great body of mounted men united with L'Estocq's 28 squadrons breaking through the thin and widely extended lines of Davout's divisions at Eylau. The vision of Seydlitz hurling himself upon the French infantry at Rossbach rises before us! Resistance to so great an onslaught would have been utterly beyond the power of the few dead-tired horses that Marulaz and Milhaud possessed.

If we probe to the bottom, therefore, we see that Prussia's chance of victoriously reasserting herself was lost, not by Bennigsen's lack of confidence and daring, but by our own faintheartedness, by the narrowness of our whole political and military conception of war and national defence. These were the fetters that forbade the leap which so forcibly suggested itself, and from which alone salvation was to be hoped for.

To L'Estocq's troops at least no blame attaches. Their behaviour on the day of Eylau deserves the greatest praise and was worthy of the famous days of old.

When we consider that many detachments had only come into their quarters late in the night, some even not before morning, and immediately fell in again, unrested and unfed, to march along the hard-frozen road to Kutschitten; that they went straight into the battle, fought with spirit and conspicuous success, camped on the field without fires and practically without victuals, and finally achieved a most orderly night-march in good, even high spirits; that they left no deserters behind them, gave vent to no audible outbursts of discontent—when we consider all this we can only regret that their devotion met with no better reward.

In action their bearing was faultless. There was no hesitation, no faltering, no trace of indecision. At no point was there any of the slackness which was in many cases responsible for the disasters on the Saale and during the retreat to the Oder. During the movement through Wackern and the withdrawal by Schlauthienen and Pompicken, everyone, officer and man, kept his place and did his duty bravely and willingly, with prudence and with decision. In the fight for Kutschitten and the attack on the little Beech Wood all the battalions bore themselves in a way that would not have disgraced Frederick the Great's infantry. At no point was there any shrinking before danger. From first to last the operation went through without a check.

The importance of this battle has been much underrated on the pretext that the losses were insignificant. Yet the forfeit paid by the corps, between 800 and 900 men, is by no means slight if we consider the short space of time in which it was incurred and the small numbers of the troops engaged.

Taken as a whole, the leading also is deserving of ungrudging recognition. On the 8th of February past mistakes were indeed retrieved by the unswerving directness with which the main object was pursued. There may seem to us today nothing very remarkable in the fact that the little corps steadily persisted in its march on to the battlefield where the die was being cast for the fate of the Fatherland, unchecked even by the enemy's cutting through the column of march. But if we place ourselves in the circumstances of that time and that moment, we are obliged to admit that it was extraordinary. When Ney appeared at Schlauthienen and Wackern the Prussian leaders might well have conceived the idea of securing to themselves credit for the result of the battle by moving off in a northerly direction to lure Ney's far superior corps away from Eylau in pursuit of them.

This alone would undoubtedly have been enough to impress

most critics—we have only to recall many a similar instance at manoeuvres and the praises showered upon the fortunate commander when his *coup* succeeded. All the more admirable, then, must we consider the manoeuvres by which the Prussians achieved the double object of turning aside Ney's corps and reaching the battlefield themselves.

Their recognition of the correct point of attack and the firmness with which they resisted every attempt to split up their forces, equally with the vigour of their attacks on Kutschitten, the rapid deployment of the corps after the taking of the village and the second great attack on the Birch Wood, are deserving of all praise.

The one point in which they fell below the highest standard was in their use of the cavalry in second line behind the infantry. It should have taken the route north of Kutschitten, following up the Towarczys and the cossacks, and with them delivered a single well-knit attack upon the French left wing.

Thus the day of Eylau, albeit held in less honoured remembrance than other great days of the nation's history, was in truth the first step towards the revival of Prussia's military glory after the bitter days of humiliation. On that day it was proved that those who lifted up their voices on behalf of the old army and protested against its defamation were right.

The spirit of feebleness so frequently displayed in the higher grades of the army and the people in 1806 had not gained any hold upon the East Prussian troops. It is a great mistake to suppose that they, like the rest, were ready to admit the enemy's superiority, and despaired of offering any successful resistance. On the contrary, as a rule, the Prussian cavalryman would have thought it "all in the day's work" to pit himself single-handed against several Frenchmen.

A Prussian musketeer or fusilier would never fail if called upon to face even a considerable number of the enemy either in intersected country or in the open field, in fire-fighting or in hand-to-hand, and in proof of this a host of instances might be quoted which are worthy of the most glorious days of the Prussian arms.[64]

It has been much disputed whether the victory of Eylau owes more to Scharnhorst or to L'Estocq. Scharnhorst's biographer[65]

---

64. Höpfner, *Der Krieg von 1806 und 1807*, iii. p. 218.
65. Max Lehmann.

gives his hero the position of leader in place of L'Estocq, whom he does not even mention. That is carrying things too far. He who bears the responsibility is entitled to the glory, however much he may have made use of another's ideas. Under certain conditions, as in this case, it is a virtue betokening strength of character to submit to wise guidance. It is characteristic of small minds to avoid the appearance of being under the influence of others, and that is why they commonly reject or only half follow even the best advice. L'Estocq's claim to the laurels of Eylau rests upon the fact that he recognized Scharnhorst's keener insight and assumed full responsibility for its consequences.

When, further, we compare him, as is right, with the men of his own generation, then his place of honour is assured. The last among the generals of Frederick the Great's school to hold a high command, he was also the only one to win a really important success in this unhappy war. He was nearly seventy, but in spite of his great age he had vigour, alertness, and daring enough to make the victory on 8th February possible. In war the responsible person sees things in quite a different light from the one who has only to advise, and his work is accomplished in an oppressive atmosphere which burdens the heart and clouds the mind. Everything he does demands a double output of strength.

But this does not detract from Scharnhorst's fame. We have only to compare the Prussians of Eylau with the Prussians of Thorn and Soldau to see that their operations were now infused with a new spirit—the spirit of Scharnhorst. In spite of his undefined position, in spite of all opposing influences, he had, by the time the decisive day arrived, succeeded in giving effect to his conceptions of war and its conduct. There can be no doubt that the idea of carrying out the glorious flank-march in the face of Ney's attempt at interception was his. No one else of L'Estocq's entourage had shown himself to possess an insight sufficiently keen for him to be suspected of having evolved such a plan.

It was beyond doubt Scharnhorst, too, who made the dispositions for keeping off the French, who chose the direction of attack on the battlefield, and who fixed the line of retreat afterwards. But it was the disadvantage of his position that he could do no more than conceive and propose these plans, and suggest ways and means of execution.

But whether we give the chief credit to L'Estocq or to Scharnhorst according to our individual feelings, the main point is, we consider, from the military historian's point of view, the attitude of the whole Prussian corps. Truly L'Estocq's troops showed convincingly that the instincts of thoroughness and courage that had distinguished the old army still existed and needed only to be turned to good account.

It was these troops who redeemed the honour of the army. The opportunity that Blücher had let slip on the 31st of October, when he held back from attacking Bernadotte, fell to them, and they made it good. They too, therefore, must have their rightful place of honour in our country's history.

Envoy

The verses which form the introduction to this work are written by no knight or warrior, no scion of ancient nobility, but by a simple son of Switzerland with a heart for Germany and a clear eye for the lessons of history.

Born of his intimate sympathy with the revival of the German empire, may his splendid song of the sword sound its grave warning note in every German province!

For that is what we need!

Again, as before the war of 1806, do we enjoy the blessings of an apparently unmenaced peace, and the idea is becoming more and more insistent in the heart of the nation that mankind will now proceed undisturbed along the path of developing humanity. It was just the same then.

What praise Prussia reaped for her policy of neutrality which enabled the country, safe from war's alarms, to advance steadily in wealth and comfort!

What enthusiasm greeted the idea of the everlasting peace which one looked to the greatest of all peace-breakers to establish!

War itself seemed likely to become milder in character. Art and science alloyed the brazen laws of its conduct.

War was to be spiritualized. Henceforward not force was to decide its issue, but superior subtlety of intellect and more abstruse chess-moves.

And how cruel was the awakening from these dreams!

One glance at the desolation of East Prussia is proof enough. The demon of war had raged over it in unchained savagery like a devastating hurricane, destroying all that human industry had for long centuries been laboriously building up.

Everyone living in the stretch of country through which both armies had passed, was ruined, if ruin means the loss of all worldly goods. There was not one head of cattle, no corn, no potatoes, no coin, no clothing, no linen left.[66]

A year of terrible mortality followed the battle. During 1807 there were five, six, and ten times as many people buried in the country round Eylau as was usual in one year.

These were the results of cosmopolitanism, the love of peace, humanitarian twaddle, and the deteriorated pre-Jena methods of warfare. Then, if ever, did history furnish proof of the fact that a nation which desires happiness must also be powerful and skilled in arms. It must neither renounce its passionate love for the Fatherland nor lose its power to regard war as an earnest, bitter thing and a historical necessity. As long as the process of reconstructing states proceeds with the changing seasons, as long as human development does not stand still, so long will there be war. But those who do not wish to be ruined by it must prepare in peace-time to endure the stern armed contest with opponents and rivals. To this end we must spare no pains in educating the rising generation in the spirit of bravery, scorn of danger, and bodily vigour; and never again, as of old before Jena, must we set a higher value upon the art of war than upon the soldierly virtues.

One thing is certain, we shall not be spared a fresh trial of our power of defence. The greater our well-being, the more refined our mode of living, the more extended our commerce, the more quickly do we arouse mistrust and envy, the more certainly will come the hour when we shall be asked whether we still have the will and the manliness to defend our all, sword in hand.

Therefore, German Fatherland, ponder well the poet's warning!

Unter Lorbeerzweigen und Myrtenreifern
Trage das Schlachtschwert!

---

66. Hildebrand, *Die Schlacht bei Pr. Eylau,* p. 34 *et seq.* We should like to draw attention particularly to the thrilling description contained in this work of the conditions which reigned after the war.

Maps

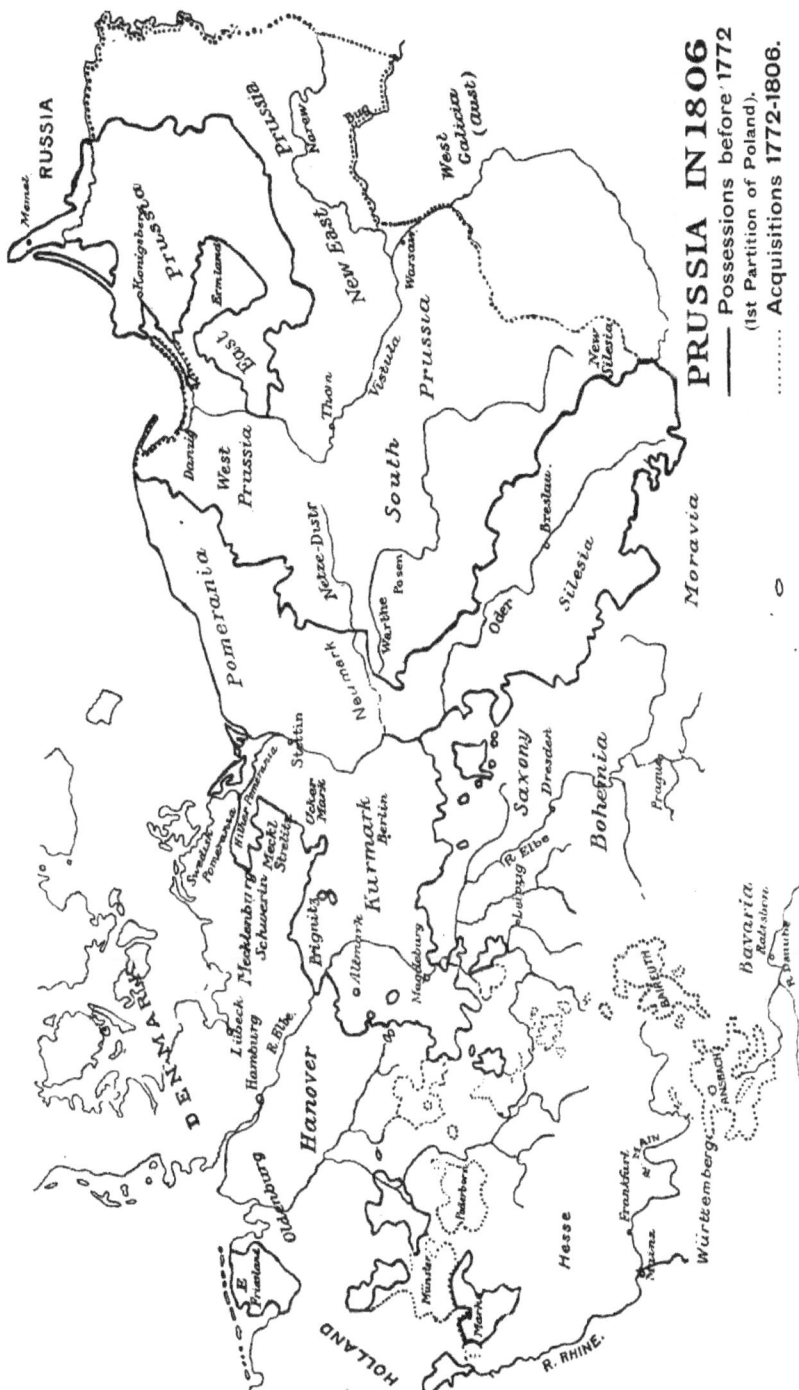

PRUSSIA IN 1806

— Possessions before 1772
(1st Partition of Poland).
········· Acquisitions 1772-1806.

MAP 1

RUSSIA

Memel

Königsberg
Prussia
Ermland
East
Prussia
Thorn
Danzig
West
Prussia
Netze-Dist.
New East
Prussia
Warta
Vistula
New Silesia
Warsaw
South
Prussia
West
Galicia
(Aust.)
Posen
Warthe
Breslau
Pomerania
Sweden
Pomerania
Stettin
Neumark
Oder
Silesia
Moravia

DENMARK
Lübeck
Hamburg
R. Elbe
Mecklenburg
Schwerin
Hither
Pomerania
Meckl.
Strelitz
Prignitz
Oldenburg
E.
Friesland
HOLLAND
Hanover
Mark
Münster
Paderborn
Altmark
Kurmark
Berlin
Magdeburg
Leipzig
R. Elbe
Dresden
Saxony
Bohemia
Prague
Hesse
Frankfurt
R. MAIN
Mainz
BAYREUTH
ANSBACH
Würtemberg
Bavaria
Radisbon
R. Danube

R. RHINE.

Oskar
Mark

191

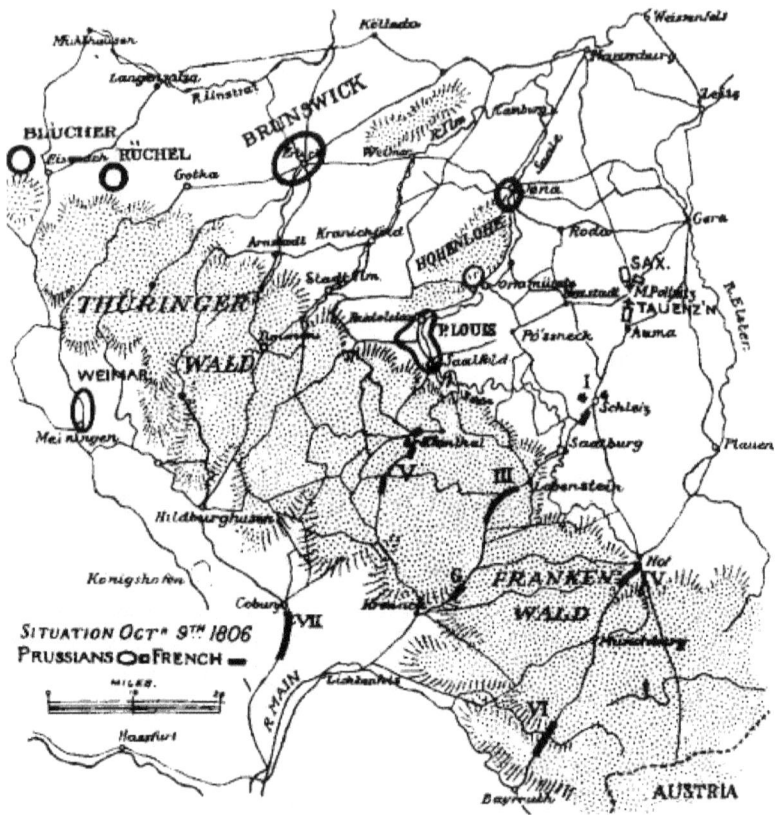

MAP 2

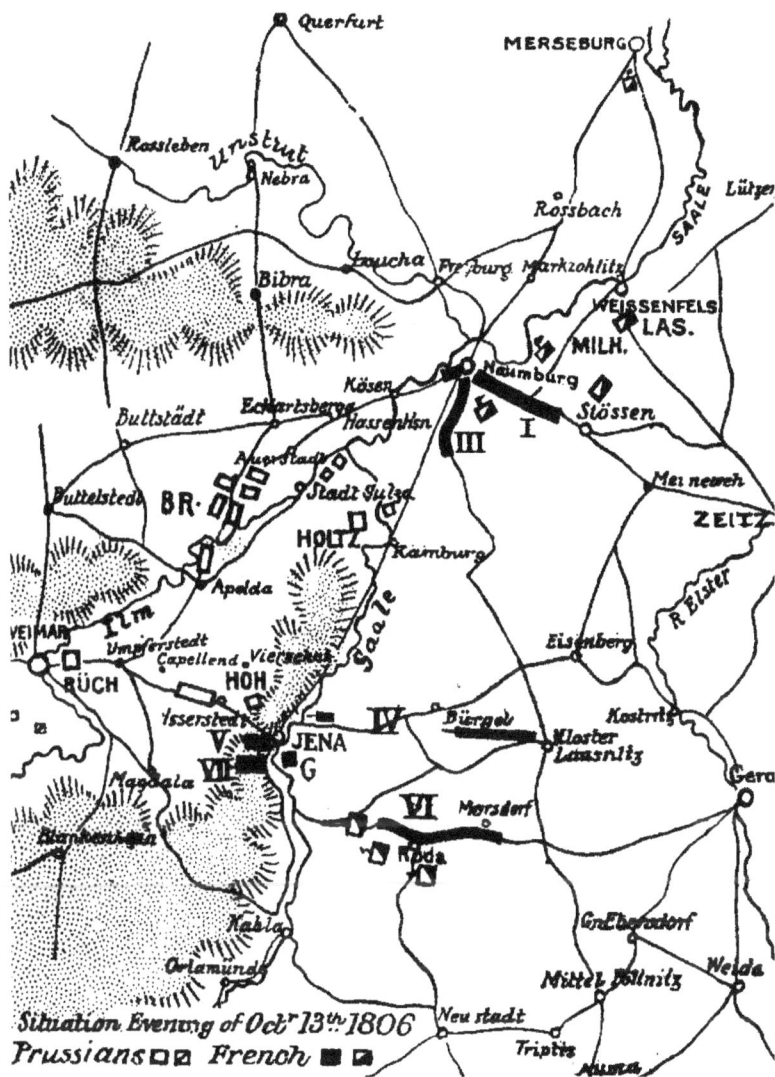

Querfurt

MERSEBURG

Rossleben   Unstrut
Nebra

Rossbach   Lützen

Zaucha Freyburg Markzohlitz   SAALE

Bibra   WEISSENFELS
                         LAS.
                    MILH.

Kösen   Naumburg

Bulstädt   Eckartsberga Hassenhsn.   Stössen
                III   I

Buttelstedt BR.   Stadt Sulza   Meineweh
                                   ZEITZ
            HOLTZ
                    Kaimburg
    Apolda   R. Elster
WEIMAR Ilm
    Umpferstedt   Eisenberg
RÜCH   Capellend Vierzehn
        HOH
    Issersted   IV   Bürgel   Kostritz
    V   JENA   Kloster
VII   G   Laasnitz
                                        Gera
    Magdala   VI   Morsdorf
                        Roda

    Kahla

    Orlamünde   Gn.Eberndorf
                                    Weida
Situation Evening of Oct.r 13th 1806 Neustadt Mittel Pöllnitz
Prussians ☐ ◙ French ■ ▣   Triptis
                                Auma

MAP 3

193

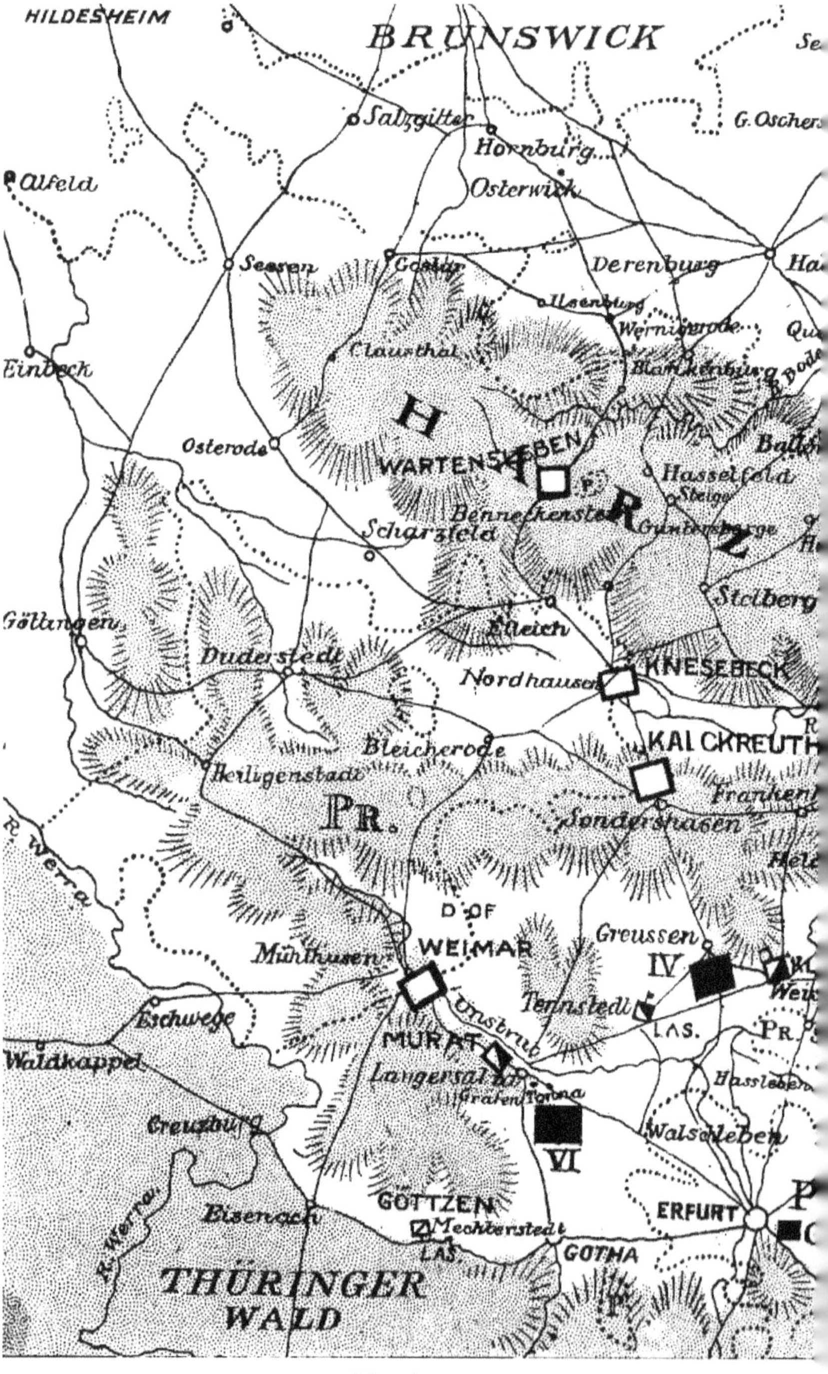

HILDESHEIM
BRUNSWICK
Salzgitter
Hornburg
G. Oschers
Alfeld
Osterwick
Seesen
Goslar
Derenburg
Ilsenburg
Wernigerode
Einbeck
Clausthal
Blankenburg
H
Osterode
WARTENSLEBEN
Hasselfeld
Steige
Benneckenstein
R
Scharzfeld
Z
Stolberg
Göttingen
Ellrich
Duderstadt
Nordhausen
KNESEBECK
Bleicherode
KALCKREUTH
Heiligenstadt
PR.
Sondershausen
R. Werra
D OF
WEIMAR
Greussen
Mühlhausen
IV
Tennstedt
Eschwege
LAS.
PR.
MURAT
Unstrut
Waldkappel
Langersalza
Grafentonna
Hassleben
Creuzburg
VI
Walschleben
GÖTTZEN
ERFURT
Eisenach
Mechterstedt
LAS.
GOTHA
R. Werra
THÜRINGER
WALD

Map 4

Situation on the evening
of 16ᵗʰ October 1806

PRUSSIANS & SAXONS ☐
FRENCH ■

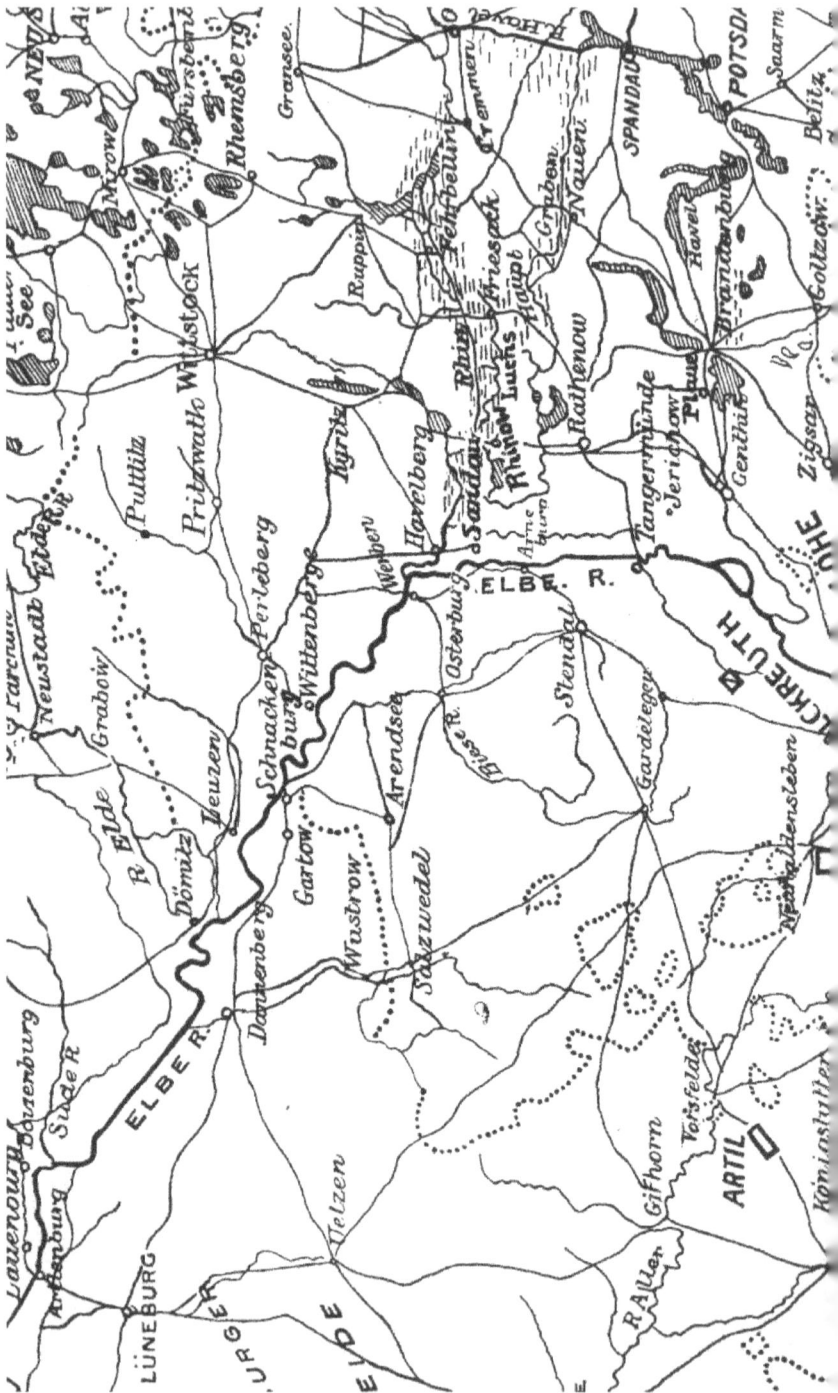

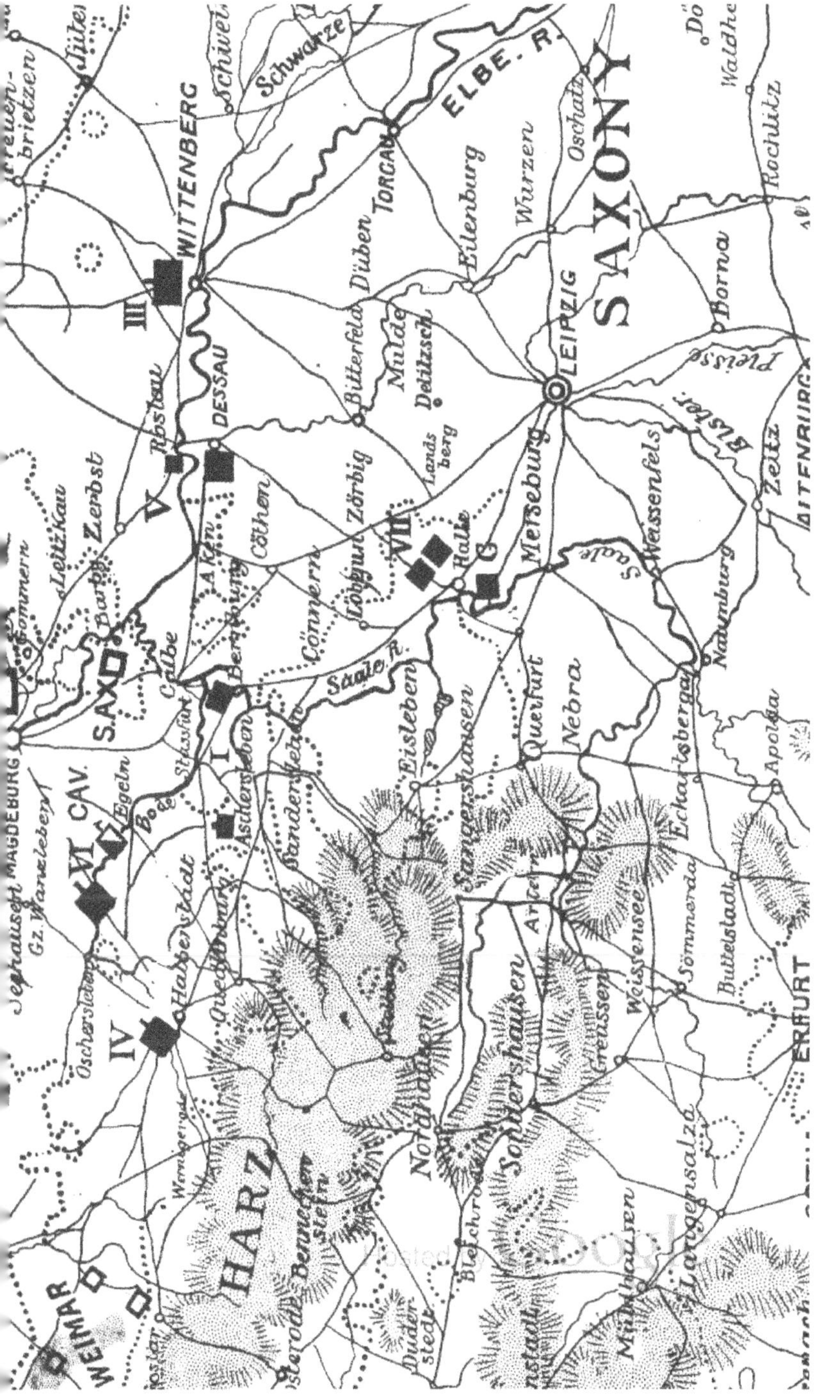
WEIMAR
HARZ
MAGDEBURG
VI
CAV.
S.AXO
IV
I
III
V
VII
G
WITTENBERG
DESSAU
Rosslau
Zerbst
Barby
Calbe
Aken
Bernburg
Cöthen
Egeln
Bode
Stassfurt
Aschersleben
Halberstadt
Quedlinburg
Oschersleben
Wernigerode
Sangerhausen
Eisleben
Saale R.
Halle
Merseburg
Querfurt
Nebra
Naumburg
Weissenfels
Zeitz
Eckartsberga
Apolda
Buttelstadt
Sömmerda
Weissensee
Greussen
Sondershausen
Nordhausen
Langensalza
Mühlhausen
Bleicherode
Duderstadt
ERFURT
Löbejün
Zörbig
Könnern
Landsberg
Delitzsch
Bitterfeld
Mulde
Düben
Eilenburg
TORGAU
ELBE. R.
Schwarze
Wurzen
Oschatz
LEIPZIG
SAXONY
Borna
Pleisse
Elster
Rochlitz
Waldheim
Leitzkau
Gz. Wanzleben

Map 5

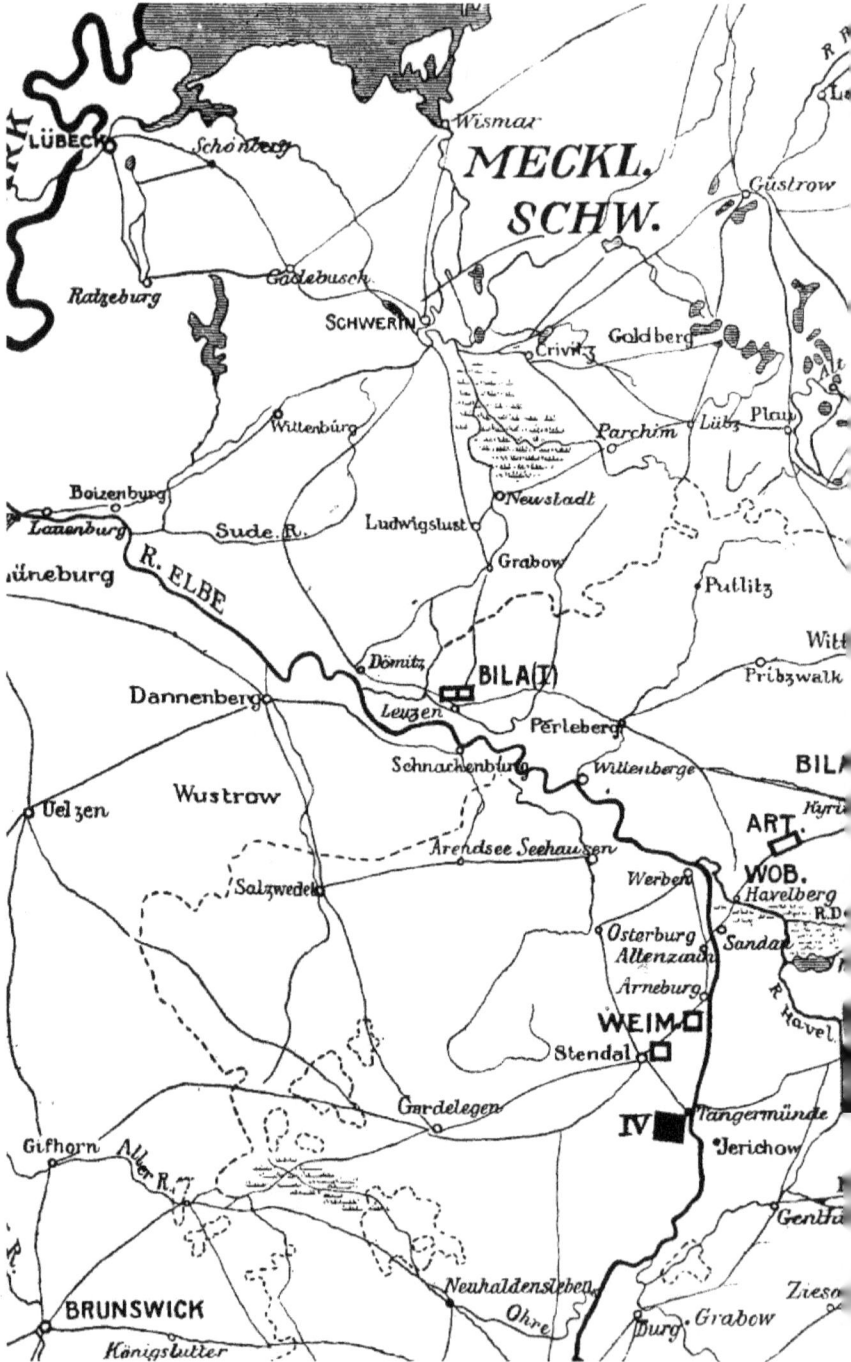

MAP 6

198

Demmin

R. Rene

Wollin I.

Usedom

Hither

Anklam

Kl. Haff

Gr. Haff

Pomerania

Malchin

Treptow

Friedland

Uckermünde

Neu

Brandenbg

Uecker R.

MECKL. STR.

Waren

Penzlin

Pasewalk

Strasburg

Löcknitz

STETT

Woldegk

Mechlin

Fürsten werder

Schönermark

Prenzlau

N. STRELITZ

A. Strelz

Mirow

Boitzenburg

Land Graben

Seehausen

Gar

CHW

Zechli

Fürstenberg

Lychen

Templin

Uecker R.

Greifenberg

Schwedt

Rheinsberg

Rhin

Gransee

Zehdenick

Angermüde

Stolpe

10H

Ruppin

Lindow

SCHIMM

Liebenwalde

Oderberg

R. ODER

Hausen

Wildberg

Finow Canal

Eberswalde

Freienwalde

Fehrbellin

Oranienburg

Riesenthal

Wrietzen

Triesack

Cremmen

LAS & GR.

Bernau

Werneuchen

CÜ

upt Graben

Nauen

MILH

Hennigsdorf

Strausberg

SAV.

SPANDAU

BERLIN

Alt Landsberg

Müncheberg

V

III

Teltow

Copenick

Brandenburg

POTSDAM

VII

Spree R.

FRANKF

I

G & RES.

Saarmünd

Goltzow

Zossen

M

Trebbin

Beesk

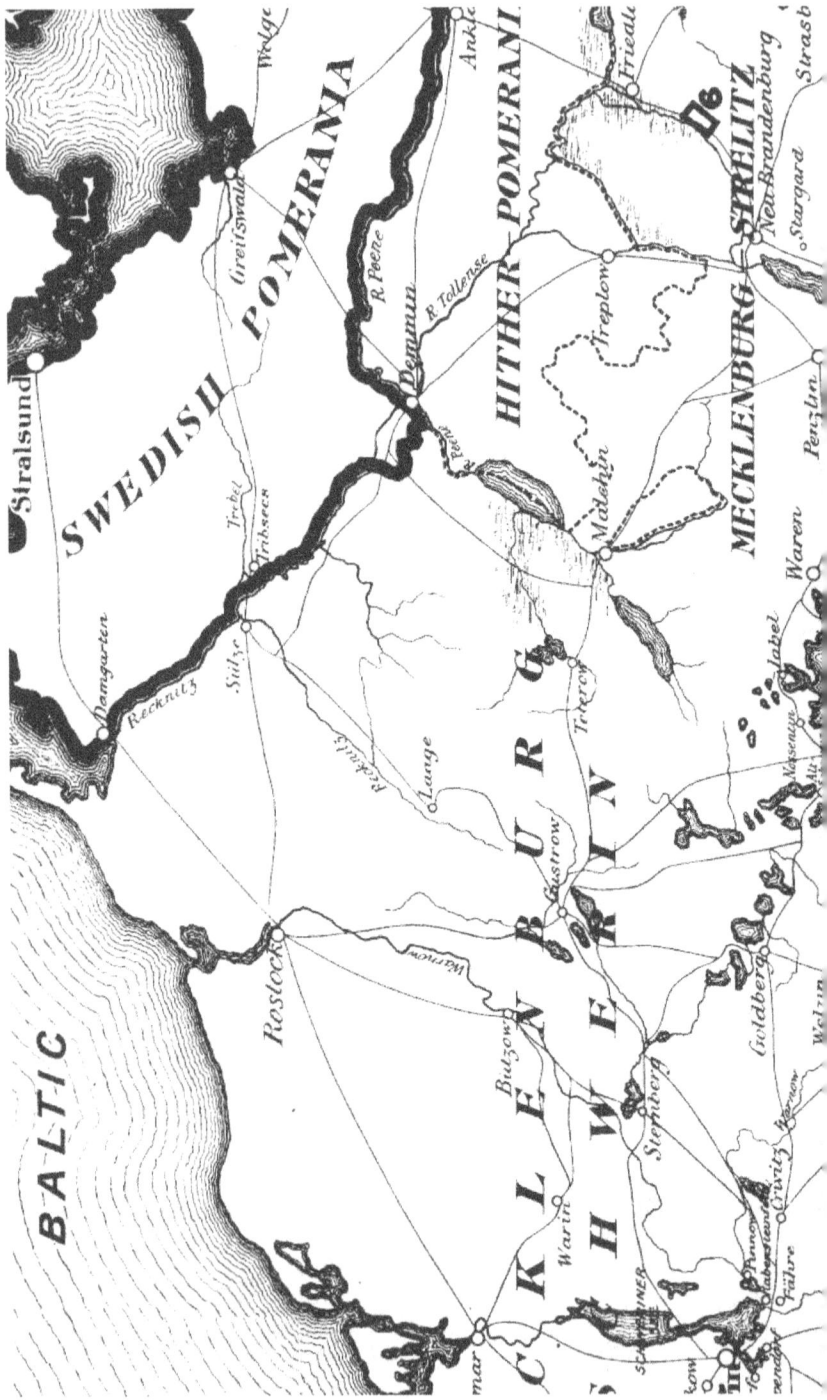

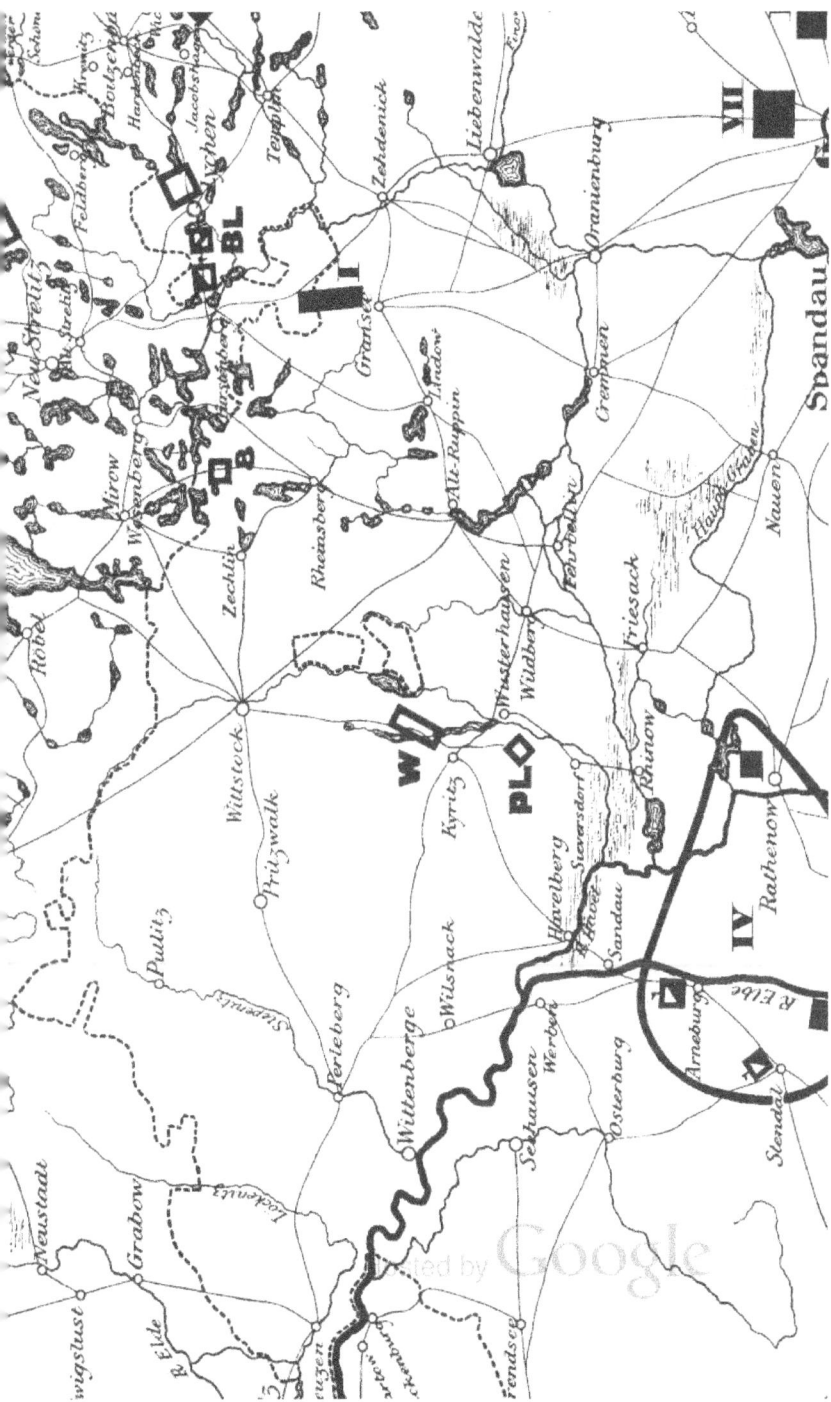

MAP 7

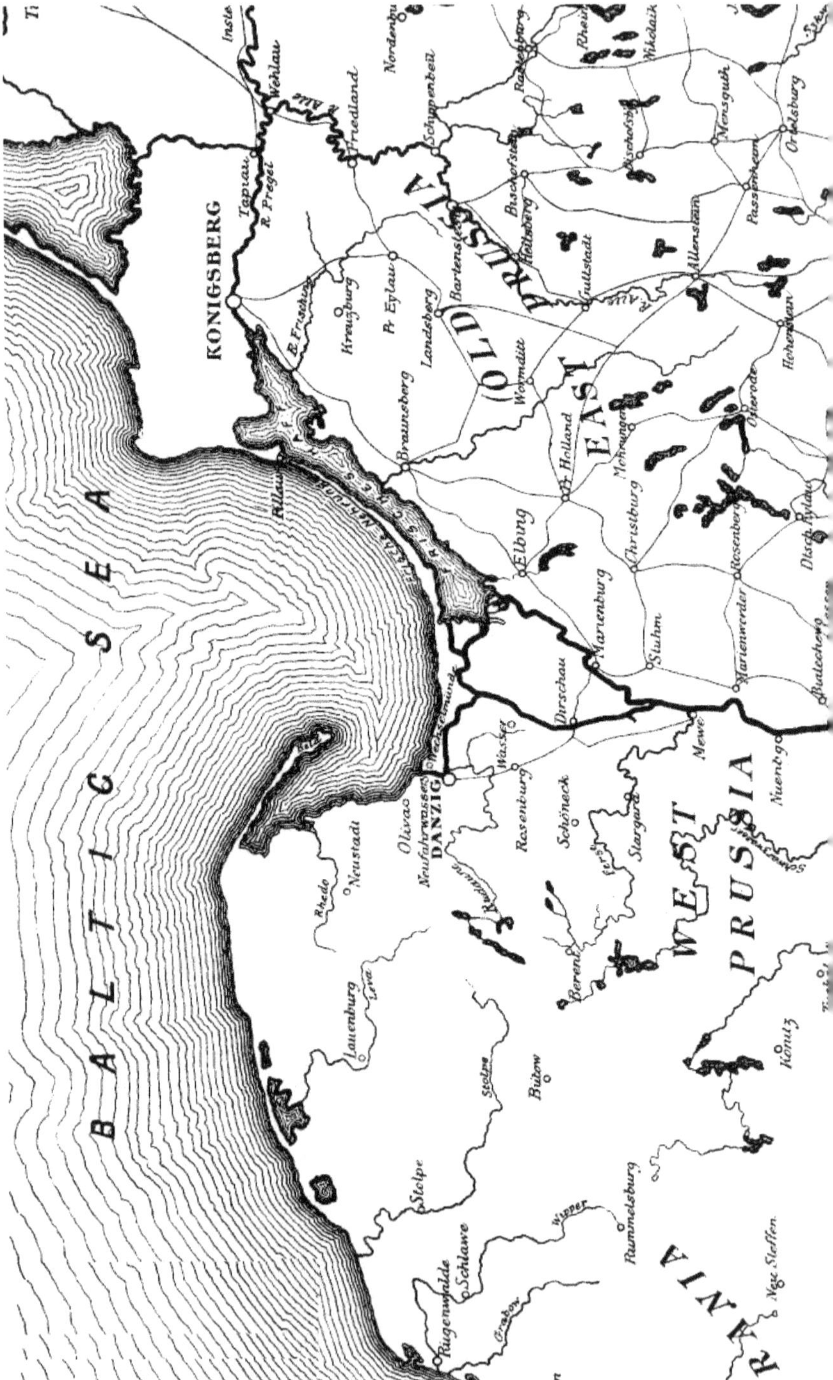
BALTIC SEA
KONIGSBERG
DANZIG
(OLD) PRUSSIA
EAST
WEST PRUSSIA
Tapiau
R. Pregel
Wehlau
Friedland
Schippenbeil
Bartenstein
Pr. Eylau
Landsberg
Kreuzburg
Braunsberg
Pillau
Elbing
Holland
Mohrungen
Wormditt
Guttstadt
Heilsberg
Bischofstein
Allenstein
Passenheim
Ortelsburg
Mensguth
Hohenstein
Osterode
Christburg
Marienburg
Stuhm
Dirschau
Marienwerder
Rosenberg
Dtsch. Eylau
Mewe
Schöneck
Stargard
Berent
Oliva
Neufahrwasser
Neustadt
Rhedo
Lauenburg
Leva
Bütow
Stolpe
Rummelsburg
Schlawe
Rügenwalde
Wipper
Grabow
Konitz
Neu Stettin

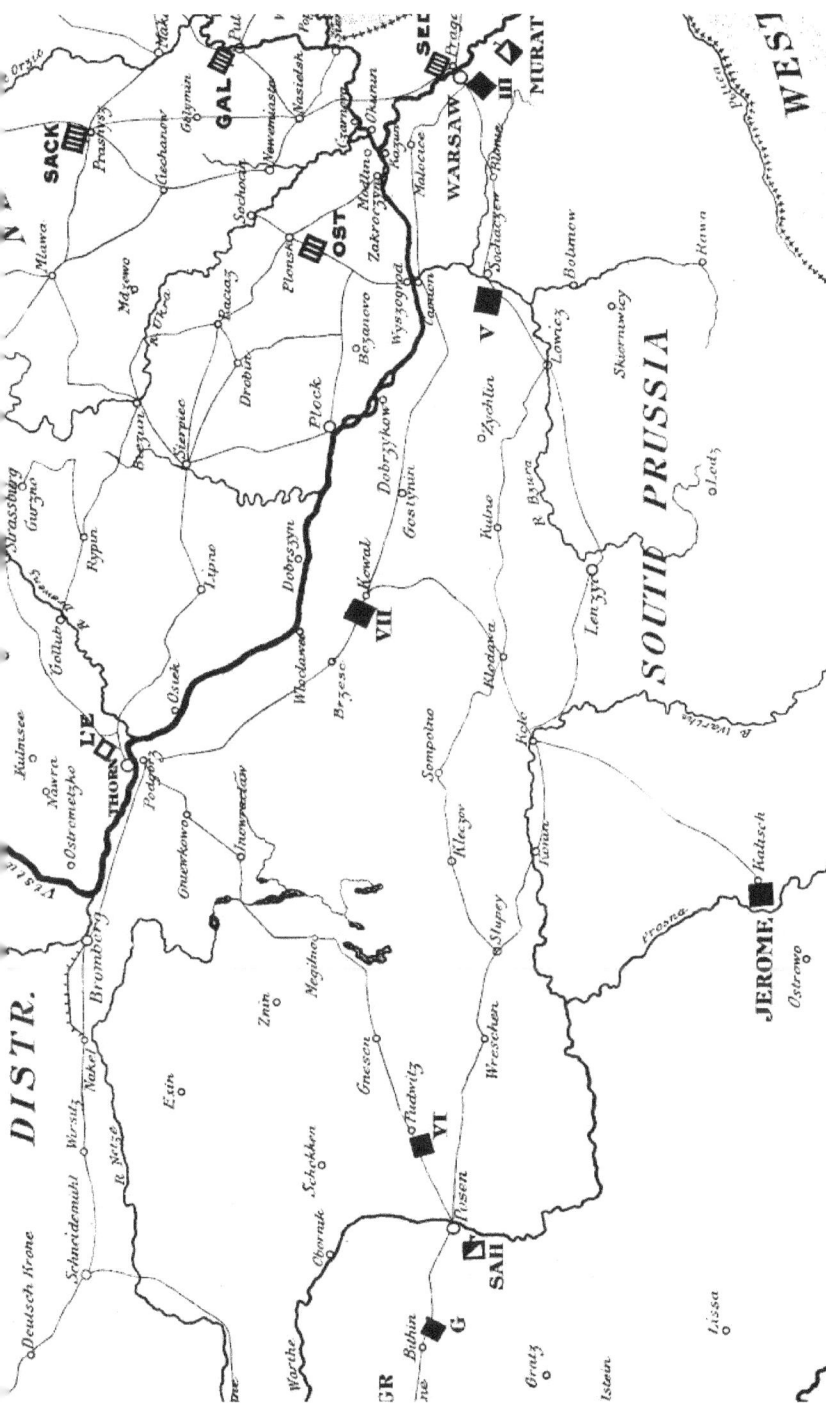

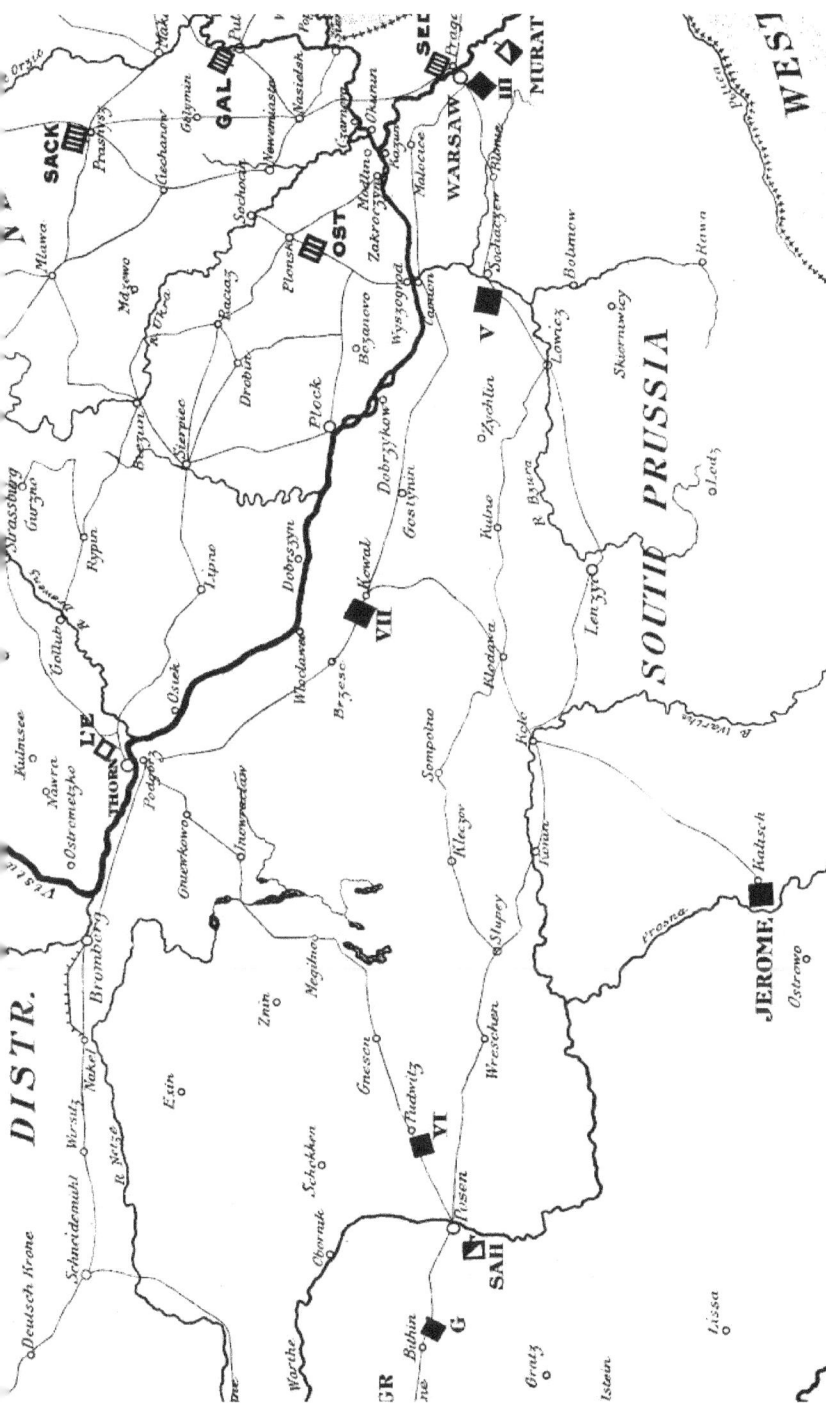

Map 8

POSITIONS ON 22ND DECEMBER 1806.

FRENCH
PRUSSIANS
RUSSIANS

Scale of English Miles.

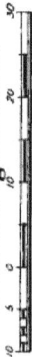

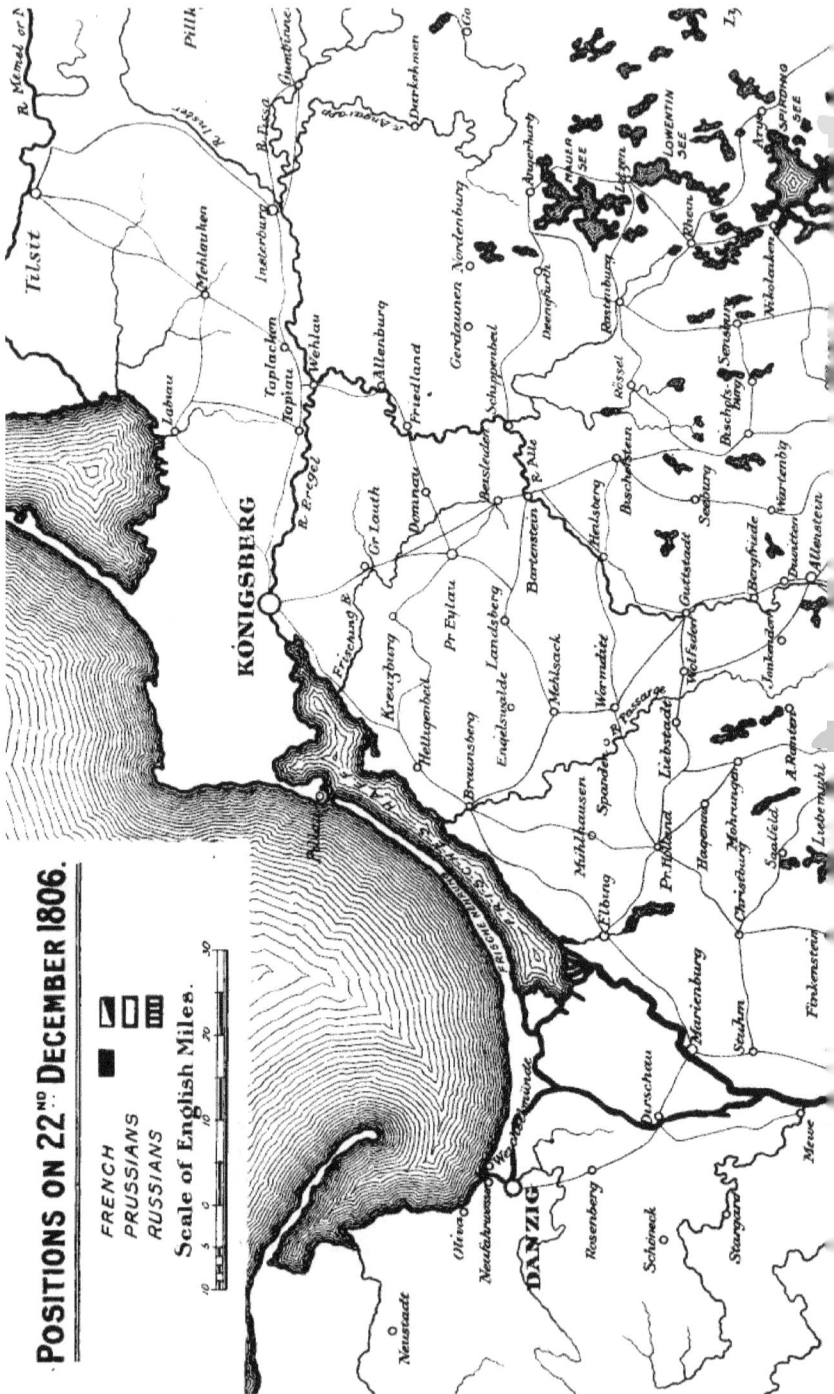

KÖNIGSBERG

DANZIG

Tilsit

PILLAU

R. Memel or N.

204

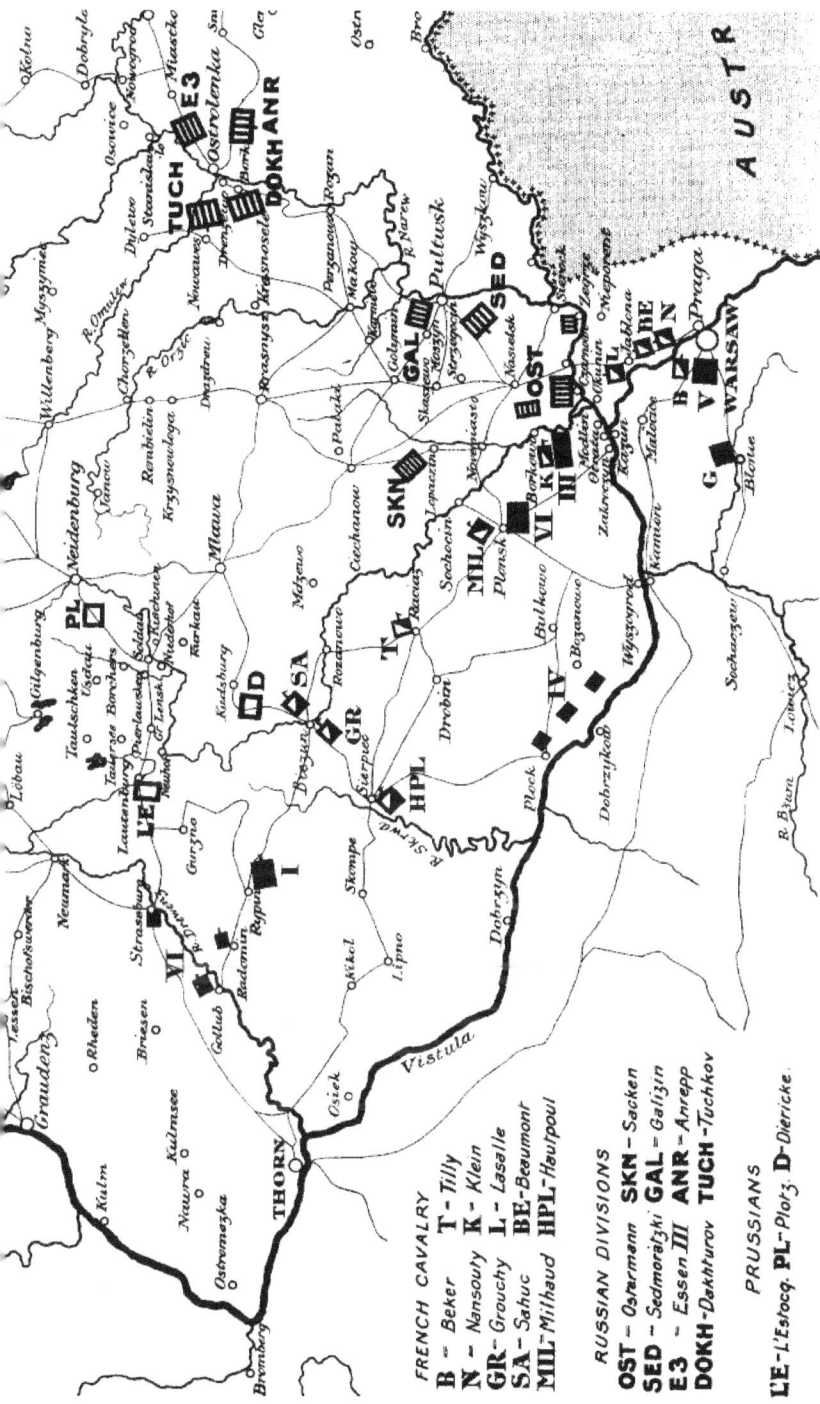

FRENCH CAVALRY

B = Beker   **T** - Tilly
N - Nansouty   **K** - Klein
GR - Grouchy   **L** - Lasalle
SA - Sahuc   **BE** - Beaumont
MIL - Milhaud   **HPL** - Hautpoul

RUSSIAN DIVISIONS

OST = Ostermann   **SKN** - Sacken
SED = Sedmoraitzki   **GAL** = Galizin
E3 - Essen III   **ANR** - Anrepp
DOKH - Dakhturov   **TUCH** - Tuchkov

PRUSSIANS

L'E - L'Estocq; **PL** - Plotz; **D** - Diericke.

MAP 9

205

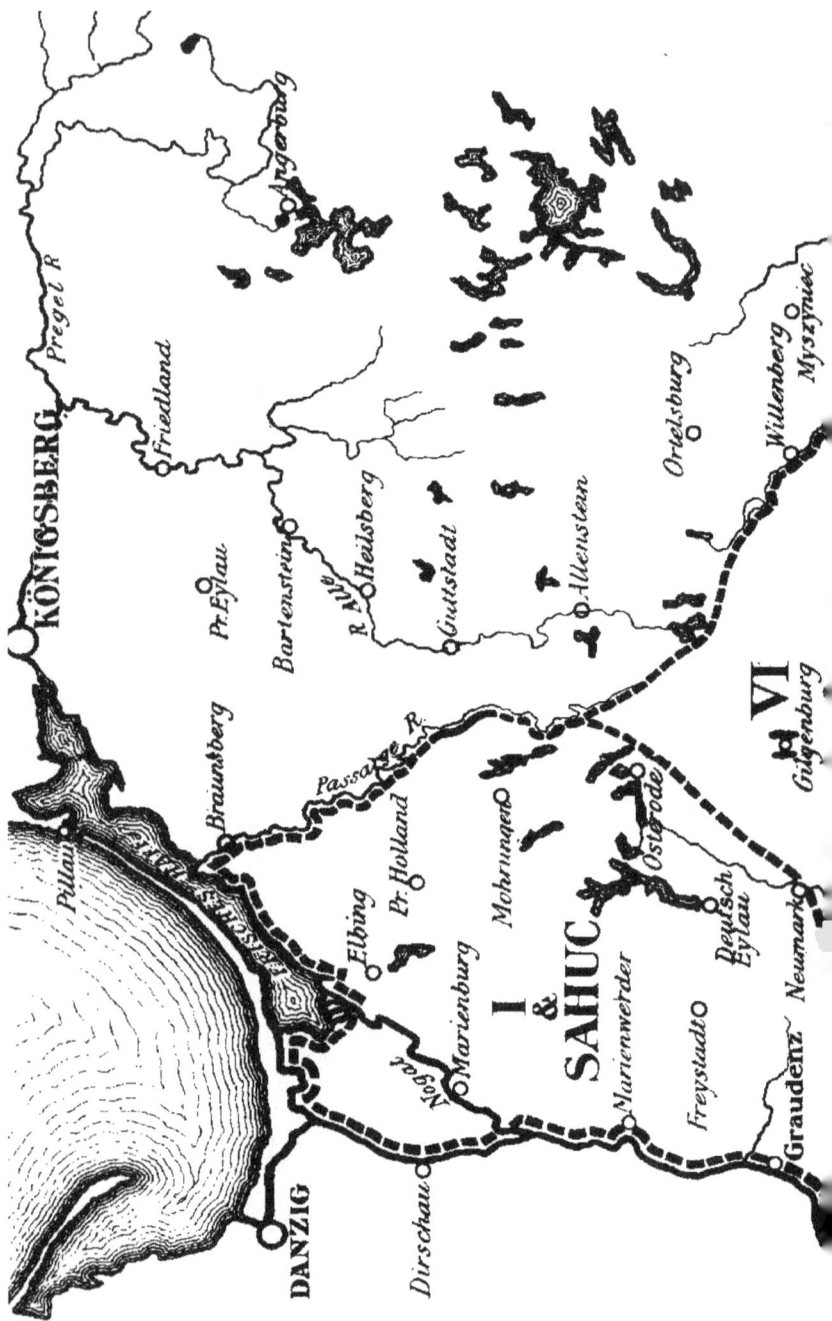

KÖNIGSBERG

Pregel R.

Argenburg

Friedland

Pr. Eylau

Bartenstein

Heilsberg

R. Ally

Guttstadt

Allenstein

Orielsburg

Willenberg

Myszyniec

Braunsberg

Passarge R.

Pillau

Mohrungen

Ostarode

VI

Gulgenburg

Elbing

Pr. Holland

I

&

SAHUC

Deutsch

Eylau

Neumark

Marienburg

Marienwerder

Freystadt

Graudenz

Nogat

Dirschau

DANZIG

206

AUSTRIA

BECKER

III

& MIL.

Brok

R. Bug

Golymin

Pultusk

Prasnysz

Sierock

V

Praga

WARSAW

G.

IV

R. Ukra

Plonsk

III

Part of V & later part of III

HAUTPOUL

KLEIN

To MIL. &

LAS.

Vistula

THORN

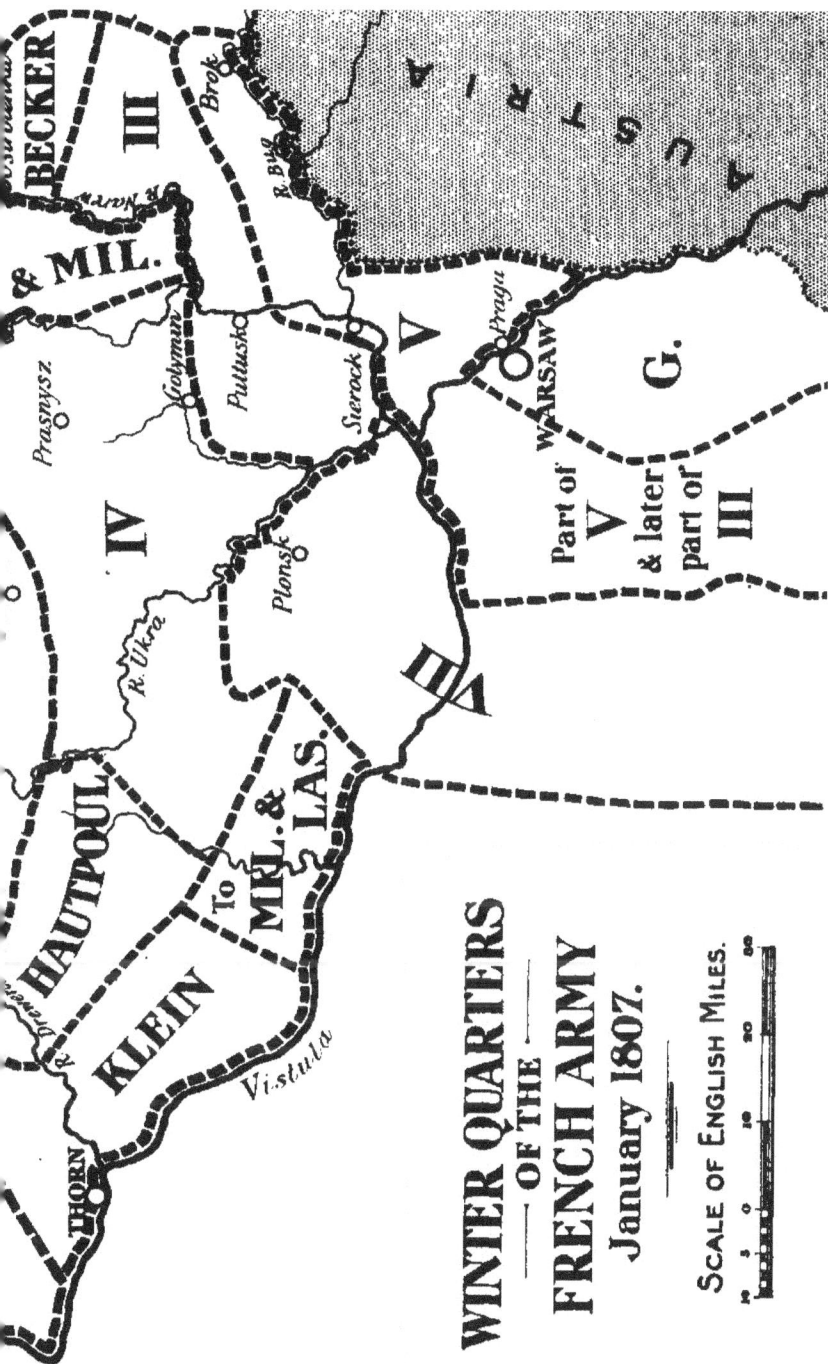

WINTER QUARTERS
— OF THE —
FRENCH ARMY
January 1807.

SCALE OF ENGLISH MILES.

MAP 10

MAP 11

208

au

burg
orf

Darkehmen

FRENCH ◼ ◢
ALLIES ▭
Positions of BENNIGSEN'S ARMY
enclosed by THICK LINE.

L'E. = L'Estocq.
MIL = Milhaud.
LA = Lasalle.
GR = Grouchy.
HPL = Hautpoul.
K = Klein.
S = Sahuc.
B = Beker.

Scale of English Miles.
10 5 0 10

aunen Nordenburg
l
Angerburg Goldapp

offstedt
Barthen
Drenglfurth
MAUER
SEE

Rastenburg Lötzen
LOWENTIN
SEE
Rhein
MEDDNER SEE SEE

Nikolaiken
SPIRDING
SEE

Johannisburg
Bialla

SEDM ⊟
Gonionds

Lyck

naun
szyniec

◼ III

R Omulew
en Dylevo

Novogrod
Lomsha
Tykocin
Bialystock

Clembock
Zambrova
Mazowiecku
ESSEN I
Rozan
Bransk
Ostrow
Brok ◼ V

MAP 12

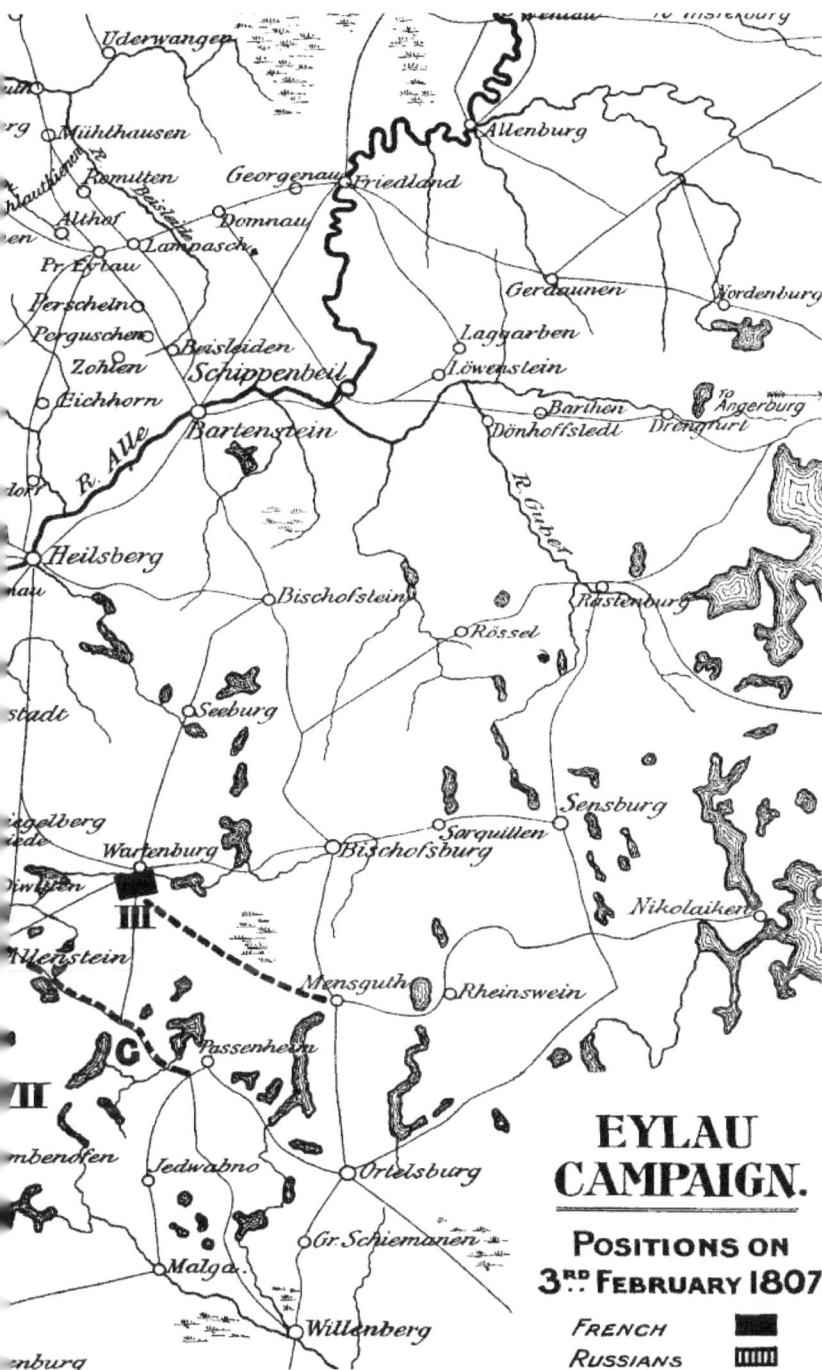

EYLAU CAMPAIGN.

POSITIONS ON
3RD FEBRUARY 1807

FRENCH
RUSSIANS

MAP 13

Uderwangen

Mühlhausen

ken

Romitten

Althof

Pr. Eylau

Lampasch

Perabeln

Zohlen

Perauschen

Beisleiden

Eichhorn

Schippenbeil

Bartenstein

R. Alle

end'f

Heilsberg

Georgenau

Friedland

R. Alle

Allenb'g

Domnau

Laggarben

Löwenstein

Dönhofstedt

Barthen

Bischofstein

Rössel

Seeburg

Wartenburg

stein

Sorquitten

Bischofsburg

Sensburg

en

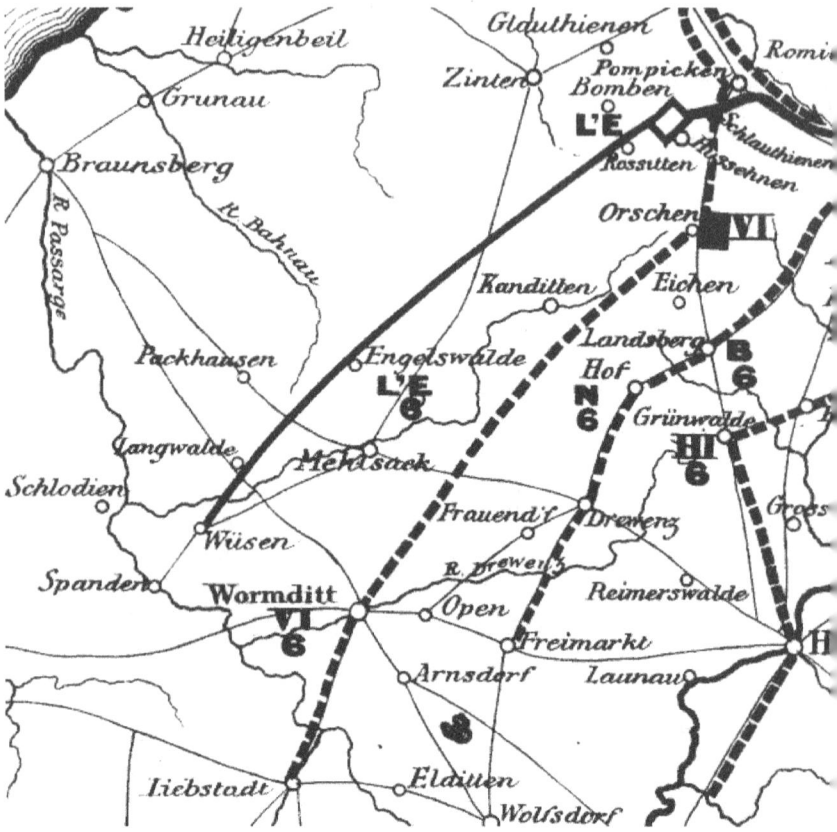

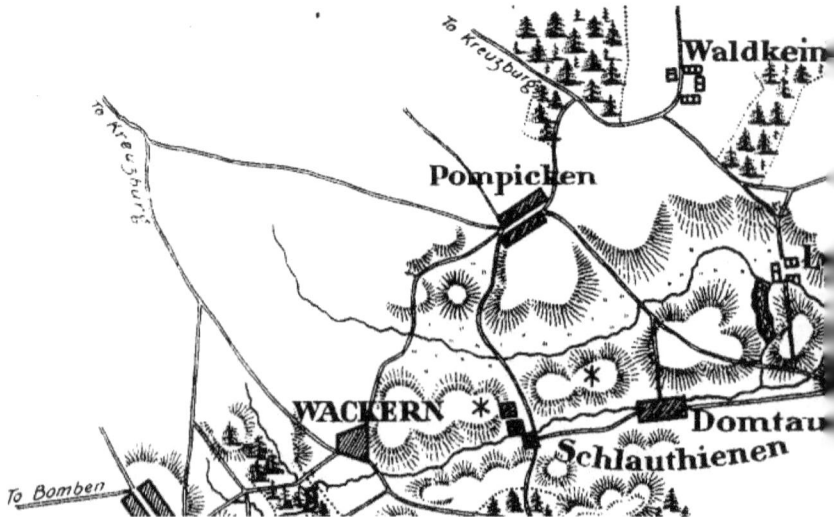

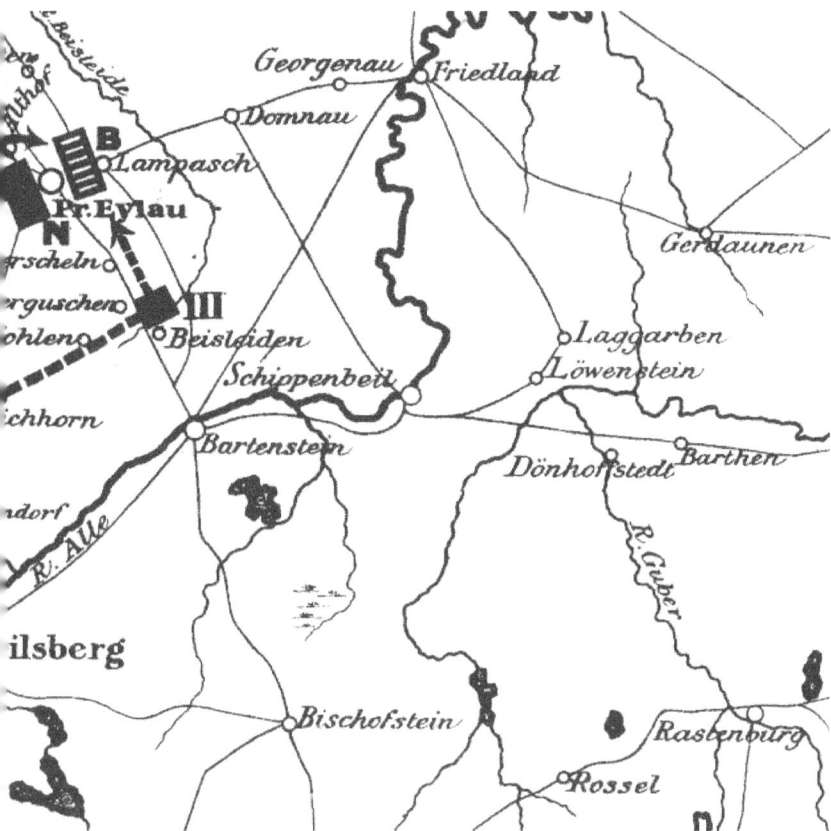

MAP 14

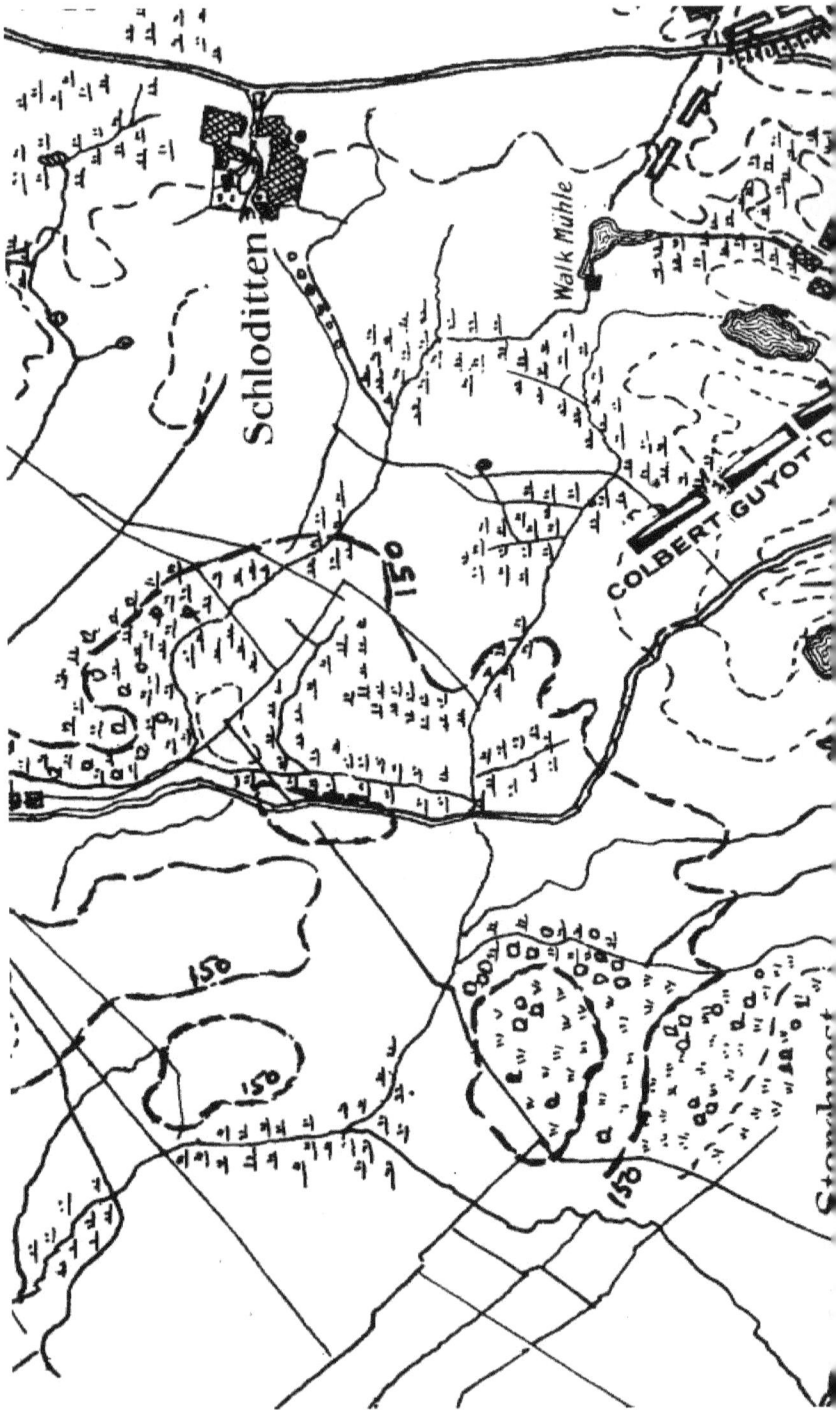

Schloditten

Walk Mühle

COLBERT GUYOT D

150

150

150

150

150

EYLAU

Freiheit

Tenknitten

ENKNITTER SEE

ASCHKEITER SEE

Torf Buch

IV

VII

G

G

G

HPL

200

100

200

200

150

150

150

MAP 15

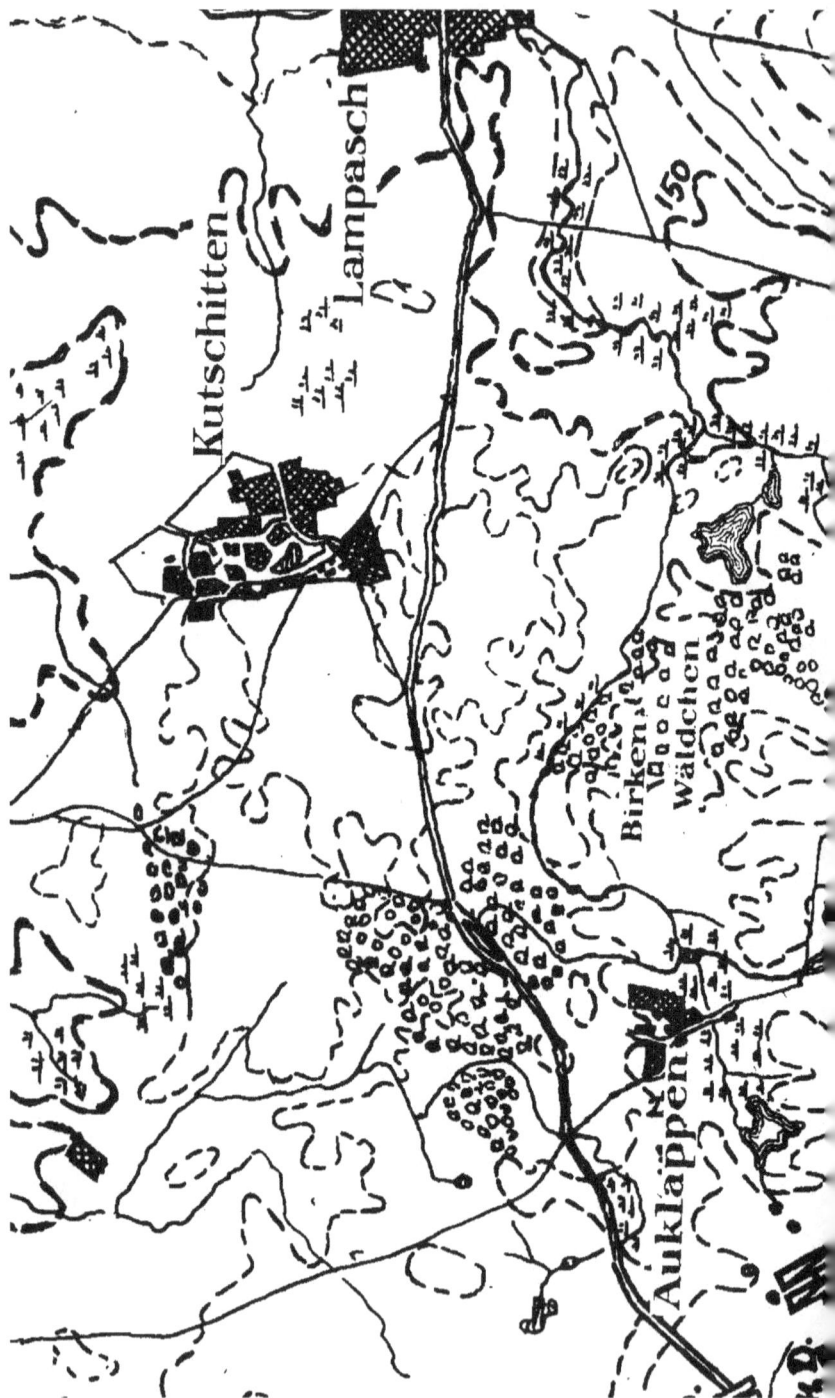

Kutschitten

Lampasch

150

Birkenwäldchen

Auklappen

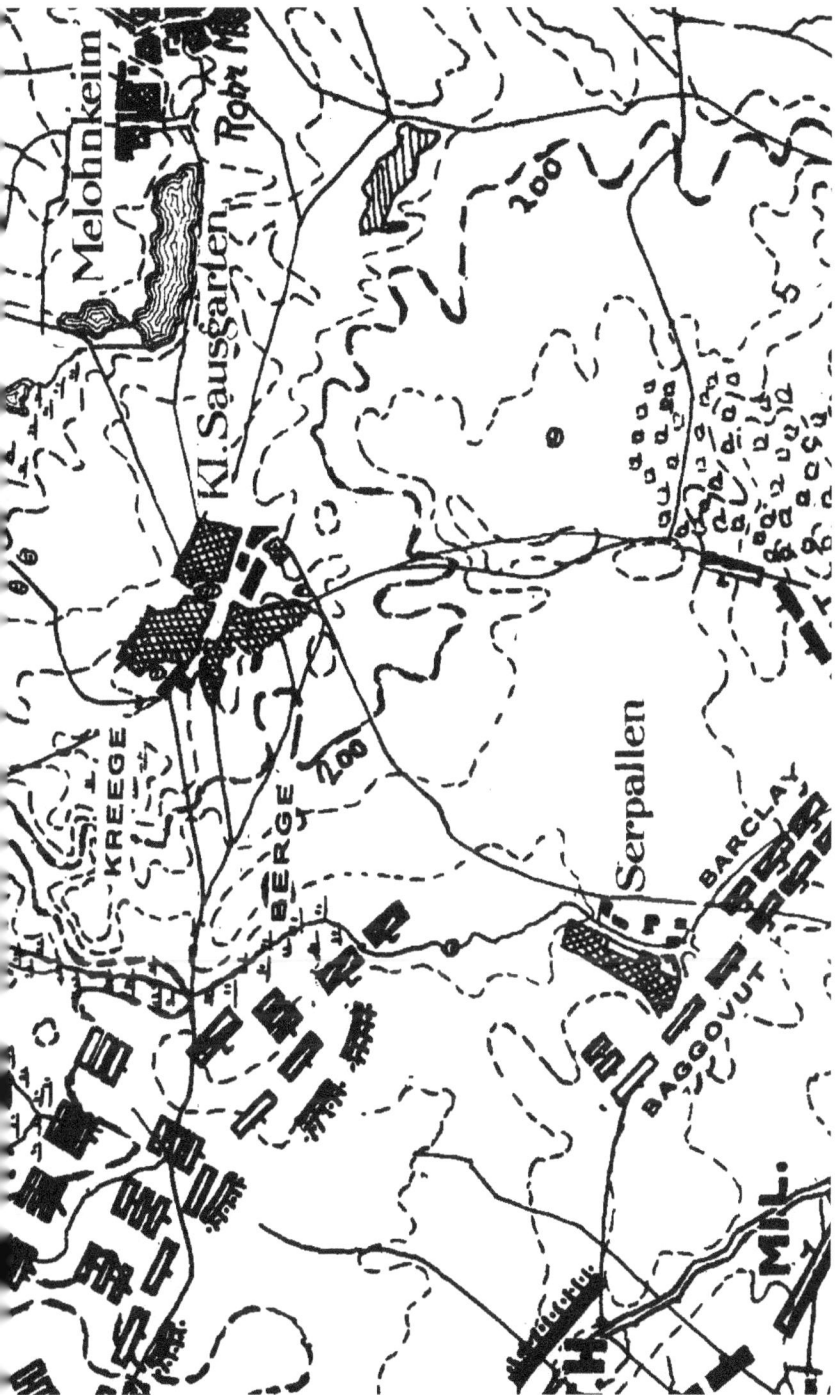

Melohnkeim

Rohr M.

Kl. Sausgarten

200

200

KREEGE

BERGE

Serpallen

BARCLAY

BAGGOVUT

MIL.

MAP 16

www.ingramcontent.com/pod-product-compliance
Lightning Source LLC
Chambersburg PA
CBHW032051080426
42733CB00006B/238